I0611754

Praise for author

"O'Toole is Ireland's best interviewer." — *Irish Mail on Sunday*

"Jason O'Toole has an extraordinary skill when it comes to Q&A interviews. He has a knack for getting the very best from his subjects; often eliciting unexpectedly candid responses to the most probing of questions." — Sylvia Pownall, *Irish Sunday Mirror*

"Indisputably Ireland's most talented and prolific interviewer." — *Irish Daily Mail*

"O'Toole's skill is getting access to important figures and being a good listener" — *Metro*

"Having been in newspapers for 25 years Jason O'Toole is the last person I'd want to be interviewed by because I'd end up saying something I shouldn't. When it comes to making people talk he's the best in the business." — Pat Flanagan, *Irish Daily Mirror*

"O'Toole specializes in in-your-face interviews." — *Sunday Independent*

"Jason O'Toole, a man with a renowned skill for convincing famous people to betray secrets they would rather not have." — John Lee, *Irish Mail on Sunday*

"Jason O'Toole is the journalistic equivalent of a hangman. Cleverly giving some of his notorious subjects just enough roof to do the job themselves." — *Evening Herald*

"O'Toole is one of our frontline interviewers, handling a plethora of headline making tete-a-tetes." — Niall Stokes, *Hot Press*

"O'Toole has developed a reputation as a journalist who gets the scoop. How does he manage to get the stars to say such revealing things?" — Chris Jones, *Dublin Live*

"O'Toole has had unparalleled access to Ireland and Irish America's greatest actors in the last number of years and his clear talent at making his interviewees feel comfortable in sharing makes for a highly interesting read." — *Irish Central*

"I love the style of interviews and the way Jason O'Toole poses the questions. It's more like radio on paper." — Broadcaster Niall Boylan, winner of the Best Schedule Talk Show in the World at the New York Radio Awards 2017 & 2019

Also by the same author

Crime Ink

Hollywood Irish

Katie Taylor: Journey to Olympic Gold

Brian Cowen: The Path to Power

The Last Days of Katy French

The End of the Party (with Bruce Arnold)

Memory Man (with Jimmy Magee)

Different Class (with Jimmy Magee)

Off The Edge (editor)

The Writing Irish
Irish authors in their own words

Jason O'Toole

BearManor Media

Orlando, Florida

The Writing Irish: Irish Authors in their Own Words
©2021 Jason O'Toole. All Rights Reserved.

No portion of this publication may be reproduced, stored, and/or copied electronically (except for academic use as a source), nor transmitted in any form or by any means without the prior written permission of the publisher and/or author.

Published in the USA by
BearManor Media
1317 Edgewater Dr. #110
Orlando, FL 32804
www.BearManorMedia.com

Softcover Edition
ISBN: 978-1-62933-834-7

Printed in the United States of America

With much love to my mother Rosaleen and my late father Gerald O'Toole, who is deeply missed. I'll be eternally appreciative of their huge support when I started out as a would-be writer. Gerald was a good-hearted man and his family's world is a much emptier place without him, but we will all cherish our many fond memories of him. Always.

Introduction

"Well, I'm Irish anyway, that's something." — Iris Murdoch

Just like the U2 song, it was a place where the streets have no name. On a dusty countryside road in Northern Spain, as I walked the Camino de Santiago, an elderly woman's eyes lit up like flashbulbs at the mere mention of Ireland.

"James Joyce!" she exclaimed.

I grinned.

"Oscar Wilde!"

I then gave her a thumbs up.

"Samuel Beckett!"

It was very touching how this octogenarian, who couldn't speak English, was able to convey such deep affection for Irish literature by simply uttering those three names with great reverence, as if they were the Holy Trinity.

Ireland has produced a disproportionate amount of notable writers for such a small nation. There's probably a plethora of reasons — such as years of oppression, the lack of job prospects before the Celtic Tiger, and the sheer boredom from being marooned on a small island in the North Atlantic with year-round miserable weather.

While, without doubt, it's a great advantage to be from a predominantly English-speaking country. It's hard to imagine too many Irish authors being widely translated and read if Gaelic was still the main native tongue.

Even so, it's impossible to fully elucidate why Ireland breeds wordsmiths in the same fashion that Brazil produces dazzlingly skilled footballers. After all, we Irish are "impervious to psychoanalysis" according to Sigmund Freud. But, as is evident in this anthology of in-depth interviews with Irish authors, we're also a remarkably candid race.

You could list a couple of dozen Irish writers from the Nineteenth and Twentieth Century and still accidentally overlook someone significant. It's easy to forget the universally acclaimed classics *Dracula*, *Gulliver's Travels* and *Tristram Shandy* were all written by Irishmen.

The fantasy novel *The Lion, The Witch and The Wardrobe* would almost certainly be overlooked because its Irish author C.S. Lewis is remembered as being an Oxford don and he was born in Belfast, which technically makes him British too.

But there are many other Irish-born authors from the Republic claimed as British too, such as Iris Murdoch and Cecil Day-Lewis, who just happened to be the official British Poet Laureate between 1968-72; even though he is probably more well-known these days as the father of Oscar winner Daniel Day-Lewis.

It's hard for certain Irish public figures to maintain their national identity on a global level because the British media has always had a propensity to claim them as one of their own. Even true blue Dubliners like Bono and Olympic champion Katie Taylor, who won a gold medal when boxing for Team Ireland, have both been described as British by respectable media outlets, such as the BBC and *The Daily Telegraph*.

I wrote two of my *Irish Sunday Mirrors* columns in 2019 alone on the matter when the actress Saoirse Ronan and golfer Rory McIlroy, who was born in Northern Ireland but opted to represent the Republic in the Olympics, were both claimed by British media as loyal subjects of their queen ... even though a Republic can't by definition have a monarch!

I'd be here all day naming Irish stars claimed as British heroes but they certainly pushed the boat by describing Stephen Roche as the "first English speaker" to win the Tour de France.

Funnily enough, the British can quite rightly assert ownership of the quintessential American noir writer Raymond Chandler (but rarely, if ever, do so) who created the iconic detective Philip Marlowe — even though he was born in the US and had Irish blood coursing through his veins thanks to his Wexford-born mother. As a young child, she separated from Raymond's father and brought him back to Wexford and then London where he was educated and later became a naturalized British citizen. He was an adult before he went back to the States. Yet he does have a much stronger connection with Ireland and, of course America.

The English newspaper columnist Melanie Philips caused huge controversy in 2017 with her ridiculous statement, "Ireland itself has a tenuous claim to nationhood, having seceded from Britain as the Irish Free State in 1922."

But Philips did hit the proverbial nail on the head because she was only saying out loud what many of her compatriots think too — that they don't perceive Ireland as a "real" country per se.

The English are not the only culprits here: I remember one American critic describing the semi-autobiography novel *The Ragged-Trousered Philanthropists* written by Dublin-born author Robert Croker — who wrote under the alias Robert Noone which was published posthumously — as "a classic of modern

British literature, that ought to rank with the work of Thomas Hardy, D.H. Lawrence and James Joyce…"

By the same token, I doubt anybody would dare describe *Down and Out in Paris and London* by George Orwell as a seminal classic of modern French literature! Looking again at that above critic's quote, it appears he was including the quintessential Dubliner James Joyce as British!

These blurring of the lines, such as arguing an Irish writer is British because he or she came from a supposed Anglo background, or was born in the 26 counties before the country became a Republic, or were born in Northern Ireland and rightfully perceived themselves as Irish and not British, does a great disservice to Irish literature.

You don't see Ireland claiming British or American authors with Irish-born parents — if we did, I'd fill many pages listing them. Even the British icon The Duke of Wellington, who ended up becoming Prime Minister a little over a decade after his victory at Waterloo, was a Dubliner by birth!

This is a subject matter probably best left for another day to tackle at length because it would take up too much space here to completely explore it. I'll leave the last word on this topic for now to Iris Murdoch, who often appears on lists of great British authors. She once stated: "Well, I'm Irish anyway, that's something."

In my teens and early twenties, there was long periods when the majority of novels I devoured were only by Irish authors and it was by no means out of any blind patriotism but rather because those just happened to be the books most readily to hand.

However, my absolute favorite novels in my youth where mostly all written by Americans or British authors, such as *The Sun Also Rises* by Ernest Hemingway, *The Sound and The Fury* by William Faulkner, *Rabbit, Run* by John Updike, and three books by John Fowles (*The Collector*, *The Magus* and *The French Lieutenant's Woman*).

I'd probably want to add into the mix a few more titles by Joseph Heller, John Irving, Charles Bukowski, Bret Easton Ellis, and Jay McInerney's *Bright Lights, Bight City*. I haven't even named *The Great Gatsby*! I need to restrain myself from mentioning many others.

But I would certainly add one Irish novelist to this list. Yes, *Ulysses* and Beckett's trilogy (*Molloy/Malone Dies/The Unnamable*) are, of course, masterpieces, but my personal favorite Irish writer has always been Flann O'Brien. He was underappreciated in his lifetime, but might've enjoyed more success if the first printing of his novel *At Swim With Two Birds* hadn't been lost when his publisher Longman's premises were destroyed in a bombing raid by the Luftwaffle in 1940.

It only sold a couple of hundred copies at the time, but it's now included in the *Guardian*'s list of 100 best English-language novels, while Anthony Burgess considered it one of the greatest ninety-nine novels written between 1939 and 1984. It's criminal that he's not as universally fêted as Beckett and Joyce because his other three novels (*The Third Policemen*, *The Poor Mouth* and *The Dalkey Archive*) are all works of genius too.

Growing up, apart from some of the aforementioned Irish writers already discussed, I read everything I could get my hands on by — deep breath before listing off such a long list — John McGahern, Brendan Behan, Patrick Kavanagh, Edna O'Brien, Kate O'Brien, John B. Keane, John Broderick, Maeve Brennan, Seamus Heaney, Brian Friel, William Trevor, Maeve Brennan, and Brian Moore, who Graham Greene hailed as his "favorite living novelist." There was a time when I would've wholeheartedly agreed with this assessment.

Then there are the many more contemporary Irish authors that emerged when I was in my late teens or early twenties who have produced great novels too, most notably John Banville, Roddy Doyle, Anne Enright and Colm Tóibín. The latter, surprisingly enough, unlike the first three, has yet to win the Booker Prize.

I mustn't forget to mention Kevin Barry, Colum McCann or Hugo Hamilton either. Nor can I overlook Frank McGuinness, a great playwright who more recently tried his hand at a novel and collection of short stories.

Unfortunately, I've yet to interview any of those magnificent seven mentioned in the above paragraph, but did once get to briefly meet Banville in The Palace Bar, Dublin. It was nice to be able to tell him that his novel *The Book of Evidence* is one of my all-time favorite reads. I was only 16-years-old when I first read it but I can still vividly recall certain passages.

But I've been fortunate to interview many authors that I grew up reading and of these I strongly believe Patrick McCabe's novel *The Butcher Boy* is one of the best Irish novels of the last 40 years. While another book I greatly admire is the Irish-American JP Donleavy's *The Ginger Man,* which is a seminal classic and justly numbered 99 in the Modern Library's 100 best novels of the 20th Century in English.

As the great man himself told me, "I guess that's better than a kick in the arse, as they say!"

I also hugely enjoyed reading Jennifer Johnston and Dermot Healy, who both have their own chapters here. Described as the Celtic Hemingway, Dermot's novel *A Goat's Song* is a masterpiece and Jennifer has written several novels that I would include in the same category. In my teens, I finished one of her books in the middle of the night and, desperate to read more by her, I was outside the nearest bookstore, which was over a dozen kilometers away, early the next morning, impatiently waiting for it open.

Another author in the book I'd also single out is Lee Dunne for his novel *Goodbye to the Hill,* which is very underrated, perhaps even forgotten now that it's sadly out of print. It's about a teenager growing up in the Dublin slums, shortly after the Second World War, with aspirations to become a famous author.

I was an impressionable young teenager when I read this novel and I credit it with planting the seeds of my own grandiose delusions to become an auteur, which is a livelong dream I'm still chasing.

I consider myself very fortunate in my journalist career to have either socialized with or interviewed some of the Irish writers I grew up reading. But I would, in particular, reserve special mention for Lee who personally encouraged me as much as possible to keep up my writing. I was 19-years-old when I was lucky enough to not only first strike up a conversation but ultimately a lifelong friendship with Lee when I went to see one of his plays and spotted him in the audience.

Sadly, Lee passed away, while I was working on the proofs for this book, at the grand old age of 86 in April 2021. He will always have my eternal gratitude. Lee was always very generous with his time and would've needed the patients of a saint to good-naturedly answer all those questions about writing, no matter how obtuse, that I bombarded him with.

Later in life, I even published two of Lee's books when I founded my very own publishing company called Killynon House Books, thanks to my late father Gerald bankrolling the venture, which was a relative success much to my surprise and relief.

One of those books included *Paddy Maguire Is Dead*, which was a follow-up to *Goodbye to the Hill* and was the last book ever banned in Ireland.

It remained out of print for 30-odd years until I had to brainwave to republish it, as my new company's first title in an effort to generate publicity for the venture, which it did.

Incidentally, Lee himself holds the dubious honor of being the most banned writer in Ireland, perhaps even Europe, with eight titles censored. As an aside, I'd the privilege of publishing Lee's final book in 2006 – his memoir, *My Middle Name is Lucky*.

Others included in this collection that have written novels I greatly admire are Sebastian Barry, John Boyne, Joseph O'Connor, Donal Ryan, and Emma Donoghue.

With regards nonfiction authors featured in *The Writing Irish*, Ulick O'Connor's biography of Brendan Behan left a lasting impression on me, as did Peter Sheridan's memoir *44* and Ian Gibson's fine tome on Lorca and his superb biography of Salvador Dalí. (As an aside, I regret never having had the opportunity to interview or meet Frank McCourt Nuala O'Faolain, or John Healy, all of whom penned wonderful memoirs too.)

The last four writers interviewed in this collection that I've yet to mention are, firstly, the hugely popular Deirdre Purcell; secondly, the current Irish President Michael D. Higgins, who is himself a poet, author and journalist; thirdly, the author of the very successful Skulduggery Pleasant book series, Derek Landy; and fourthly, Leland Bardwell, who was considered one of Ireland's greatest poets and a fine novelist too, but sadly underappreciated.

I just realized I've somehow managed to write this introduction without once citing the great talents George Bernard Shaw and William Butler Yates! I'll no doubt be left hanging my head in shame when somebody else more than likely points out my failure to reference others. As I said earlier, there are too many to mention, but I feel this collection offers a good representation of the writing Irish.

Chapter One: JP Donleavy

A stern warning not to enter "without prior notice" hangs on the corroded wrought iron gates at the entrance to JP Donleavy's 180-acre estate. It forewarns ominously of "roaming bulls, wolfhounds and high voltage electric fencing" waiting unwelcomed visitors.

However, there was a far worse repercussion facing trespassers' who dared step onto the property when JP was still with us: that of the legendary author brandishing a shotgun that he was certainly not adverse to using if called upon.

"I remember once someone breaking into the house. I noticed some cold air blowing throw a doorway somewhere. He ran to the window of the dining room and jumped out the window. So, I left off a couple of shells; one on either side close to his ears — enough not to come here again," JP recalled.

"I was being very careful, but I made a point of letting someone know what the situation would be. I may have become a target. People thought maybe I had money or something. But I was a focus in some ways of trespassing people. So, that was my reaction."

Needless to say, Westmeath denizens' never stepped onto the property without prior permission after discovering how JP dealt with that particular intruder.

Having been cautioned about JP's no-nonsense approach to uninvited guests at Levington Park, I joked in one of my newspaper's articles that I had taken the precautionary measure of walking up the elongated driveway waving a copy of the *Irish Daily Mail* to ensure there was no confusion about my identity.

I was met at the entrance of the Georgian home by Bill Dunn, an American journalist. The then 63-year-old proclaimed himself to be an enthusiastic fan of the notorious author, having struck up a friendship after interviewing him for *USA Today* back in 1990. Dunn voluntarily came over for a month to help with the cataloguing all the master's manuscripts to sell on to a university.

He ushered me into the gargantuan parlor. It was elegant but, like the rest of the mansion that was built in 1742 by the third Baronet of Parwich, Sir Charles Levinge, it was unadorned. The room, which was full of old newspapers and magazines because JP detested throwing out reading material, consisted mainly of a big open fire, two chairs, an ancient floral sofa, and a grand piano in the far corner. The walls were adorned with works of art.

While waiting for JP to arrive, Dunn told me that James Joyce once visited the house and wrote about it in his semi-autobiographical novel, *Stephen's Hero*.

A few minutes later, the then 83-years-old author entered the room. I was instantly struck by how healthy and fit he appeared. JP told me how he spent his mornings attended to upkeep of his cattle. A portion of the herd was now down on Lough Owel and just getting there — climbing the hills and going over fences — and back was almost two miles.

"That's a good work out," he said.

Right up until the end, JP spent his afternoons working on his latest opus, entitled *The Dog on the Seventeenth Floor*. He worked in longhand and then had his secretary types it up on the computer.

To demonstrate his remarkable robustness for a man of his age, JP started shadowboxing in front of me.

"How many punches was that?" he asked rhetorically, as all the imaginary punches landed only a short distance from my ribcage.

"You can't even count them. Six punches there. Each one a knockout. I'm busy all the time and I physically work out every day."

JP explained that he learnt how to box at the New York Athletic Club where he was trained by some of the top coaches around.

"The famous referee Arthur Donovan was one of my coaches. He did all the Joe Louis fights. So, I knew nothing but the best boxers in America. You'd be working out with these people."

JP had "a terrible reputation for getting into fights" when he moved here to study at Trinity because others would pick on him because of his "beard"!

"There was nowhere I could go because I had a beard. People would say, 'Why are you growing a beard?' And I'd say, 'I'm not doing anything, you're shaving every day.' It wouldn't take long before there would be a fight.

"But people couldn't fight. Fights were over so quickly. Nobody ever lasted more than, I think, 30 seconds; that would be a long fight for me. In those days I could throw five punches in a second. All landing with my body behind it, so my fights were over so fast.

"I got a reputation. Some man came from Belgium. He'd heard about me. He was one of these paratroopers who'd been in the middle of the war. He travelled to Dublin after hearing this thing that evidently someone was so tough in Dublin. He was going to challenge me to a fight.

"He came over to Davy Byrne's, which was packed, and he said to a guy coming to the doors, 'Where is he?' 'He's that guy at the end of the bar.' He said, 'That little guy!' The guy said, 'That's what everybody says!' Somehow the way this was put to him he decided to shake hands with me, rather than challenge to a fight."

Did you ever lose a fight?

"No, I don't think I ever did."

Did anybody come close?

"No. 15 seconds was normal for my fights. I had a habit of worrying about what I would do to my fists. I still have injuries to my fists from fights. You could knock them out and they'd smash their heads on the ground, but if you hit them in the stomach you bent them over and they fell better!" he said.

Perhaps unsurprisingly, JP became acquainted with Brendan Behan after challenging each other to a fight.

|He was calling me a narrowback in Davy Byrne's and I was very sensitive to any kind of anti-American statements. It took no time at all for me to tell him

to step outside the pub and we'd see who was a narrowback. I looked upon it as a derogatory description," JP reminisced.

"So, we squared off outside. The traffic stopped either side of us. But no one bothered to come out of the pub to watch us fight. And Behan said, 'Here we are out here going to have a fight and not a single one of them has come out to watch. So, why the hell should we put on a fight?' We became great pals after that."

JP said the perception out there of himself being a heavy drinker was inaccurate as he was "careful and very conscious of the damage to the body and stuff." However, he did nostalgically recall many a boozy night out with Behan.

"One occasion he fell, just like that. Crashed. There was a newly married couple in the flat below and the ceiling came off with the impact of falling. There they were lying in bed with the ceiling half-covering the newlyweds," he said.

"I was then giving the job of taking him away. I had to pick him up and put him over my shoulder. And Behan was no lightweight, but I had a farm and was strong enough to do this.

"I went down the stairs with Behan over my shoulder. I thought that Behan was unconscious. And, as I went around the landing, the couples were standing there with plaster and watching us come down, and Behan's head was facing them directly and I heard Behan come alive and say, 'Would you ever fuck off you pair of eejits!' Jesus! Behan could be a real devil.

"I got down to my car, which used to belong to the Bishop of Meath, and I opened the back door and I threw Behan off my shoulder into the car and closed the door. I forgot he was there and I drove all the way back to Wicklow.

"I went into my place and I woke up at about eight o'clock the next morning and I heard this voice — and it was Behan. He'd crawled out of the car and he was going up to a bull to feed him some grass. I luckily saw this and ran out of the house and said, "Behan, get out of the way. That's a bull preparing to attack.'"

Was JP aware that Behan was bi-sexual?

"No one was safe with Behan. Oh, he would (try) with anybody. I always had some lady around, so it didn't crop up. But there's no doubt that Behan would make overtures."

JP stared at me again. Shaking his head, he said how I remind him of a young

Behan. I am ashamed to admit that I was considerably heavier back then, as this was during a period when I didn't exercise and I drank like a proverbial fish.

"Oh, yes, indeed. It took me aback when you first walked into the room," he said.

He then brought me into his study, with its floor covered in boxes from the archiving project at hand, to show me a drawing of Behan. We agreed to disagree on any resemblance. I felt I was much handsomer — even if I was rotund at the time!

"Behan was the first one ever to read the manuscript for *The Ginger Man* and he said, 'That's a great book. That will go around the world." I thought, 'God! Behan, you are such a bloody exaggerator!'" JP told me.

But that premonition back in 1955 came true. Donleavy's controversial debut novel, which was ranked 99 on the list of 100 best novels of the 20th Century written in English, has sold over a staggering 45 million copies.

This salacious book was banned upon its release in Ireland, as were several of his subsequent works. The book is also famous for its decades' long legal battle with Olympia Press over copyright infringement.

JP told me how he was required to write to the Department of Justice and An Post to request permission to have copies of his own books posted to him from the US or UK.

"I was allowed 24 copies or something like that. Banning anything means you'd increase your sales, so I wouldn't complain," he said, laughing.

However, JP admits to being upset when stage adaptation at the Gate was sensationally cancelled after three performances because the Archbishop of Dublin John McQuaid ordered it to be stopped. The play's leading actor Richard Harris told the press he wanted to fly over to Rome with the script to show the Pope.

"It was unpleasant business. It didn't go down well with me. On the first night, someone shouted up from the audience, 'This has got to stop!' But they were frightened of Harris, who is such a big guy. They were terrified Harris might come off the stage.

"The church sent an emissary to the theatre and threatened the owner that

5

if he didn't close this play something would happen. At the time, Richard Harris was standing in front of the theatre and had his back to the wall. I was talking to Harris and one of the theatre door opened and one of the priest's came and as he passed Harris said these words: "There goes a battleship!'"

Recalling his visit to Harris's London flat in the run up to the West End production of The Ginger Man, JP said: "He showed me there was a fist imprint in the top of the refrigerator. It was Harris losing his temper and hitting the refrigerator and you could see the shape of a fist in it. That takes something."

There were talks now of the book being finally adapted for the big screen. The Hollywood heartthrob Johnny Depp, who has starred in the Pirates of the Caribbean trilogy, had two meetings with JP to discuss his desire to play the book's protagonist Sebastian Dangerfield.

However, despite reports to the contrary, JP told me that Depp has not yet bought the film right. And nor did he visit Levington House last year, as some tabloids had suggested. But he did visit JP shortly after this interview.

"He's interested in playing Dangerfield. He was planning to pay a visit here and one thing lead to another and finally I was in New York City and we met up for the first time. He was delightful company," he said.

"He was like a cowboy showing up at my hotel room. I couldn't understand this but somebody explained to me that if anybody spotted him the traffic would stop. There would be sieges everywhere. So, he had to really make his way into the hotel just as he was in this curious outfit. I remember one of his people saying to Mr Depp, 'How did you get here? Did you wear a bag over your head?'

"If he were interested to play it, he's a very fine actor and a major figure, and the combination would be tremendous. If he wants to precede with it than one would let it go ahead, encourage it."

Despite having a reputation of something of a ladies' man himself, JP insisted that he was not promiscuous in his formative years. Prostitution, he said, might have been "rife on the Quays in Dublin, but I was pretty cautious about one's life in that regard" because he feared contracting STDS.

Nor, JP insisted, did he have an endless string of brief love affairs.

"It wouldn't be in the dozens. Anyone who did come around it was always a rather longer-term business, I would never have any brief situations. I never indulged in that at all! I was very careful of my behavior," he told me.

"I've always liked the company of women. Mostly for their intelligence and their attitudes. But they are difficult to find these days suitable for an older gentleman. So, I can't remember finding that many who'd want to spend them around and the loneliness of the place.

"I don't have any contemporary lady friends who seems to be ready to take up any residence here. No one these days wants to waste time coming to a place where there's no one else present. At a certain age, women certainly don't want to be burdened with somebody who might be entering a deep decrepitude."

But JP married twice. The first was with an Englishwoman named Valerie Heron, whom he married in 1948 and, after having two children, got divorced in 1968. The second marriage to Mary Wilson Price in 1970 lasted until 1989.

"Unfortunately, all my wives were such great beauties that they were besieged by men all the time," he sighed.

Did he have any regrets about his marriages not working out?

"Well, only from the point of view that they'd be pleasant company and so on. I was never restrictive to any degree about what, you know, (the) women want to do. What I did not want to have was anybody round me who didn't want to be there. That was very important because you wouldn't be at ease and so on," he explained.

"I made a point of (saying this to) anybody who had any doubts about wanting to be around ... a lot of them would be interested in not leaving the house and all the things, that freedom around the place was here."

After almost an hour of talking in his study, JP then took me on a tour of his mansion to show me his collection of paintings. Since his Trinity days, JP had many exhibitions of his art; the most recent being at the Molesworth Gallery in 2006. His watercolors today can fetch several thousand euro.

"I was doing this along with writing things. I had lady friend Phyllis Hayward, who was a painter, and she would come along to my rooms in Trinity and she would declare, 'Looking at this pictures I know that they signify you're in your cellulite penis phase!' I laughed at it."

7

Walking through the vast rooms, we eventually come across some nude portraits. "Sometimes people posed (naked), but usually I did them from my imagination quicker," he said, laughing.

After showing me his sauna and an idle swimming pool badly in need of maintenance, we eventually found ourselves back in the main parlor. Like the protagonist out of his Dracy Dancer novels about a writer living the life of Reilly in his country estate, JP asked his good friend Dunn: "What could one have, Bill? Is there anything one could have... what kind of stuff does this place have?"

Bill replied: "There's wine and beer. Would you like a glass of wine?"

"What kind of wine is out there? Is there white stuff? Maybe a little chardonnay. Is there anything to chew on out there? There must be something," JP said.

"Cheese, biscuits?" Dunn replied.

"Yeah, that kind of stuff."

As Dunn headed out to get our refreshments, JP asked if I liked his unusual looking leather jacket. He explained that normally it wouldn't be his style, but it was a gift from a multimillionaire lady friend.

"A pal of mine said, 'You know this jacket would cost about $5,000 if you went into a shop to buy it?' This is dear skin, you see. If you feel this, it's unbelievable soft. I didn't realize the jacket cost a fortune."

On the subject of money, JP had often been described as "miserly" in some previous profiles. I told him how I heard he was supposedly switching off all the lights in his mansion at exactly 9pm in order to penny pinch.

He laughed, saying he'd never heard that particular story, which he insisted is fictitious.

"I'm not exactly scrooge-like. You're walking around this place here and it has a couple of hundred acres. This house alone has 25 rooms. It's un-scrooge-like," he said.

He then recounted how his second wife was always throwing lavish parties at Levington Park. He recalled Mick Jagger and his wife Bianca coming along for one of their soirees.

"My wife was the one that did all this partying. I would make an appearance for about three or four minutes, walk around and just leave and not be seen again. No one missed you if you made one appearance," he said.

"I'd be just on my own somewhere in the house, up above. I wasn't a great party person. These were all gatherings that I didn't find myself standing around and talking."

JP bought this Georgian mansion in 1972. Prior to moving back to Ireland in 1969 to avail of the Artists' Tax Exemption scheme brought in by Charlie Haughey, JP had divided his time between the UK and US.

"I had three different places in London where I would hold up. One I referred to as Tax Dodgers Towers! I had one in Fulham and another place in Kensington. I also had a place in the Isle of Man and I also had a place in New York. I'm not sure which places I have anymore," he said.

"I remember the tax inspector had to call me in and say, 'We noticed that you have listed seven different addresses all over. You can't make all of them tax deductable.'"

On the wall of one of his downstairs bathrooms there's a humorous map of Ireland that declares JP Donleavy is enjoying a tax-free existence because of the Artists' Tax Exemption scheme. The poster was obviously put on the wall as an act of self-deprecation humor.

JP was highly critical of the idea of scarping this tax exemption scheme for artists. He said it "has no significance here at all. It might amount to a few pounds here or there."

He added: "It's so ridiculous that it doesn't bare even discussing. In fact, it became worth millions and millions and millions in publicity for Ireland. That's what it did. Millions. And to think now of striking it out would be like cutting your own throat.

"Ireland would be absolutely the laughing stock of the face of the earth to cut that out. It means nothing to the government. It means nothing to anybody because writers can go anywhere to be tax free if they want, if they make enough money. So, it's a total nonsense."

Getting on in years, JP admitted that he quite frequently thought about death.

"It worries me often because if you are totally healthy and have no signs of dying — knowing about how the body works and all the rest of it — at what stage will I recognize that death's encroaches?" he confessed.

"My mother, for instance, lived to be 96. I am conscious of that. I still drive. I don't have — touch wood — any infirmities that I could recognize at present. I know that they must come and will come. And so I just go on. I do my exercises every day. I do my shadowboxing.

"I'm in favor of religion, but I don't apply it to myself in any way. To me it's aesthetic at its best. Religious ceremonies in the Catholic Church are very impressive things, quite stunning to watch this elaborate thing. I'm in favor of all of that. I don't believe in any of the Catholic doctrine things."

JP told me he didn't believe in the afterlife. But, as his friend Bill Dunn added philosophically, "The work lives on."

— 2007

Chapter Two: Sebastian Barry

Hot Press magazine were not the only ones in Ireland celebrating a 40th anniversary in the publishing game in 2017 — 1977 was also when Sebastian Barry started seriously bashing away at the keyboard of his battered old typewriter, harboring dreams of greatness too.

2017 turned out to be another memorable year for one of our greatest living writers: back in February, he became the first ever novelist to twice win the Costa Book of the Year for his superb novel, *Days Without End*. He was inspired to write the insightful novel about a gay character then after his 16-year-son Toby came out to him.

The Dublin-born writer, who now lives in the wilds of County Wicklow, hails from a creative clan and could've ended up going down a number of different artistic avenues. He first toyed with the idea of becoming a painter, when his grandfather took him under his wing as a young boy and taught him about watercolors and acrylics.

Barry might also have followed in his famous mother's footsteps and trodden the boards of the Abbey Theatre. In later years, before her death in 2007, his mother Joan O'Hara was best known to younger viewers for her role as the busybody neighbor, Eunince Dunstan, in *Fair City*. But to our more mature readers, she'll be fondly remembered as one of the finest stage actresses of her generation.

In his student days at Trinity, Barry was always passionate about music and dreamt of following his aunt Mary O'Hara into showbiz. The soprano and harpist had the world at her feet, back in the so-called good auld days. She performed at the likes of Carnegie Hall in New York, before retiring in 1994. In his memoir, the late, great Liam Clancy wrote about how she was a major inspiration to those in the vanguard of the Folk Revival.

But Barry decided to follow in his father's footsteps instead, and to try his hand at writing. He started out as a poet, moving on to short stories and plays — before eventually establishing himself as one of Ireland's leading contemporary novelists.

Q: What do you make of Hemingway's famous saying that the best training for a writer is an unhappy childhood?

A: It's essential. I don't see how you could get your ticket franked for the job without it. I think that's the experience of a lot of writers. Well, certainly this writer.

Q: You once hinted at a "darkness" in your childhood during an interview with the *Guardian*, but didn't expand.

A: I don't go into it, not because I wouldn't be happy to talk about such a thing, but whenever I sat down to write something there's always this shadow book — the marriage of my parents — and I'm always sitting down to write that book, but I never do.

Q: Why not?

A: I would have to wait for people to sadly pass away, but maybe I would have to pass away myself! So, it would be a truly posthumous book because the author himself would be posthumously writing it! It's not only the impossible book but it's the impossible subject for many families. The thing that's almost impossible to talk about — and maybe there isn't even a lingo for it, there isn't even a language, words don't even exist yet really to talk about properly — is the trouble that happens within families. The greatest trouble for an ex-Catholic, or as they call it, a recovering Catholic, like myself, is that commandment: honor my father and my mother. It's an atrocious and ill-advised commandment. And yet it haunts us all. It's very hard to talk negatively about one's childhood.

There isn't really a tradition of a writer hammering their parents in Irish fiction.

Not only that but in Irish literature — apart from the very great John McGahern who did go after his father, long after his father was dead, in his fiction and memoir — there is an elevation of the parent. It is because we are in a predominantly Catholic country. You get those wonderful poems by John Montague or Seamus (Heaney) about his mother. I feel such a wretch for not being able to share in that. I literally envy people who have had and have always had a close relationship with their parents.

Q: Did your parents spend much time with you as a kid?

A: My mother was a famous actor and she was very busy. In the old days, in the Abbey, you rehearsed during the day and played something from the repertoire in the evening. So, you were literally never home. The business of being a parent is being at home. My good father would stray off in the evenings to do whatever he did, as a man about town. We were a little bit unguarded. That's as far as I'll say. And that created a sense of danger for us. We didn't feel safe when we were kids. And my own experience as a father, I was trying to give them a sense of safety — that's why we bought this house here in the mountains — to try to guard them.

Q: Your mother worked with you in later life on one of your plays. I heard it was an uneasy experience.

A: We weren't right together. Something had a thorn at the roots of everything and we didn't know how to fix it. We weren't the gardeners of that sorrow. We all think we speak English in Ireland — and sometimes we mourn that — but sometimes parents and children may seem to be speaking the same language but, in effect, you're not. Almost every word you're using has a different meaning for your listener. If you're estranged from you're parents, even the moment they try to say they love you can be vexed, because the child is stupefied by not hearing it. So, to hear it is almost a moment of resentment.

Q: Was the resentment ever eased in your mind?

A: We were a bit messed up together. At the same time, I revered her. She was the most magnificent grandmother. The kids adored her. When I was a boy she was a terrific entertainer of her children. And that was all true. And it remains even more true now that she's gone. Just the last years were very complicated. So, as you can see, I'm saying two things at the same time, but isn't that how we talk about a lot of things? I think about her a lot. I remember the day she died.

Q: How did you feel when she died?

A: It wasn't a moment of sorrow. I thought she'd gone away, like Billy the Kid. Pat Garrett hadn't got her. She'd got down into Mexico and she's free. I had a sense of her scooting around the galaxies and having a lovely time. It was a relief for me to feel that she'd been just let go, because her body was closing down and she was in those awful chains of illness. I've seen the sorrow of people when they lose their parent and it's not regretful, it's a total feeling of loss because the relationship was so good. I always say to them, "This is terrible. And this sharp pain will pass. But I do envy you your sorrow, you know?"

Q: Was there closure?

A: You know in plays where you get to these resolving scenes? Many people never get to those scenes. I often thought with my mother it was tragic really, when you think she was an actress and had often played those scenes in many an

14

Irish play where there's a reconciliation. And the audience can go home feeling that life is worth it, hard as it may be. I tried to stir her towards them. Because she probably knew the lines from some ghastly play by somebody or other — even myself! — but she didn't. We never got to speak them. It's important to speak them. A person of good heart knows that.

Q: You describe your father as a "man about town." It sounds like he was a drinker. Was that part of the problem?

A: That's always a problem. My mother had come out of an alcoholic family: her father stopped, but her mother died of alcoholism. She died of liver cancer when she was 53. My father's still alive. He's 87 this year. But, yes, there was a lot of drinking in his generation and he partook in it. I don't know how you separate that out from parenting, but I didn't think he managed it, ultimately. It can be very destructive.

If I was an advisor to parents, one of my commandments from on high (*laughs*) would be: give up the sauce in the years where you're parents. So, to answer your question: yeah, that did create a certain amount of trouble. But there's lots of things you can survive. I'll throw in that as well.

Q: Did you ever suffer from depression?

A: I was very seriously unwell — and it's worth talking about. I so admired Prince Harry for coming out and talking about these things. We're obliged now to be open about these issues. Because it's so incredibly painful. If your friend had a gaping wound, or the knee was shot out of him by a bullet, you'd rush in to help, wouldn't you? And bind the wound and bring them to hospital. But mental pain is invisible. People might say, 'Snap out of it.' But it's such an enormous pain. People don't get it. People need to get it.

Q: When did depression first come to a head for you?

A: In '99, I was at the end of an American book tour. By the time I got to San Francisco — it sounds like a song — it was a terrible year where my poor brother, who was 13 years younger, had become mentally unwell and he had to be briefly sectioned. And Donald McCann died. It was one of those years and I didn't deal with it very well. A book tour is very weakening in every way. I really had a meltdown in San Francisco. I suppose I — because we're all so ashamed of these conditions — should've rung somebody and said, "Will you come and get me?" Or, "Can I book in somewhere?" But I didn't: I struggled on. I wasn't sleeping. And that level of suffering, no one can tell you unless you've had it yourself.

Q: It's horrendous…

A: You can't describe it. It's as if somebody has poured acid into your brain and melted it. All the resources that you used to have, tiny little things like coffee in the morning, nothing works — there's no taste in your mouth. I had that for about seven months.

Q: It's not called the black dog for nothing…

A: The black dog, exactly. You're probably too young to have read Beano. There was a wonderful story in those comics. I can't remember what it was called: they lived in a man's head and they stirred him around. It's like some bastard has got in there and killed all the good-hearted preachers in your head and he's taking over and driving — and you want to get him out. Maybe a witchdoctor! A witchdoctor would work just as well for some people, I think.

Q: What finally helped you?

A: My doctor said, "I don't know what's wrong with you. We can try Prozac. I think it is anxiety and it is very painful. You're 44-years-old, why don't you try running every day?" We were living in Mayo at the time. Running in Mayo on those hills, almost anything was better than running (*laughs*). It was a great cure (*laughs*).

Q: Do you keep it up?

A: I run every day, every city I'm in. I'll get up at six to do it. If public schools are an evil in England — I don't know if they are or not — at least the motto is true, "Mens sana in corpore sano": A healthy mind and a healthy body. There is a truth in that.

Q: Did you try meds to deal with anxiety?

A: Well, let me be really honest about it: I did try Prozac for a couple of weeks.

Q: Why did you stop?

A: I started to feel a bit high. I don't really drink, so that was bizarre. I didn't feel very sober, strangely enough. I rang Ivor Browne. He once gloried in the title of chief psychiatrist of Ireland, which I think is wonderful and amusing. And I said, "I'm not functioning at the minute anyway, but this is even worse." I was in great distress. He was very concerned. I just wanted to be able to do something; for instance, like go walking with the babies, or whatever you're supposed to be doing with the children. And he said, "You work out a lot of your stuff in your work. Come off that Prozac and do the running intensively. And see where that gets you. And see if you can get back to work. And maybe that's your balance again." So, that did work for me. Different things works for different people.

Q: Prozac unfairly gets a bad rap...

A: Donal McCann drank because he was very depressed. He told me, "If I had Prozac when I was a young man I would never have bothered drinking." That was the power of that amazing drug. It literally freed Donal from his particular demon. Some people worry that if they take Prozac it'll affect their creativity — it's a load of bunkum. Donal did his greatest work as a sober man. Ivor said when somebody's in crisis it's very important sometimes to make interventions that are highly medical. And also incredibly valuable is a doctor who knows about it and can fine tune things. But look at the outcome: for people to be restored. And, even if one is a little bit vulnerable the whole bloody time, not to be pitching over that goddamn cliff every so often is an immense advantage.

Q: It sounds like Donal's death hit you very hard?

A: It was a rather Greek experience. He brought a little bit of me into the underworld with him. I had to go and retrieve it. I had to bring myself back into the world. I had three small children, so it was an utter emergency and a disaster. And my wife, of course, was probably terrified, if she would ever admit the word.

Q: And then you had to go through that all over again when you and your wife's friend Alan Rickman died.

A: The Gods are either really stupid and don't know what they're doing by taking these people, or are really astute and want these beautiful examples of humanity around them. So, they take them young. Like Alan Rickman, our other great friend. He was the total opposite of what you might expect a great star to be: a very thinking man, rather like Donal. And he worshipped Donal. And Donal hugely admired him.

It's almost unimaginable to think that they could actually leave the earth. I mean, where is that door? How does that happen? And that does engender anxiety because all the things that had you moored, that you didn't even know where mooring you, like a ship doesn't know that there's two ropes at the stern and holding it to the key, but if you take the ropes away it soon finds out. It's like that, isn't it? You feel literally unmoored and you're drifting off, and there's no sailor onboard to help you.

Q: Starting out, was writing a form of therapy?

A: It wasn't therapy: it was like when the hawk goes down for the mouse, that feeling of doing totally the thing that you could do. Even if you could do nothing else, at least this one thing you could do gave you that shot of joy.

Q: You were the editor of the student mag during your time at Trinity.

A: I know on my Wikipedia page they mention that, and I often see it cropping up in things, but it was really nothing to write home about. I did one issue of Icarus. I outraged my fellow editor to such a degree that she detached from the project. I wasn't a great editor in any sense, in that I was already alienating my co-editor. I loved doing it, but it was only one issue. That was my glorious career (*laughs*).

Q: What was university like for you? Were you off boozing and chasing women?

A: I was very odd. I was a bit of a curiosity, old fashioned: a young person that acts like an old man. Also, I wasn't particularly sound, I would say, in the ways that are properly understandable coming out of that childhood. I was a bit rattled. So, I took refuge in certain attitudes, which I regret now. I was fairly arrogant. At the same time, if you're going to be a writer, you do need to have an enormous self-belief and that can come across as arrogant, even to yourself. It's very necessary.

I'm not as arrogant as I was in my twenties — it's beaten out of me (*laughs*). Actually, now that you mention it, they were lonely years at Trinity — until I met somebody right at the end of college. And then we lived together for a couple of years.

Q: Was she your first serious girlfriend?

A: She wasn't actually. My other rescuer (*laughs*), my first girlfriend — again they come to me like Gods in memory — was probably 13 and I was 14. We were together for four or five years.

19

Q: How old were you when you lost your virginity?

A: I can't remember (*laughs*)! That probably doesn't speak well for the occasion! And what is virginity anyway? I actually don't remember. It was probably around 16. But that's good. It's the right age. I'm a bit worried for people who say earlier or later, because both of those things can be a bit dicey riley.

Q: After Trinity, you moved to Paris with your girlfriend.

A: We were there for half-a-year and then we went to Hampshire. It was that very pathetic life where you're wandering around broke. I was literally a kept man. And very happy to be so. There was that glory of getting up in the morning and start a short story on my Olivetti Traveller Deluxe and by evening you'd have seven or eight pages of a story. I mean, such excitement and pleasure. And this lovely girl was very interested in that and hugely supportive. Although it was all a bit kind of vulnerable and mad as well, that was the compensatory thing.

Q: Didn't you meet your wife because you asked her — a total stranger — for a loan?

A: I don't know how true it is anymore! She has her version of it, I'm sure. Well, I had this lovely friend in Dublin, Roger Doyle. We knocked around together intensively. I was writing and he was composing. He had a theatre company and he would get CVs — and one of them he opened it in front of me and this picture fell out, which I looked at in his hall and I thought, "Oh, there's trouble!" It was the first same thought I had when my first son was born: "This is wonderful. There's trouble."

She was incredibly beautiful. Truly beautiful. She was gorgeous. And, you know, most men think they're not worthy of a really beautiful woman — that's the truth of the matter, and that's what I always used to think. If she was beautiful and sane there was no chance!

Q: So, what happened next?

A: A couple of days later I rang Roger and I said, "You wouldn't have a lend of a fiver?" A fiver was a lot of money in those days. I wanted to go to Tobin's. He said, "I don't have any money. But Allison Deegan is here." I said, "Who's Allison Deegan?" He said, "You saw her picture the other day." I said, as if I could see your picture and meant I could say the following, which was: "Well, ask her (*laughs*)!"

Q: So, you really did have the audacity to ask a total stranger for a fiver?

A: It was a kind of a joke. So, my whole happiness is actually based on this moment of levity, you know? And he said, "Ah, ok. Alison, do you have a fiver?" And I could hear her distantly on the other side of the room: "Yeah!" Like really dubious: What the hell is this? Because she was just coming to meet him for work and she's getting this weird (request). And he said, "It's Sebastian Barry: do you know who that is?" And she said quite crossly, "No!" Anyway, we arranged to meet in Bewley's and she would give me this fiver. I think I was two hours late! And they were coming back down the stairs because they were leaving. She was very angry because I was late.

Q: She was probably wondering what the hell she'd gotten herself involved in.

A: She thought she had fallen in with two lunatics. She possibly did in my case! I hope I said I was sorry. Anyway, she gave me the fiver. And then I can't remember how it happened — this is ancient history — the Pink Elephant was a nightclub and Roger went there with people, so he brought me that evening. And she happened to be there and we arranged to meet.

Q: The big question is: did you pay her back?

A: I never directly paid her back. I hope I have in some form or other given her good interest on her fiver. A life out of that moment of daftness really: 'Well, ask her?'

Q: I was reading an interview with Allison in which she said that the first time she met you was like a chemical attraction.

A: (*Sounding surprised*) Did she? God bless her. She's in France. She's on the way home. Now I'm looking forward to her coming back (*laughs*).

Q: Your aunt Mary O'Hara was a huge singer back in the day.

A: She was so gifted that at 17 — at 17 now — she had her own BBC series. She became incredibly famous. She had this most amazing voice and extreme gift. When she sings Archie Cooan (Ardaí Chuain) in The Quiet Land O' Erin she holds a note for about, well, it sounds like a minute-and-a-half. I remember her doing that in concert and smiling right through the note. Very, very beautiful.

Q: She famously walked away from it all to become a nun.

A: Her husband Richard Seling had Hodgkin's Disease — and he died after about 18 months of marriage. So, they never had a bloody chance. She completely lost heart. And she was deeply religious even as a young woman. So, she didn't just become a nun, she founded an enclosed order. I really loved her when I was a child. I thought she was the bee's knees.

Q: Why did she leave the Order?

A: She's stopped singing. And it was as if because she'd stopped singing she'd started to get unwell. And, after maybe a dozen years, she simply had to sing to live. She might disagree with me, but that was my interpretation of it. And she came out. Now, that was like 1973 or '74. And when she came out she had literally never heard of anyone in the '60s.

Q: So she hadn't an iota about The Beatles or Dylan?

A: She'd never heard of Bob Dylan! I remember playing her Bob Dylan. She had actually been on the moon! "What's that? It's like a very old man singing." I said, "No. He's 19. This is his first album." She barely knew who The Beatles were. It was quite extraordinary. It was surreally fantastic. It was like a magic realism trying to talk to her about these things.

Q: Did she like Dylan?

A: I worshipped at the altar of Dylan. I was very distressed when she didn't care for it. She became mega famous again in the 1970s and '80s, but walked away from it again. She stopped because she hated performing. She said, "My voice is still good — I'm going to stop now."

Q: It's funny that you played Dylan for her considering he cited the Clancy Brothers — who'd actually had collaborated with your aunt — as a major influence.

A: Exactly. When I published A Long, Long Way, which obviously is from the song, Liam Clancy came down to an event in Galway for the festival, for the book. I was absolutely thrilled. He spoke so highly of Mary and had known her very well in the '50s.

Q: Did you ever dream about becoming a musician?

A: I wanted to be a singer. I could play the guitar really well, but I couldn't compose.

Q: You're basically a rock star in the literary world these days. You made history this year by becoming the only ever novelist to win the Costa Book of the Year twice.

A: Isn't there an Oscar Wilde quote: 'To lose it once is understandable, lose it twice sounds like carelessness'? Whatever the opposite of that would be. I was told that you can't win it twice.

Q: So, if you weren't expecting to win it, you mustn't have been nervous at the ceremony?

A: I thought I was going to faint — I was so stressed. But when I got down to the floor and I saw the other writers there, and having been told you couldn't win it twice, I suddenly became quite the opposite: I felt lightheaded in a happy sort of way, rather childish actually feeling of I can't win it twice, so it's fine.

Q: You gave a humorous acceptance speech.

A: The first thing I said when I got up was, "You nearly had your first posthumous winner because you gave me such a fright!" It was intensely happy, almost dangerously happy, because it's a feeling of release again of being catapulted, of just being manumitted. It's hard to say what the experience is, but it's also that when you've been through being a parent and you've been in the highs, and the lows and you've done your stupid running because you're half-bonkers, and all the rest of it — all those things become gathered in a little maelstrom of happiness. It's like not only an award for your book, but a little reward for being alive. Writing books is probably not in the scheme of the universe a very important thing to do. But in that moment it seems like the loveliest, brightest, most bedecked circus you could ever be in. The bearded lady is kissing you, the strongman is lifting you up — it's lovely.

Q: Days Without End is an extra special book for you because you took inspiration from your son coming out as gay.

A: Yeah. I was going to write this book anyway, but it coincided with a rather difficult time when Toby — he's at Maynooth studying music — became a bit depressed. I could see that he was suffering, even if, thank God, moderately. But still that's a serious business. And I live in a part of Wicklow where there has been a number of absolutely unimaginable tragedies of young men taking their lives. So, when it happens obviously all parents will then mobilize themselves, they will try to find out what's the cause. Now you're in a realm far beyond language, or ever attaining the language to describe it. So, I moved everything around. Was it his piano studies bothering him? Was it girl trouble? What could it be?

Q: It was obviously a very difficult time...

A: We weren't sleeping, Ally and me. It was a terrible time. He was suffering. And I was terrified. Eventually, he spoke to his sister Carol, who said, 'Toby, just go in and say'. So, after this period of silent suffering he came in with the immense courage required of all young people who have to go in and say something that is not just grown-up but is a sort of immensity all in its own category. And he said, "The thing is, Dad, I'm gay."

Q: How did you feel?

A: The sense of relief when he spoke was so profound. A deep-rooted sense of relief. And I praised his valor. And I made it my business to try to understand as a stupid straight man what this could be. I studied as much as I could. He told me everything he could. We sat and watched RuPaul. It was a PhD in being gay and the professor was my son. I was just about to start the book when all this was happening. I didn't put it in the book, the book drew it into itself in a magical way. Partially because Toby had released us from this crashing worry and it was the beginning of a renewed happiness for him, I wrote that book with a sort of almost unlikely happiness. It was one of the experiences of my life really. It all comes from him, so I dedicated it to him.

Q: You wrote a letter to *The Irish Times* supporting same sex marriages.

A: I wrote a little letter because he wasn't 18, so he couldn't vote. I wanted to help if I could, so I wrote a letter. The default reaction of the middle class Irish male is to write to *The Irish Times* in a moment of emergency (*laughs*). He said to me, "Dad, if this isn't passed I don't think I can live in Ireland." So, there was a lot at stake for me. I mean, maybe he'll go anyway, but I didn't want him to go for that reason because I would've been so ashamed of my country I probably would've had to go too. Certainly, I would follow where he was going, that's for sure. But, anyway, the people of Ireland passed it.

Q: What was Toby's reaction to the letter?

A: He did shed a tear. I thought, "If I can make Toby Barry cry maybe the letter's okay." So, we sent it off and it went viral, which is rather magical. This letter went to many corners of the earth. It was read out in the Australian parliament by the leader of the opposition, because Australia hasn't quite got there yet with this matter.

Q: Did Toby ever experience any nasty homophobic jibes?

A: He was on a train somewhere down the country. And his lovely boyfriend Jack was getting off the train, so they kissed goodbye, as you do with your beloveds. And three or four sons of bitches — I think it was three women and a boy, sitting beside him — seemed to think they had the license to mock him and intimate him because of this kiss! Instead of reverence and happiness to witness such a kiss between two human persons, this was their reaction!

Q: What ran through your head when Toby told you?

A: I did want to go and find them and beat them with a stick, rather than remonstrate them with words. That's how I felt, I have to be honest. I was afraid it would pitch him over back into this really terrible misery. But it didn't. He was resourceful. He mobilized himself. But I could see it had truly hurt him.

Q: It's appalling that anybody could act like that in a so-called civilized society.

A: It is literally a crime. It is a hate crime. I hope it's in the legislation. I imagine it is. Would you let anyone say anything to your child to dismay them in the great innocents of being 16? Would you do that? Would you allow that for any reason? So, why would you either allow it in this case or even engage in it. It's a form of criminality to do so. These incidents of human love are so important that they must be held up. We must hold it up to children in school and everywhere else that this is a great state of being and it has to be celebrated. And if anyone feels otherwise there should be a law passed that they immediately (shouts) shut up (*laughs*)!

Q: I interviewed the Primate of All-Ireland, Archbishop Eamon Martin in *Hot Press* last year and he basically suggested that being gay is not a sin but the act of homosexuality is a sin. Isn't that a load of medieval nonsense?

A: Yeah. Shut up! We do admire him and he said some good things. But, in this instance, I respectfully tell you to (shouts) shut up already (laughs)!

Q: Could you see yourself writing a similar letter to the *Irish Times* in support of taking the Eighth Amendment out of the Irish Constitution in order to legalize abortion?

A: I certainly could. It's not just that every woman's body is their own concern, which is beyond dispute, it's that every woman alive is the concern of all the other people around her to assist in the decisive and difficult business of being alive. Happiness is to raise each other up. And when you're cast down by an emergency to feel yourself being lifted by the arms of the people who love you. That priest saying what he said to you, I mean, how dare he involve himself in the love of my son? I'm trying to keep expletives out of these responses. But how dare he even think for a moment, or try to get a picture in his head of what that might mean, and to tell us what he means when he knows not only nothing about it but he's trying to impose his murderous ignorance on somebody else — and he's supposed to be a caring priest! How dare he trot out his nonsense. I've been at the coalface and I can tell him what he's saying is potentially murderous.

Q: Speaking of murderous behavior, some theatre-goers and critics wanted to kill you — you got a lot of flack over the Charles Haughey play, Hinterland. I read you felt like leaving the country at the time.

A: No, I was told to leave the country! I certainly felt like leaving the country, but also told for a change (laughs), in a letter to the *Irish Times*. You see, it is the default mode of protest. It doesn't really matter if the play was good or bad — it was more the nature of the reaction: because it was just a play and plays have a right to fail. But this was very little to do with theatrical terms: this was a reaction. Mr Haughey was still alive; his wife was still alive. So, it's something that moves into a realm.

Q: How did you feel being at the centre of such a maelstrom?

A: It was very frightening. Of course it would be. Naturally it would if people are talking about suing you, especially if it's a former prime minister. It was sort of a thing I had to process. It was very strange experience and very surreal. And it was something to do with what are the boundaries of literature, how free can you be? Can you write about anything you want? Can words talk about anything? And the answer seemed to be for a lot of people: No! There are boundaries.

Q: And are there?

A: I do think that as long as the writer's heart is true there is no boundary to it because if there is, then you're starting to move into a realm actually that I think Donald Trump would rather like. It was an attempt to say that this had crossed some line, but in literature there are no lines. And societies at various times have tried to draw lines for us. You have to be very careful with all that and, I think, the best role is just let it be; let there be a total freedom of speech and the written word. That's what I would conclude from it. But it's almost as if it happened in another time or another life, in a funny sort of way.

Q: I wouldn't envy you going though such an experience...

A: It doesn't toughen you up because you can't be toughened up as a writer. It does create extra resilience, if only to say to yourself, "Even with this I'll go on." It's nice to find that within yourself the ability to go on. And then a few months later I published a little book called *Annie Dunne*, which was received in a lovely way. What can I say about that?

Q: Nobody's asked what was your deep-rooted motivation for wanting to write this particular play in the first place?

A: Hinterland was an effort to write about my father by not writing about him, pretending it was somebody else, because it's not a portrait of Haughey at all. It's certainly not a portrait of the late Mrs Haughey because the woman in that play is inept attempt to portray my mother. But, anyway, for the purposes of social survival you probably are safer in some ways writing about the past, or what seems to be the past.

Q: Any plans in the pipeline for a movie adaption of *Days Without End*?

A: They're going to make a film out of *Days Without End*, I hope. They're just doing the contract at the minute. They haven't quite announced it.

Q: Are you mapping out a new book?

A: I'll read for a year now and then, hopefully, in another year, I'll get going on something that's as structured as I can make it. I'm sure it'll be a novel of some sort — if I've ever written a proper one!

Q: You swore blind you'd never do another play, but you had one on at the Dublin Theatre Festival.

A: Although I swore that I would never write another play, I did just very naturally. It's called *On Blueberry Hill,* like the Fats Domino song.

Q: What's it about?

A: Let's go see it together and you tell me.

Q: What advice would you give to young writers?

A: In a funny way, young writers don't need advice because they cannot stop themselves doing it. They're unstoppable. In a way, if you need advice you're in the wrong profession (*laughs*). Because it's a mystery. A young writer, young painter, a young composer will, by definition, be not only unstoppable but probably beyond advise. Because it's not a sensible undertaking.

Q: Why?

A: Hopefully every parent now who is told that their son or daughter is gay knows how to deal with it and will be happy and exult and give praise. But maybe it'll never be true when a son or daughter comes to a parent and says, 'I want to be a writer (laughs)'! Maybe running for the hills is the proper reaction, or some form of therapy for the poor child! Because, obviously, the poor child has gone mad and wants to throw their lives into the flames of the uncertain!

— 2017

Chapter Three: Patrick McCabe

Trainspotting author Irvine Welsh once observed that if Roddy Doyle was the Irish literary version of The Beatles then Patrick McCabe had to be the less clean-cut and more rebellious The Rolling Stones.

"It was a nice thing to have said about you," acknowledged McCabe. "But I don't really know if it's true, because sometimes the books are actually apprehended as kind of sparky rock 'n' roll impertinent — and I really never intended them that way, you know?"

"But it's nice. I appreciate the positive review of anything that I do. The Rolling Stones/Beatles thing is fine by me, but I wouldn't see them that way — Irvine's books are more like that than mine."

As a major music fan, McCabe has read *Hot Press*, which is Ireland's only music magazine with a mixture of current affairs, since his teens. "I discovered it long before it was called *Hot Press*," he recalled. "I remember *Scene* magazine, it was edited by Niall Stokes at that time. I used to read that. It was like an NME kind of format and then it became more stylized. *Hot Press* was the beginning of something worthwhile, something valuable."

Pat seems to have an almost encyclopedic knowledge of *Hot Press*. At one point in the interviews, he recalled one of my major HP interview from over a decade ago with former Sinn Féin leader, Tomas Mac Giolla.

On the subject of what has been dubbed the Troubles, Pat confessed that, as a teenager, he did contemplate taking up arms to fight the Brits.

"Back then, at 17, everybody considered joining the IRA. First of all, because the kind of anti-establishment aspect of the freedom fighters was very attractive as a concept," he revealed.

"It was also only ten years after what used to be called the Border Campaign, in 1958. I was around five or six when that happened. The feeling around that time of the Border Campaign — it was why the IRA split in two afterwards — was that the Border Campaign people thought they were going to ignite a revolution and drive the British into the sea, because the Irish Catholic Northerners would rise up. But they didn't. In fact, it was a complete disaster.

"So, when the Official IRA split with the Provisionals they realized — and their thinking was correct - that you were only going to cause a sectarian bloodbath. Politically they wouldn't have been sophisticated enough perhaps in '72 to realize, but I think it was kind of inevitable — that there was going to be an awful lot of bodies in the ground for very little return.

"So, while I had a lot of Republican friends — and still have — I didn't think that it made any sense to fight in a war that you couldn't win. But I thought about it."

As a self-confessed hippy back then, Pat probably was the type of character that Irvine Welsh would've loved to have put under the microscope. Was he dropping acid?

"Ah, I was doing all that stuff, yeah."

Did he experiment with drugs as a way to help shape him as a writer, or is that a nonsensical idea?

"It's the air you breathe when you're a particular age," he reflected. "I think that it's as important as knowing about football or knowing about your neighbor. Psychedelia was just another aspect to it. It was around, it's gone now. And you kind of place it in the canvass of your work wherever you will — it might be foreground or it might be background, but at least you experienced it and you know what it is. But it's no more important than walking the dog, as far as I'm concerned."

What about non-psychedelic drugs?

"What are they?"

Cocaine, I suppose, I said.

"No, I have no interest in that at all. The interesting thing about psychedelia was that it altered your state spiritually — there was something interesting in that," he said.

"But anything else, even hash, or anything like that, used to bore the fucking arse off me! I used to love drinking because at least people loosened up when they were drinking. I never heard such bullshit talked as when I was hanging out in Rathmines, when people were rolling up numbers — I just used to fucking hate it. And I still hate it. But, by and large, I think these were just adolescent entertainments: I wouldn't have any interest in them beyond adolescence."

A story appeared in certain newspapers that Pat was a teacher when he met his future wife — when she was actually doing her Leaving Cert. It is a myth that Pat debunks.

"People are always saying these things. It's just wrong. She was not, indeed, a student. You'll get me arrested! She was not. She lived in the same town alright, but that was it. It's ridiculous," he said.

Originally published in 1992, *The Butcher Boy* is rightly hailed one of the most important pieces of fiction to emerge from this island in the last 50 years. The book was made into a critically acclaimed movie by Neil Jordan and there was a stage adaption entitled *Frank Pig Says Hello*, originally done for the Dublin Theatre Festival in 1992. Now, Pat has written a companion piece *The Leaves of Hell*, which will run alongside Frank Pig.

Pat got the idea of staging the two plays together from watching movie double-bills. He remembers going to the long-defunct Cameo Cinema on Abbey Street in Dublin.

"It was a good kind of dive cinema," he recalled.

"The Cameo had a disinfectant, disreputable quality to it that I liked. It was very common, where you got an arty movie, you get a Bergman mixed up with *The Attack Of The Giant Spiders*.

"It was a kind of a grindhouse culture that, it's very common in America for the Fellinis and the Bergmans — they used to be known as continental cinema, and a bit risqué, so you'd have them mixed in with, as you say, *Police Academy 6*.

"It's kind of in that spirit. *Frank Pig Says Hello*, which was first seen about 25 years ago, and the other one *The Leaves Of Heaven*, is a kind of companion piece to it.

"The two plays are very cinematic. *Frank Pig Says Hello* is very influenced by Fellini. The Leaves of Heaven is a mixture of Fellini and Hammer (Horror) movies, which are the quintessence of trash, really bad taste, or disreputable kitsch. They are very influenced by cinema. Joe O'Byrne is a very cinematic director as well, and he's very informed."

Has Pat ever been tempted to write a sequel to *The Butcher Boy*?

"I couldn't actually write a sequel because I don't really know if I could spend that amount of time inside a mental hospital really! I'd have to do it some other way," he said, laughing.

(Incidentally, Pat did indeed go on to write a sequel entitled *The Big Yaroo*, which was only published two years after this conversation in 2019.)

While there's a lot of black humor in Pat's books, there is also a darkness at its core. "Ireland's a dark place. Let's not mince words. Ireland, you know, has a very troubled history and it was very poor for an awful long time. And it's all very well now with the high-kicking Riverdance optimism, and everything else, to forget that when you went abroad and you opened your mouth, you brought a whole load of history with you that you didn't necessarily want to carry but you hadn't much choice," he said.

"I'm glad that that's all gone and it's very European now. And that's good, but it wasn't always the case. So, there were a lot of emotions that you had to work through and I often worked through them through the characters. I would say that they're very Irish books, in the sense that there's a lot of hilarity and a lot of melancholy. That's a very Irish thing."

There's a lot of oddball characters in Pat's books. Do people think he is one himself?

"Well, you probably would these days because we're living in very conservative times," he said. "When I grew up the place was full of oddballs. People who didn't know what the rules were. Kind of hillbillies, psycho, Jerry Lee Lewis types. And you don't really have those people now, or if they do they're kind of subsumed by X Factor or Celebrity Bake-Off, or something. I don't know, but the machine gets them very early.

"Whereas in my time, there wasn't any structure like that, there was just a kind of rockabilly, I suppose, anarchy in a way, the rural kind of thing — people who don't like being boxed-in by rules that suit the corporate ethos."

What type of music is Pat listening to these days?

"I would be out of touch now. I am a grandfather," he said, self-effacingly. "I'm really fond of Lisa O'Neill. And I like The Strypes. I loved U2's last album. I don't know what everybody's complaining about something being fucking free for! But the songs are magnificent on that album. It's so well constructed. It's really amazing, I think, at this stage of the game to make songs like that.

"I see that Prog Rock is getting kind of rehabilitated now. It went out of fashion. I'd suggest that that was always my favorite kind of music. I would've been a unreconstructed hippy, a sort of a culchie hippy, I suppose you would call it."

Pat has signed a new book deal with New Island and aims to have two novels out, the first was planned for spring 2018 and the second in April 2019, which ended up being the sequel to *The Butcher Boy*.

"A very musical book this one," he promised. "I'd describe it as a redneck opera! I'm serious!"

— 2017

Chapter Four: Jennifer Johnston

Jennifer Johnston was one of my favorite authors in my late teens.

I read the majority of her books during the course of one long summer. I remember after finishing *How Many Miles to Babylon* late one night, I got up very early the next morning and made the hour-long bus journey into Dublin City centre to buy another one of her novels. I can still vividly remember arriving about ten minutes before the bookstore on O'Connell Street opened and standing there stamping my feet to keep myself warm, as I waited impatiently.

During the five years I spent writing a weekly interview for the *Irish Daily Mail*, I thought it was a good opportunity to write to Jennifer and ask for an interview. I was thrilled when she phoned me a few days later and agreed to meet me. I had sent her a couple of newspaper clippings of previous interviews and Jennifer told me she really enjoyed the one with JP Donleavy.

That phone call actually wasn't the first time I had ever spoken with Jennifer — in my late teens, I went to a talk she gave at the Dublin Writers' Museum and I managed to ask a few questions from the floor.

The grand dame of Irish literature was 81-year-old when we met for lunch at a restaurant in Galway city. Happily, time had been kind to the award-winning author who — apart from a walking cane, which she needs since a nasty fall a couple of years back — certainly had the appearance and vitality of a woman much younger than her age would suggest.

During our lunch, she kindly signed my hardback collection of all her books. She was astonished to see I actually had every single one of them. If I had to pick my favorites, I'd opt for *The Captains and the Kings*, *Fool's Sanctuary*, *The Railway Station Man*, *The Invisible Worm*, *The Old Jest*, *Shadow on Our Skins*, and *How Many Miles to Babylon?*

For someone in her twilight years, the Dublin-born author was remarkably as prolific as ever and clearly hadn't lost any of her enthusiasm for the written word. Back then she still wrote every single day. She's now ninety and I haven't spoken to her since that lovely lunch, but I like to imagine she is still writing. I hope there is another book or two still to come.

Q: You once said you were much more interested in acting than writing because of your mother.

A: Oh, yes. When I was at school we were always acting. We were always doing plays. I saw myself going on to become an actress — that was from a very early age, yes. It just seemed to be a wonderful thing to be. Actually, I was quite good. My mother hated the thought that I was going to be an actress for various reasons of her own. And we used to pick rows about this. And then suddenly when I was leaving school she said, "You can either become an actress or you can go to university — but you're not going to go to university and go on and be an actress." She had all these thoughts in her head. So I said, "Oh, I want to go to university." I did some acting in Trinity, but not much and then I gave it up.

Q: Your mother sounded very stubborn.

A: She was domineering and bossy. She used to have little temper tantrums. You spent a lot of your time avoiding the temper tantrums. You just did what you were told. She was a temper tantrum lady. I think that was one of the reasons they separated because my father didn't like that either. But she was a great, great, great lady, absolutely splendid and you could have nothing but enormous admiration for her and what she did and how she was, but she just had her own views about how she wanted her children to be. So, we disappeared and did our own thing.

Q: What did you study in Trinity?

A: English and French.

Q: You met your first husband in Trinity. Was it love at first sight?

A: No. But it sort of grew over a couple of years really. He was the year ahead of me. He was also doing English and French.

Q: And then you got married and moved to France.

A: We lived in France for a year.

Q: How did you find that experience?

A: It was really very soon after the war, you know. It was like '51. The war hadn't been over all that long, so Paris was very run down and nothing worked and the plumbing went bang, bang, bang, bang. But it was fun. It was not Dublin — and that was very important. Dublin was getting smaller and smaller and smaller and smaller at the time, the rules and regulations were very boring and it was just such a relief not to be there anymore. People breathing down your neck — whether it was your mother, or whether it was the church, or whatever it was, there were so many things and you didn't have much freedom and the censorship and all that sort of nonsense went on.

Q: You didn't grew up a Catholic.

A: It wasn't an Anglo background — it was a protestant background. My mother's family was totally mixed. Some of them were Catholics, some of them

38

were Protestants, some were Jewish and some of them were nothing which was pie-eye. And we lived a fairly privileged life — there's no question about that. We didn't have any money, but we had lots of books and lots of friends and we did what we wanted to do and that was ok, except for the fact that there were always people breathing down your backs saying, "You mustn't do that. You mustn't do that," and "You mustn't do that."

Q: You got married in Dublin prior to moving to France.

A: Yes, we got married in Dublin and then we were in France for almost a year and then we came back and moved to London and we lived in London for a long time

Q: You had four children.

A: Yes.

Q: At around the age of 35 when you started to write, I read about how you felt a frustration.

A: Yes, I just felt what was the point on being on this world spinning around if you don't really do something. And I wasn't going to be an actress. I left that too long and I never wanted to be second, I always wanted to be first and if I was going to be an actress I was going to have to start carrying trays, you know. I didn't want to do that. I would have loved to have played star parts — or forget it. So, I thought, "I'll try to see if I could write." And, low and behold, I could, which was some pretty well magic.

Q: But I understand there was a lot of material which didn't see the light of day at first.

A: Well, I threw it all away, so, yes, it didn't see the light of day. It's in the dustbin.

Q: Were there many works that saw, as you just put it, "the inside of the dustbin?"

A: No, because I never finished anything. That was the first sort of thing I thought myself, "You had to finish something." And so I stopped writing unfinished novels and throwing them away and I finished a novel and I sent it to a publisher who wrote me back a very nice letter saying, "This is not quite publishable yet but please send us the next novel you write."

So. I was pleased about that and it was a novel about an alcoholic actor, the idiotic things one does! The next one I wrote was a play, it was a very bad play and it was about a friend of mine, she never knew I'd written it, luckily. And my mother read it and gave it to Norman Rodway who was then in London and he read it and he rang me up and he said, "Jennifer that's a ghastly play!"

At the same time that my mother sent it to Norman, she also sent a copy of it to her agent in London and he rang me up and said, "You know, this is a terrible play. But your writing (shows promise). Go away and write a novel and send it to me when your finished with it."

Q: Which novel was this?

A: And that was *The Gate* which, again he sent to every publisher in London and they all wrote back and said, "No," except the publisher who I finally went with. But by that time I was working on the next novel, *The Captains and the Kings* and he sent it to Hamish Hamilton and they said, "Yes, yes we do like this, thank you very much indeed."

I was terribly lucky that that happened because it won a prize for being the best first novel of the year, which was a prize given by the *Evening Standard*. And it was wonderful. Oh, the joy and excitement of that was absolutely extraordinary. And once you get a prize, you see, then it means the critics read your books and how else do people get to know you've written a book unless critics review them? And the critics reviewed my books from then on and it was absolutely wonderful. So, I was terribly, terribly lucky.

Q: I mistakenly presumed you wrote *The Captains and the Kings* first.

A: *The Gates*. But then Hamish Hamilton rang and said, "Have you got any books hidden under the bed?" And I said, "I have this one." And they published it. And I wasn't very happy about that, but I couldn't say no because I thought perhaps this is never going to happen again. But I don't like *The Gates*. I think it's terribly messy awful piece of work. But then it got published and, within a year, I had two books published. And I had to get a new passport and I put writer on it and that was something else the day I got my passport; I thought, "Yes I'm a writer, it's in my passport."

Q: How long did it take you to write *The Captain and the Kings*?

A: About two years.

Q: So you do a few drafts?

A: No, I just take a very long time.

Q: How many words of a draft would you do?

A: I don't know about numbers of words. Of course, then I had my kids and there were an awful lot of other things happening and I probably only wrote for a couple of hours a day and a lot of that time spent chewing the end of the pen.

Q: I was wondering how you could write a couple of novels while raising children.

A: They'd go to school at 8.30 in the morning, so that was really when I worked.

Q: Was it a burden in anyway having a famous father as a writer starting off?

A: No, because I knew I was never going to be writing anything remotely like him. So, no that, was absolutely no problem.

Q: What about your mam, as was a well-known actress and director as well?

A: No, I didn't feel overshadowed in the beginning of my career not at all. I never felt that they were famous because you don't as child think, "My parents are famous." In fact, I remember once my mother's middle sister had a daughter who was a film star called Geraldine Fitzgerald and when the war was over, my aunt, granny and my mother used to go out to visit her, she used to go on one of these wonderful (ships), The Queen Elizabeth or Queen Mary. And one year she came back and she'd bought herself a mink coat and my mother borrowed this mink coat to come to a school play.

And I remember our school had a long narrow garden and at the bottom of the garden there was this sort of theatre — it was really our gym but it was turned into a theatre when we did our school plays and there was steps down from the school — and I remember seeing my mother coming down the steps with this wonderful mink coat.

And I rushed up to her and said, "Where did you get the wonderful mink coat?" And she got so angry with me; she kept saying, "Shut up! Shut up! Shut up!" She wanted to make out she wore the coat all the time. But I was shaken. I wanted to say, "Look at my mother's wonderful mink coat." And she had borrowed it from her sister and she was so cross with me because I didn't just sort of act in a blasé way.

Q: You once commented, "The pain I felt at the age of 35 troubled me. I wanted to see if I could write the pain out of myself."

A: Yeah. You go on having the pain inside, that is one thing I really discovered. You can write bits of pain out of yourself, but then something else always comes and fills the hole. You must know that?

Q: Yes, I do indeed. I can see it in your writing.

A: Yeah, well, you think, "Well, now this time." I suppose most of my problem was as I got older and as I lived in London and things in Ireland had started to change, but there were always the people who would say to you, "Of course you're not really Irish!" And this used to drive me absolutely out of my mind. And I'd say, "What on earth are you talking about? Of course I'm Irish." Both my parents are Irish, all my ancestors are buried in Ireland and I'm as Irish as anybody else.

Q: Do you think that's true what Hemmingway once said that the best early training for a writer is an unhappy childhood?

A: Well, yes, it would be vaguely true. You have to be capable of feeling pain and knowing why you're feeling it. And I just thought, "Maybe I can sort out the problems in my head by writing them out." And, of course, you don't. But you do understand why people do the things they do and that's important.

Q: As a teenager, I attended a lecturer you gave. I remember you said, "When I start a book I have an image in my head." And this one image you were talking about at the time was that the person was terribly impressed and couldn't get out of bed. You said that image was staying in your head. I think with that particular story you also had an image of a man with birds.

A: Yes. Well, I've always hated birds. And that particular book I really worked on that one. I hate birds. And if a bird was to come in here now, I would have to leave. A real phobia. Absolutely. I don't have any idea where it came from. I don't think anyone has any idea where phobias come from.

43

Q: So all these books start with an image and then you progress from there, trying to figure it out as you go along?

A: As you start writing more and more, ideas come like as if you were holding up a magnet, you know, and bits of metal were flying at it. I don't understand how this happens except it's all coming out of your subconscious and, somehow or other, it turns itself into a novel. I usually know by the time I get to page twenty how it'll end. But I don't know what I'm going to write; I don't make any outlines.

I was so relieved the other evening, the woman who was introducing Dermot Healy to the audience and the guy who wrote the book *Skippy Dies*, Paul Murray. But this woman asked him how many rewrites had he done on this book and he looked absolutely astonished and he said, "None." And I thought, "Good on ya, Dermot." Because so many writers are endlessly rewriting and rewriting — and I can't do that at all. I finish a book and then I'll probably go back through it and then I cut bits out of it, but I can't rewrite. So, I was greatly relieved when I heard him say this, but his books are slightly longer than mine.

Q: His latest book is 420 pages, while your books are usually around the 150 pages mark.

A: It's very good.

Q: It's certainly different. I read the first 200 pages on my Blackberry during the train journey to visit him. He brought me to his local bar and we bumped into the poet Leland Bardwell, who graciously invited me over to visit her the next day.

A: There's a little sort of nest of writers who all live within spitting distance of each other.

Q: How do you take criticism like the trashing of *The Christmas Tree* by the *New York Times*?

A: Yes, it got the most terrible reviews in the *New York Times* — this was so terrible that all I could do was laugh, because it was just too terrible, it really was like a sort of serious personal attack on me by this man who's name was Anatole Broyard. And I asked my American friends about him and they all laughed and they said he's slaughtered an awful lot of people. He wrote about his bad review — and it was after that that they (US publishers) stopped publishing my books.

Q: That must have been frustrating.

A: Yes, it's annoying because I think they thought I wasn't writing Irish novels really, they didn't like what I was saying about Ireland and the American-Irish were not buying my books because they were different.

Q: You're books are different. *Fools Sanctuary, The Captains and the Kings, The Dawning* — all those early books have the theme of the big house with the protestants and the Anglos. You're writing about a different Ireland than perhaps they want to read about — the Irish-American audiences want the John McGahern types, I suppose.

A: They may want John McGahern. But there are other people who they infinitely prefer to me and that's ok. But it did mean that my sales never grew in the States.

Q: But you had a falling out with the publisher in the States?

A: No, not that I'm aware of no.

Q: I love many of our books, such as *The Railway Station Man, The Old Jest, The Captains and the Kings, Shadows on Our Skins*, and *How Many Miles To Babylon?* I read *Truth or Fiction* again this morning, the whole book on the journey up here to meet you. I particularly love *The Invisible Worm*. I also think it also has the best jacket of all your books. It's a beautiful painting.

A: Is that the one with the woman swallowing —?

Q: You're referring to *The Illusionist*.

A: I'll tell you who did that painting was Ralph Feines mother. She's dead. They lived in Ireland for a while. And that was one of her paintings. And when that book was being published my publisher — and she was a great friend of his — said, "I know exactly the jacket for this book."

Q: Did you know her?

A: No, she died then — I think she probably died before the book came out.

Q: Are you working on another book at the moment?

A: I have a book coming out in November and I'm working on the next one.

Q: What's the one coming out next November called?

A: It's called *Shadow Story*. Well, it is a very shadowy story and it's written in rather a shadowy way.

Q: Is that true the character in *Shadow Story* is inspired by your father because there's one scene or two scenes that are similar to interviews in which I've heard you talk about your father.

A: Well, in a way. It's not my father, but the possibility, it's his house, my father's house. Everybody stopped reading his plays — and he did consider himself to be the great forgotten writer.

46

Q: One of his plays I think really cemented Hilton Edwards and Micheál Mac Liammóir reputation at The Gate.

A: That play he sent to the Abbey and he got the script back with "No" written on it. And that was the first play he wrote. So he changed the title and it was called *Shadow Dance* and that's why I've called this book I've written now, *Shadow Story*.

Q: Is there a connection with the new book and your father?

A: No, not at all. It's about Ireland in the '40s and '50s. And it's the voice of a woman looking back at her childhood which was just after the war, her father was killed in the war and her mother marries again and she has a small brother and sister and she never really… well, she loved them all, but she didn't feel totally at home with them any longer. She spent all her holidays with her grandparents in Co. Clare. She becomes a writer and she ends up by writing this book about her own childhood and that's all it is. Nothing happens. There's very little drama in it.

Q: In *Truth or Fiction*, there is a lot of your dad in there, isn't there?

A: Well, not him personally, no. But my son Patrick wrote that bit in *The Irish Times* about it.

Q: There's a scene in the book where the character Desmond, the writer, sits down with his daughter and he tells her about his unrequited love and his regrets in life and that sounds similar to a conversation you had with him.

A: Oh, yes. Well, there were things but he never turns into my father actually.

Q: From what I know about your father, I think this character is similar but different: they're both playwriters; they both went to war; they both married to an actress and he was a rascal but I don't think your dad would have been as bad as this character?

A: My father wasn't good!

Q: But I don't think he was that bad as a character in your book, or maybe I'm wrong?

A: He wasn't like that character — as far as goodness or badness goes there's not much between them both.

Q: I understand you'd a lot of admiration and respect for him growing up until you read his diaries.

A: I wasn't able to read his diaries, but the one bit that I did read was referring to something that had happened to me at home. And his vision of what this was, was so totally and utterly untrue that I thought, "I'm not reading anymore of these diaries because they are the way he wanted life to be, not the way life really is."

Q: It must have angered you?

A: Well, it annoyed me yes — because people really believe that when you sit down and write a diary that it's a true story and he put the truth as he wanted it to be.

Q: He was rewriting history, which a lot of writers do that as they get older. I've seen it with other writers that I know they've rewritten their history to suit themselves. I think it's a natural thing in some ways, isn't it?

A: Well, he wrote these diaries a long time ago, as they were happening more or less.

Q: Your parents separated by the time your father went off to report on the frontlines of the Second World War. How did it affect you?

A: More or less. But you don't know any of these things when you're a child — I was eight — because the War started and my parents perhaps, with the best will in the world, didn't tell us that they were separating. The War was on, so it was a very good reason for my father not being at home — nobody ever told us why when he came home on leave he didn't come to us, he stayed with my grandmother and you sort of get used to it.

It wasn't until I was about fifteen that I was told — I was told at school that my parents were divorced, (by) somebody else whose parents were also divorced and she was very pleased to find out mine were too. Because everybody else and all the adults in Dublin knew, I was raging, absolutely raging because it seemed so unfair that one had been lied to for all these years.

Q: He went off to America and had another family. You've two half-brothers. Were you able to have a relationship with them?

A: No. I feel quite bad about that. Michael (my brother) was much better than me; Michael used to go and stay with them in America. So, he actually knew them better. But I've been lazy about that and really haven't. One of them is dead and I didn't see either of them much at all. But we were always very polite to each other. But that was all — we never became pals.

Q: Did you ever talk to your father about your own work?

A: I suppose it would have been in the '80s, we had been out somewhere or other and he came in and switched on the television set in the way one does and I suddenly heard my father's voice. It was RTÉ and he was being interviewed. Suddenly, this man said, "What about your daughter's work?" And my father said, "She is the most wonderful writer." And I was taken totally aback.

I know when it was: it was just after I had written *Shadows of our Skin*. And he said, "There are just bits of her writing that are absolutely wonderful and I'm so proud of her." And I just burst into floods of tears and the whole thing ended then. And I just sat there sobbing, looking at the television set.

And he never spoke to me about my work never, neither did my mother. My mother used to do awful things like push me into a crowd of people and say, "This is my daughter, Jennifer Johnston who's very famous." So, basically it was much easier when neither of them talked about my work. But he never did and that was the only time that I was aware of how he might or might not have felt about it.

Q: It's peculiar how he could say it in public but yet he couldn't say it directly to you. When both your parents were at the end of their lives, did you get on well with them?

A: The last five or ten years of my father's life, I really got on quite well with him. He didn't want to talk about my work, but we did become much more friendly and he was always terribly nice and kind and chatty, and appeared to like my kids and they loved him. I never had any problems with my mother at all. We had the same slightly turbulent relationship always, but she was just a wonderful woman — she just was a strange mother.

Q : You've wrote a scene between a father and daughter in which he's talks about his regrets in life. Did that that really did happen? Was there was a moment where you sat down with your dad?

A: There was a moment where he invited me out to dinner when I was in Dublin. And I was terribly pleased because basically my brother, my own brother, not one of the half brothers, is the person who I have always envied, because he was the one my father really seemed to get on well with better than anybody else. And they both had been in Cambridge and they used to go back to Cambridge once a year. And my brother would drive my father in his car and I thought, "Oh wonderful and they would have talked and talked about everything, absolutely marvelous, this car all the way from Dun Laoghaire to Cambridge and back again." So, I said this to Michael once and he just burst out laughing and said, "We never say a word. We hardly ever speak!"

But my dad invited me to dinner and we had a very nice dinner. And as we were munching on, he suddenly said, "There's something I would like to tell you." And he started to tell me about the great love of his life. I really didn't want to know about the great love of his life. I really didn't, but he told me and I felt terribly sorry for him. I said, "Oh God! You poor man. This is very sad."

Afterwards, looking back on it, I thought, "He was a bastard. He just wanted to hear me say those sort of things to him: 'Oh! I'm so sorry.' And, 'How wonderful.' And, 'How sad.' And, 'How blah…'" And it wasn't true, you know. I don't think it was true like he told me; I don't think his heart was broken; and I don't think he had spent the rest of his life grieving. She married somebody else and this had all been going on while he was married to my mother and was having an affair with Betty and the great love of his life was happening at the same time — for God's sake, you know!

Q: So he had two affairs?

A: Two affairs and a wife. And, you know, this is one reason why I wrote that book; I thought, "I can't keep all this rubbish inside myself anymore."

Q: I was going to ask you about your own regrets in life. Do you have any?

A: Oh, yeah. Everybody has regrets in life. But I mean they're not earth shattering regrets. I'm not going to tell you what they are — all you can do is ask.

Q: Your mother got to see your work on stage.

A: She went to a couple of my monologues — that was kind of embarrassing because one of them was on in The Peacock in Dublin and it was done at lunchtime, it was an hour long and it was one about an actress. It wasn't totally a monologue, there were a couple of other people in it too, but it was mainly a monologue. And the woman who was playing the old ex- actress, who was a very good actress called May Cluskey but she had decided that I had written the play about my mother, so she did her act on my mother — and I hadn't seen any of the rehearsals!

David and I were going to Venice, just after the first performance. And I went down to the dress rehearsal, which was the night before, and I was just shattered and there was nothing then that I could do; I couldn't say you know, "For God's sake! Stop pretending you're my mother. This is not about my mother." And it was a very full audience and they all thought that I had written a play about my mother. And my mother thought I had written a play about her too.

The woman ends up the play by tearing up all her reviews, which she's got in a big box. After it was all over, my mother swept out of the theatre, refusing to stay for lunch or whatever. And she said, "No, my darling, I'm going home to tear up my reviews!" So, I was so relieved that we were going to Venice — I couldn't get out of the country quick enough! She was furious.

Q: Did she ever forgive you?

A: Oh, yes. The great thing about my mother was she used to get furious quite easily but then she'd stop being furious. And when we were children, if she had one of these furies she always gave you presents the next day. My mother never remarried. Marriage was not for her, but she did love her two children very dearly and she would have been a very different sort of person if she hadn't had Michael and me. But unless everything went exactly the way she wanted it to go… she and my father would never have made a go of it. Eight years was pretty good, I reckon. Well, nine years. My mother was the youngest by 17 years, of a large family. Well, she and her brother; there was a couple of years between them. Then there was 16 years and then there were the others. My mum passed away in '85. My father died in '84.

Q: It must've been a very difficult time for you with both of them dying within such a short space of time.

A: Yes. It was strange the difference of their dying. My father was in hospital for a long time and his second wife had died in March. He was in a nursing home in Dalkey/Killiney and we used to go and visit him. We went everyday. The last week of his life, I was down in Dublin and we would sit there and Michael and I used to sing songs to him. And he sort of drifted away and he died with us in the room. And we were there, just Michael and myself. And the other two boys were not in the country even.

But really, you know, crowds of people didn't go to see him or anything like that; occasionally people came; Victor Griffin who was the Dean of St. Patrick's Cathedral came to see him, other people were just occasional.

My mother for the last two weeks of her life was in a nursing home and she had cancer and there were just queues and queues of people. It was the way they related to other people. My mother was a very warm, loving person and my father had no emotions. He had lots of friends but no emotion. And she was a very awe embracing person and this sort of manifested itself in the way they both died. It was strange.

Q: When did you move back to Ireland?

A: '74.

Q: Did you move back with your first husband or had you broken up by then?

A: That was why we moved back.

Q: So you separated after your fourth child was born?

A: Oh yes, he was seven or eight at the time.

Q: That must have been very difficult.

A: It was yes. I don't want to talk about it.

Q: I don't mean to pry but was it a sudden break-up or was it something that dragged on?

A: No when it started, it happened quite quickly.

Q: How did you meet your second husband?

A: I met him in Donegal. He had a cottage up there and I just met him there. He lives in Derry.

Q: How long after you broke up did you meet your second husband?

A: No, I met him before.

Q: Oh, I see. When did you get married the second time?

A: How long was it? It wasn't very long, got divorced and got married then immediately just like that. There was no sort of hanging about. What's the point in hanging about, you know? We all thought that.

Q: Then you moved to Derry. Your second husband had a big house there. I didn't know about it until I looked up your address to send you a letter, but I've seen a photograph and it looked fabulous — so you've been living there since the mid-70s really. Did your children moved there with you as well?

A: No. The two oldest ones were grown up. The next two were 12 and 9, or something like that, and they lived with their father in school term time and they came to me in the holidays. And the older ones just did what older children do. I mean, they were both in Trinity by then.

Q : That must have been difficult for the younger children; they were in London at school.

A: Yes they were in London — well it was indeed but they bore it very well, God bless them.

Q: What was it like moving to Derry like in the 1970s?

A: A little scary, but it was ok. Everybody was very nice to me. And I knew that part of the world quite well, because my first husband came from Strabane, which was only just down the road.

Q: You've obviously got a thing for Northern Irish men!

A: My mother was very cross about that!

Q: Did you ever get any nasty letters, or death threats or anything like that?

A: No, no. The nearest thing I got was when I was still in London, but there was some idiot who blew up some army barracks in England and blowing this up they killed four or five waiters or something like that — two of them were Irish. And I wrote a furious letter to the *Irish Times* saying, "This is quite ridiculous." And then I got a threatening letter from somebody or other over here and I brought it into the police and gave it to them and they said, "Well, we'll keep an eye on your house." And that was the nearest I got so far to death threats.

Q: Did you feel living in Derry has influenced your writing much? *Shadow on our Skin* was about the North, but then you started writing about Dublin more recently.

A: Oh, yes, that's where I know best. And the people in the North are very different, even *Shadow on our Skin* they all talk like people out of a play by Sean

55

O'Casey rather than the real Derry people. I mean one thing I have written was a monologue called *Twinkle Toes* and it's about a Derry woman. I wrote it after I had been working in Long Kesh for six or seven months and it was about the wife of a prisoner and that really has got a real Northern voice. It worked but otherwise I can't do the North at all.

Q: How long were you in the prisons?

A: About eight or months. It would have been the beginning of the '80s sometime — the prisons were full and I was asked by the welfare people would I go and talk to the men and I said yes and I went up for about eight or nine months, about twice a week.

Q: Did you enjoy it?

A: Oh, I didn't enjoy it, but I really liked it. It was very, very, very interesting and the men were very, very, very nice. And then I had to stop because I think I was working very hard on something and this was taking up an awful lot of my time and an enormous amount of my energy mentally and so I stopped, but it was great.

Q: Who were your own favorite writers growing up, because you have your own unique style, short paragraphs but I've noticed they're getting a bit longer. In the books you wrote in the 1970s and 1980s, the first ten books anyway, the paragraphs were extremely short, almost one sentence. Where did that come from?

A: It just came out of my head the way it came, you know. That's the way it happened and that's the way it seemed to me that it was right. And I know that lots have laughed at this but that's the way I would do it.

Q: I love your style. I remember picking up *The Railway Station Man* and the first line is simply the word "Isolation." It was as if the words were dancing off the page…

A: Well, when I started to write first I wrote till I was about 18 and then I stopped and the people I suppose I liked best — you know, once you leave *Alice in Wonderland* — were, well, Jane Austen, Ian Foster. I love Ian Foster. I love people who are sticking their barbs in — and wit. (John) McGahern obviously much later because he was such a wonderful writer and such a wonderful man. Oh, he was just wonderful.

Q: He was another person who wrote in short paragraphs — but not as short as you. You also mix first person and third person narratives together in your novels, which I really like too.

A: Well, it seemed to me to be the only way to express things that I wanted to express and to be able to try and put down what somebody's thinking while they're talking at the same time, you know, that sort of role of a ranged personality I couldn't think of another way of doing it, you know, except like that.

Q: Also, you move stories forward via dialogue, which is unusual. I was reading *Truth or Fiction* this morning and in one scene the old writer is coming into the pub and Caroline is sitting with his first wife and she says, "Oh there you are, come over to us?" — rather than describe him walking into the room you lead him in through dialogue, which is unusual. There's a lot of dialogue in your work. The stories move forward with dialogue.

A: Yes, I love dialogue. There's a French writer who has written a couple of novels, which are just nothing but dialogue — they're absolutely fascinating.

Q: And when you where in your 30s who were you reading?

A: I loved Salinger. (I read) *The Catcher in the Rye* when I was about 20. I thought, "This is wonderful." It was just written then. In my 30s, I was reading everybody. I didn't start writing till I was about 35.

Q: You were saying if you were to be an actress you'd want to be the star — was it the same for writing?

A: No. I knew if I was writing I'd be doing it all on my own terms. And if I didn't get to be a star — there was nobody to blame but me. And that's the way I've always wanted to be. I've never ever, ever wanted to work for anybody else or do anything. I mean, it's piggish of me I know, but it's the way I am I just want to be me.

Q: You've managed to make a good living out of writing as well, haven't you?

A: Yes.

Q: Which is highly unusual for an Irish writer today. A lot of writers nowadays supplement their income by doing journalism.

A: Oh yes, but I happen to be married, which means I get a lot of bills paid.

Q: How do you spend your days now?

A: Writing everyday, not very many hours. John McGahern once said, "You couldn't write creatively for more than two hours a day!" And when I heard him I thought, "I love you so much." It was wonderful; it was just Manna from heaven. He's probably right. He said you can do other things, correct things, but you can't write creatively. And you see more people who say, "Oh, I get up at six and I write till nine thirty and I have breakfast and I go back and I write till lunchtime and then I have a cup of coffee." And I think, "God! You are a bullshitter!"

58

Q: Is this true: there was a story — and I'm not sure if it's true — your first novel, maybe it was *The Captains and the Kings* or the first written book, *The Gates* — that the publisher brought you in to a meeting and he said, "It's a good book but we don't see you as a writer!"

A: Oh, that was the very first one. *The Gates*. And that was not my publisher, that was one that rejected me: Jonathan Cape. It was a man called Tom Nasher and he summoned me in to go and see him and it sort of become an idiotic story in my mind. In those days, people were wearing flares and I had this ghastly (attire) — what looked like a bus conductors suit on — and it was horrible. And I thought, "This is what I'm going to wear." And I brushed and combed my hair.

And I went off the Primsbury Square, or wherever it was. And the door was opened by a sort of vision in a beautiful dress and high heel shoes, looking absolutely a million dollars. And she brought me up to his room, which was enormous. And he was sitting at the desk right over there dressed in pale blue; everything was pale blue and he was doing this (tapping) on a pile of papers, which was my manuscript. And he was just horrible, absolutely horrible. I've written about it in one of the books. I can't remember which one.

Q: I understand you're not a religious person, but do you believe in Heaven and Hell and that type of stuff?

A: No. I spent my childhood days — well my adolescent years rather — saying, "Will I rush out and become a Catholic? It seems to be the right thing to do." And, of course, when people used to say, "Well, you're not Irish — you're not a Catholic!" All these things go into your head and they stir around inside, you know. I thought, "Well. maybe I have to be Irish, maybe I have to be Catholic?!"

My elder daughter became a Catholic at the age of 20. She's terribly un-Catholic now. She was received by the Jesuits. And David and myself and my father went to the service. And my father was intrigued but furious. And I was amused but I also thought, "Good on her. That's great." She did remain a Catholic for about five years and then the Protestantism came back, but I don't think she's anything now.

Q: You're one of the most distinguished Irish writers — perhaps you should have written a memoir.

A: Me? I haven't got anything to write about!

— 2011

Chapter Five: Dermot Healy

Dermot Healy was often hailed as the Celtic Hemingway and even described as "Ireland's greatest writer" by Roddy Doyle. But when I met him only two years before his death, Dermot acknowledged that most readers had "forgotten" about him because at that stage he had been almost a dozen years in the literary wilderness without publishing a single book.

"But I'm slow anyway. I am a slow writer. This new book took me 11 years," he told me in 2011 when he very generously invited me to stay overnight at his home in Sligo to interview him for a profile piece I planned to publish in the *Irish Daily Mail*, which he was doing to promote his last novel aptly entitled *Long Time, No See.*

"I had it finished practically in 2002. And all of a sudden, I went off to do a play, came back and I couldn't find my way into it. Then I went to the poems and they took the same period. So, one was against the other, if you know what I mean?" he explained.

"The head would go into the poems, then the head would go back into the novel. But I returned to the novel about a year-and-a-half ago and got it finished. And it was actually finished. It was just a matter of cruising to the end. I was trying to find a way of getting out of it, that left it to the reader. And, all of a sudden, I found one day I had finished it. *A Goat's Song* did take long, but not as long as this!"

What inspired him to write *Long Time, No See*?

"The novel is about the thing of having something happened to you once upon a time and being haunted by it. I wanted to do the dialogue," he said about the novel written in a style that's heavy on dialogue.

"The dialogue was driving me mad. On the train to Dublin, I'd be filling books and books of dialogue. And here I'd be writing late at night, so all of a sudden the shape of it began to take place.

"I didn't have a clue where it was going to end up. I was pursuing the thing of oldness and youth and the two different speaks that come out of them. The funny thing is there's no sex in the book, as someone pointed out, which is unusual for a long novel."

It was quite understandable that the award-winning author was desperately hoping his latest opus (and sadly last) would get tongues wagging with excitement when it was released. Sadly, the publicity generated during its first week was for all the wrong reasons — with his book at the centre of a literary catfight after a war of words between critically acclaimed authors John Banville and Eugene McCabe.

After it was savaged by one of the country's then leading literary critics, Eileen Battersby, an incensed McCabe felt compelled to lash out in *The Irish Times*' letters page to accuse her of disgracefully "disemboweling" Dermot Healy's work. He also insultingly described one of her own creative short stories as "shite and onions," to paraphrase a poem by James Joyce. It prompted the Booker Prize winner Banville to fire back a missive for what he described as McCabe's "ad hominem and scatological assault" on Battersby, who tragically died in a car crash in 2018.

This controversy blew up about a week after I had visited Dermot.

"I didn't know anything about Eugene sending that letter," Dermot told me when I phoned him about it. "I only heard the whole thing because I was in Dublin doing the launch. It's nothing to do with me."

But surely Battersby's scathing review must have left him reeling?

"It's just two visions of the book," he said. "Someone who doesn't like it and someone who does. Simple as that. The review is her account — that's her reader's view, and then you have someone else's view. Reviews are reviews — a bad review, a good review, it makes no difference."

One can't help but think that the Sligo-based author must have been putting a brave — and, indeed, gracious — face on things. Certainly, according to sources close to him, while he may have taken the review on the chin, publicly anyway, Dermot was apparently miffed by how other prominent authors failed to jump to his defense in light of the awful book review.

But this was far from the only storm surrounding his latest novel. When we met, I put it to him that I heard an ex-partner was so concerned that a character in the 400-page novel was based on her that she got a solicitor to go through the manuscript.

Reluctantly, the then 63-year-old defensively conceded: "Yeah, but we can't enter into that. You better steer clear of that. People do read themselves into things and you have to fight it off. I don't want to go into it. It's all wrong and it's over. No, you can't bring it up."

Dermot was noticeably touchy about the subject because he had been accused of doing exactly the same thing to another ex-partner. When his critically acclaimed novel, *A Goat's Song* was published, the literary world was fueled with speculation that the protagonist's love interest — an actress in the book — was based on his former girlfriend, a prominent journalist.

"But that wasn't true," he told me. "And she realized that when she got a hold of it. No, it's a con that. It was a myth. It was never based on anyone."

But wasn't it true that his ex-partner also hired a solicitor to demand changes to the manuscript of *A Goat's Song*?

"No. That's not based in truth. One change in it was, I changed from Donegal to Mayo. I can't go into that. You're bringing up a legal thing. There would have been a thing because it was set in Donegal. But, anyway, it didn't, it went through," he insisted.

When I ask how long he was with his ex-partner in question, he responded, "Ah, Jesus, you're not putting this down in the paper? No, you can't go into that. It's not a good place to go into. Leave it. The thing is with novels people read themselves into the parts. That happens."

Regardless, the book in question is rightly considered to be an Irish masterpiece. But Dermot appeared very modest about his success, which spoke volumes about the man.

"It did well, I suppose, in terms of sales. I can't really speak about that — I can't value judgment about my own books. I leave that to the reader," he said.

The Westmeath-born writer, who grew up in Cavan, had lived out his final years with his second wife, Helen, their dog, Tiny, and horse, Lucky, on a picturesque acre-and-a-half site by a jagged precipice that looks down on the Atlantic. He had a son, who "lives down the road" from him in Ballyconnell, from his marriage to his first wife, Annemarie. He also had a daughter named Inor from a different relationship, which he was reluctant to discuss.

Speaking about the break-up of his first marriage, which lasted "about eight years," Dermot said: "We broke up, but we're still the best of mates. It was lonesome. For the pair of us. It was a lonesome drifting apart. We didn't really separate, you see? Because we remained friends."

But obviously they got divorced because he is now married to his second wife?

"No, we didn't get divorced. We got married in a registry office, myself and Helen. So, no divorce," he insisted.

He must have got divorced or had the marriage annulled? "You can't be legally married twice?" I pointed out.

"No, I didn't. Ask herself, she'll tell you. No divorce," he said, stubbornly. (Thankfully, it turned out that he wasn't a bigamist. For the record, Helen clarified her husband was divorced when they married!)

He met Helen, who worked for Bank of Ireland, back in 1988 when a friend introduced them outside his favorite pub in Sligo town. Was it love at first sight?

"Ah! Whatever you call it. We got on," he said.

Though a reluctant talker about himself, Dermot is undoubtedly a man of words. It was, he admitted, "a lie" that propelled him to first carve out a writing career. "The first time I walked myself into it. I used to be at it (writing) and people would ask me, 'Are you doing anything?' And I told a lie one time and I said that I had a play coming up in London," he said.

"I said it to a fella in the *Anglo Celt* newspaper. And, of course, he put it in the paper. I ran and started writing! So, all of a sudden, I was pressurized by a lie into performing."

Dermot first started writing as a child, but he became more focused on it after his father tragically died. He recalled: "My father died when I was quite young, about 14. He'd been ill for a couple of years, so I used to do my school exercise by his bed. It left a deep impression. He died on Christmas Day. Twenty years later, my mother died on St Stephen's Day. It had a strong effect and a sense of loss."

He believed his schoolteacher introducing the class to Dickens' *Tales of Two Cities* was the inspiration behind his love for the novel.

"The Dickens thing helped enormously because for the first time you got the shape of a novel, of that type that you wouldn't have read at that age, 14. It comes to my mind as a great debt," he told me.

"I think another thing that was very helpful was reading comics from about ten, the classic series, which did all the famous novels with pictures and they became an insight — a visual one, plus a literary one. So, they were a great help. I just enjoy doing it. And I enjoyed writing in Irish as well, at one stage. I suppose I started in primary school. I just enjoyed it. I did a lot of reading," he said.

Dermot's "real breakthrough" as a writer came when he was noticed by a British publisher after one of his short stories was published in the now defunct *Irish Press*.

"I started off with the short stories and the poems and I never thought that I'd reach a novel. It was purely the publisher in England published the first (collection) of short stories and then said to me, 'A novel?' I turned to the novel but I didn't think I'd be able to make it. But I did it in about two-and-a-half-years. It's one called *Fighting with Shadows*. It did fairly well," he said modestly.

Ironically, Dermot, who had been toiling away in London doing different manual jobs and had even "painted the publisher's office prior to publication."

He continued: "We were going around painting houses at the time. I lived in London for a good few years, doing various things — insurance, security, building sites, everything. I had worked in all kinds of things — supermarkets, bars, everything — growing up.

"One of the images that I always have of working in security is driving up the middle of London, piles of people on the streets, and me sitting inside with a million pounds, in my underpants — because it was so warm, I used to take my clothes off in the back of the van! Coincidentally, I ended up renting a room from a family called Healy and the youngest was Dermot.

"I was over and back to London many times. I came back, I think, in '82 and I went to live in Belfast and then down to here, Sligo. That's 29 years ago. So, take 29 away from 63, what do you get? I was in my late 30s."

Why did a Westmeath man pick Sligo, of all places, to settle down?

"Pure chance. I came down and I didn't even know I was going to stay. Didn't know at all. And all of a sudden I realized that my great grandfather and grandfather on my mother side came from Sligo," he recalled.

"And of all a sudden, I felt, 'I can stay here.' And I worked for a while in Ross's Point with the boats. I worked fishing boats for a few years. Then, all of a sudden, moved out here. That was about 23 years ago."

Dermot never became rich from his stellar writing career. I was shocked when he told me he had only received an advance of £20,000 (which I can't recall if it was in Irish punts or sterling) for a three-book deal. It was then Dermot's turn to express surprise when I mentioned I had earned more than double that figure for my previous two non-fiction titles, which were never going to set the world on fire!

(Incidentally, over half the Irish writers consulted for a survey (58.7 per cent) said they earned less than €5,000 from writing-related income and more than a quarter (or 27.9 per cent) of respondents said they earned less than €500 a year, according to Irish authors' incomes, which was published by the Irish Copyright Licencing Agency in 2010.)

"I think I'm very fortunate to be a member of Aosdána," he said in reference to the Irish association of artists that offers a year stipend to allow its members to work full-time as artists. The annual sum was reportedly €17,180 in 2015.

"Would I have made...? No, you wouldn't. There's times you do and then there's a long period of nothing. I've workshops, readings, there's all type of things to make the money come in. But you wouldn't be (dependent) on anything...

"There's times when I would have only had the £12,000 Aosdána had. That would have been my only income for maybe a couple of years. And then when I get an advance I'd step down from it. When I got the advance for this it was so long ago, it was burnt out in about, I'd say, eight or six years. But I try to keep it going."

Did he ever worry about money?

"Oh, I would have been. But not to a bad extent, no. The spending wouldn't be too big anyway, you know what I mean?" he said.

"And doing the work here meant we were able to do the house cheaply. And he (the builder) was great the man I worked with. So, yeah, there would have been periods. But I don't remember anything like poverty or anything like that."

On the publication of his first book, Dermot remembered being so broke that he could barely afford the train fare to one of his first major book-signing events.

"My publisher from Ireland was to meet me at Heuston Station. I was late and he was gone. I had just the amount of money to buy the ticket and a bottle of Guinness and I was standing there thinking, 'Ah, Jesus! Is there any way out of this?'" he said.

"I got a tap on the shoulder from a fella I knew. I told him the story and he said, 'Here, I'm a registered lunatic! Go over and buy your ticket with my pass.' So, I took his discount pass and bought the ticket. He said, 'I'll take the pass back because I'll need it. But if on the train they ask you where's your pass, say Mammy took it from me!'

"So, I got on the train and ordered the bottle of Guinness and sat down, with a man opposite me reading *The Irish Times*. And we started chatting. There was another four people on the left; they started chatting to me. Enjoying myself. Bag full of books; my first publication; on my way to my first launch and feeling great.

"And the next thing is, "Tickets!' I handed him up the ticket. 'Can I have your pass please?' I said: 'No! Mammy took it from me!' *The Irish Times* boy shot up the paper; the other people looked. 'Jesus!' He asked me if I had any identity. I looked into the bag and I saw the books and I said: 'No!' I couldn't.'

"He said, 'You're to get off this train at the next stop.' When he went into the next carriage, I walked up and went in and said: 'The people were so upset with you that they gave me the money to buy the ticket.'

"He said, 'Aren't they great, now.' I arrived in Listowel with six pence in my pocket. And John B Keane put up a pint for me and said, 'That's a great story.'"

Dermot roared with laughter, partly from embarrassment, when I then told him another anecdote I heard about him from one of his acquaintances involving him leaving a hospital in his pajamas to go and recite poetry at Yeats's grave!

"Not at all. No. that's madness! No, I never read in my pajamas — for Jaysus sake!" he said.

So, what about his reputation for having a wild streak at one time? "Ah, I've still wild streaks," he joked.

However, he dismissed rumors about him having a problem with alcohol. "Big boozer? If someone was to say to you. 'Are you a big boozer?' what would you say?" he asked me rhetorically.

"There would be times when you would be at it, maybe when you were a student. There would be times when you might be over in London, going for the Sunday morning one. But no. There's in and outs of it. The same as everybody else."

But did alcohol influence his writing?

"Ah, yeah, it would and it wouldn't. You don't write when you're drinking. You can't. So, therefore it's the escape from it. But I find (with) the isolation, sometimes out here working, I'll jump in the car and drive to Grange (pub) to get a breakfast, just to be among people," he said.

"I find the isolation sometimes gets to you. I'll hop over there and come back and sit down and do another bit. But now me head is empty since the two books have came out. I have nothing left in me. I'd love to get back in working."

Did he ever turn to drink to escape from the writing?

"No, no, no. Because that won't work. It's the comfort zone. It's the thing for doing the work — the pint in the evening. I go up (to the pub) for a half an hour. That's the gift for doing the day's work. When you're working, writing, if you did that you'd lose the book. The novel is a funny one, you have to work every day," he said.

So, he was never as bad as Brendan Behan with the booze?

"Ah, no, no, no. I'm not going to go into…there's a value judgment on Behan. I can't go into value judgments. I don't enter into the area. It's a kind of an escape route," he said

He never had a problem with booze?

"No."

So he could control it?

"Well, can you control anything? It's a social one and it's meeting a few people," he insisted.

When he did venture out to Sligo town, Dermot was often mistaken for the Nobel Prize winner Seamus Heaney. "It happens quite often. This man came up and said: 'Ha! Ha! You can turn your arse to them now! The Nobel Prize.' I said: 'No, that's Heaney.' 'Oh, Jaysus, are you not Heaney?' I've been introduced on stage as Seamus Heaney! It's unbelievable. The name sounds the same. It never happens to him, of course. He's never called Healy," he said.

He rued not taking up an offer of a place at the Abbey School of Acting as a young man. "I went to London instead. I always regret it. I think the dialogue that's floating in the books is coming from the actor in me," he said.

"I made a movie with Rock Hudson but it was only a small part. It was great being with him. He was very friendly, very upfront. We'd have conversations in the early mornings," he said.

Dermot appeared in several other films too — he was in the award-winning film *I Could Read The Sky* with Stephen Rae and Maria Doyle Kennedy.

"Timothy O'Grady wrote *I Could Read The Sky* and, pure chance, suddenly I was in it. And that was an extraordinary time because it was one week in London. In a big shed. With me in my pajamas and they all wrapped up, the cameramen and everybody wrapped up. Freezing!" he said.

"And I got through the week and I came home and I had the worst flu I ever had in my life. I lay in bed for three weeks. So, it was a hard one. And I never saw any other actors — I had to do it on me own. So, the soundman gave me his eyes, so I used to look at him.

"And (my wife) Helen was there one time and I had to do a love scene. She stood at the far end and I was able to look over at her. But I enjoyed it!"

Dermot also had cameos in *The Butcher Buy* and in a scene opposite Don Cheadle — of *Hotel Rwanda* and *Ocean's Thirteen* fame — for *The Guard*, which also starred Brendan Gleeson. He also starred in John Michael McDonagh's short film *The Second Death*.

Dermot confessed that he had never even heard of Don Cheadle before they met for that scene in which he "gives Don a sideways look."

He added: "A taxi brought me down to Galway (to do my scene). I had to do this walk. I had to walk by this black actor, who I didn't know who he was. Don, as it turned out. I had to walk down and give him a sideways look.

"They asked me to do the walk again. The whole shot was four or five minutes. I went back up into the taxi. I was giving back the pair of wellingtons to the wardrobe person and I said, 'Can I have those wellingtons? You see, I'm from Cavan!' And Brendan Gleeson roared fucking laughing. I got into the taxi and went back to Sligo. Your man said, 'I've been doing movies for 30 years and I've never driven someone to do four minutes!'

But it's another confession about how he managed to spend an entire evening with one of America's most iconic figures, without realizing who it was, that did stretch credulity. Dermot claimed he mistook Frank McCourt for Arthur Miller! It was a story my then editor said couldn't have been true.

"I was down below in Galway to give a lecture the following morning to a workshop of American writers. I went up for a drink in Nochtans (bar) and this lady came in who looks after writers and said, 'Come over please, you have to join Frank McCourt. He heard you were here.'

"We were talking for a while. He said, 'Please come to this play.' As we were walking up the street various different people joined us.

"One man in a blue coat and large glasses joined us and introduced. On the way he said, 'Would you mind sitting beside me because if I misunderstand any of the play you can let me know what's happening — because of the Irish accent.' I said, 'Sure.'

"So, he sat down and I gave him the odd whisper. At halftime we went up to the bar. After the play, he said, 'Please come on with me.' We went back into this room in the theatre and wine (was) served, all the actors came. All the actors went over to shake the hands of the man in the blue coat. After one pint, I said, 'I have to go now.' He said, 'Stay where you are'. (I said). 'I have to get up in the morning.' (He said,) 'We all have to get up in the morning.' There was this argument. So, I took off.

"The following morning I was entering the university when a lecturer said to me, 'Haha! You were with the big rats last night!' I said, 'Old Frank McCourt.' 'Frank McCourt not at all! You were with Marlon Monroe's ex!' (I said,) 'Who are you talking about.' 'Arthur Millar!' I was with Arthur Millar for the evening and I didn't know it."

After the laughter died down, the conversation turned back to his writing. Prior to his last novel, he wrote a critically acclaimed memoir entitled *The Bend For Home*, which was published in 1996.

"You don't know what's hidden in your memory. But there was one day, I remember putting down the line: 'It was a half day in Cavan town.' I wrote it down and four days later I was still on the one sentence — this half day in Cavan town! Still moving on. And walking down main street naming all the things I'd totally forgotten and all of a sudden it piled up," he said.

"So, four pages later I was still doing it. And it became a kind of a thing that there's a whole load buried, you put down a line that you think is going to be nothing and the next thing out comes all of this. So, it was great doing it, travelling back into the past and rediscovering again whole lots you'd forgotten."

At the time of writing, Dermot had no idea what his next book would be about, but his ideas could come from anywhere, he said. "*Sudden Times* just came from a funeral. Someone turned to me and said, 'These are sudden times.'"

But he was longing to get back to writing. "This new book took me 11 years. But I'm slow anyway. This book could have been finished in 2002. I just couldn't find my way to the ending."

Sadly, before he had time to pen his next magnum opus, Dermot died in June 2014.

— 2011

Chapter Six: John Boyne

John Boyne had already penned a clutch of novels when he wrote his first book for young adults. Published in 2006, *The Boy In The Striped Pajamas* went on to become a literary phenomenon, selling seven million copies. But behind that remarkable success lies a very different kind of life story.

Now, with the publication of his latest novel, *The Heart's Invisible Furies*, the best-selling writer feels that he can talk honestly and openly about his past: about growing up in Ireland, his sexuality, the break-down of his civil partnership, depression, drinking and a lot more besides.

Whoever said nice guys finish last obviously never met John Boyne. He is one of Ireland's most successful ever writers, having sold an astonishing seven million copies of his widely loved novel, *The Boy in The Striped Pajamas*. The book, written for younger readers, went to No.1 on the *New York Times* bestsellers list and was turned into a Hollywood movie. Yet there was no ego about the man: not when I first met him back in 2009; and not when we spoke again for this interview.

Like many other would-be authors, John started writing while working behind the till at a Dublin bookshop. The now 45-year-old Dubliner has gone on to sell over nine million books in total, an incredible achievement, unmatched by many of the literary heavy hitters from this neck of the woods. John is a prolific writer too, to date having penned ten novels for adults, five books for younger readers, and a collection of short stories.

This interview was conducted while he was promoting his then latest novel, *The Heart's Invisible Furies*, which was not only his best work to date, but also his most personal. For the first time in one of his novels, John explored the subject of homosexuality. For a man who once refused point-blank to discuss his own sexuality in a newspaper interview, it was a breakthrough moment.

John was on a break in Australia when we did this interview over the Christmas holiday period. It might've been summer Down Under, but it wasn't your stereotypical sun-drenched morning. The overcast sky matched John's reflective mood, as he opened up for what is undoubtedly his most candid interview ever.

Q: What do you make of Hemingway's famous saying that the best training for a writer is an unhappy childhood?

A: I wouldn't be able to agree with it. I had a very happy childhood. As a kid, I was — I still am, in a way — somebody quite solitary, quite isolated. Even from a very young age, books were the thing that got me out of myself.

Q: I read a piece you wrote in *The Irish Times* a couple of years ago about how you were beaten in school by a priest.

A: It was a Carmelite — not that it matters (*laughs*). When I published *A History of Loneliness* a couple of years ago, which was about abuse in the Church, I confronted a lot of that: the ritual beatings.

Q: But weren't you so badly beaten that you needed two weeks off school?

A: It was a priest who had this stick that he kept up his sleeve and he called it Excalibur. He had a metal weight taped to the top of it and that was his weapon of choice. In those days, if you were coming home beaten up, parents would maybe feel, "You probably did something to deserve it." You know: that inherent fear of going up against the Church. Ireland has changed for the better because those things don't happen anymore.

Q: When did you realize you were gay?

A: Oh, before I even knew what the word meant, like eight- or nine-years-old. At around eight or nine, generally people feel some sort of attraction to somebody without understanding what that attraction is. I would've known from then. And then when I was about 11 or 12, I started to understand that better — and I felt quite terrified about it really, to be honest.

Q: Why terrified?

A: As a teenager in the '80s, one of the most prominent news stories was Aids. As the Aids epidemic started to grow — and so many people were dying — it was so connected to the gay community. It would've been really frightening.

Q: What ran through your mind?

A: I can remember being in the car going to school, hearing news reports about the terror of it and — not telling anybody I was gay — thinking, "Oh God! Is this going to happen to me? Am I going to die? Is this some kind of biblical punishment?" We were uninformed. I think even straight people struggled because sex was something that was not talked about as much back then. People were intimidated and frightened by the idea of it.

Q: Things are very different these days…

A: It's terrific for kids today. But one can also feel slightly envious of how free they are, in the way you think, "God! I wish I was like that when I was 15, instead of terrified of what people would think." I have a friend who has an 11-year-old son and she recently told me about a kid in his class, also 11, who has already declared himself to be gay! I know! I thought it was a bit odd as well (*laughs*). But can you imagine somebody saying that when we were kids? You would've been beaten out of the place with a stick (*laughs*).

Q: Some younger readers might not realize that it was illegal to be a sexually active gay person when you were growing up in Ireland.

A: That's another thing! I was in Trinity when it was still illegal. When I tell people that in other countries, that's shocking to them. But that's all part of the mindset of feeling there's something wrong with it: that there's something wrong with you, and that you're deformed in some way! And that does lead to an inability to have relationships when you're younger. It definitely did with me. There would be people who were fine with it, but I struggled quite a bit.

Q: How old were you when you lost your virginity?

I was 17.

Q: Were you very nervous?

A: I guess. Excited (*laughs*)! Everybody's a bit nervous, I suppose, but I was excited. I wanted to do it (*laughs*).

Q: Were you ever curious about sex with women?

A: Oh, yes, certainly. I should've pointed out that when I lost my virginity it was to a woman. So, there you go! A lot of gay people have probably been with girls when they were younger. It's a normal thing to do because you're still trying to figure everything out. You're still trying to understand your sexuality. So, I tried it out with a couple of girls at that age. It wasn't really for me, but it was fine for the two-and-a-half minutes it lasted (*laughs*)!

Q: How old were you when you first had sex with a man?

A: I was about 19 when I first had sex with a guy — and that was much better (*laughs*)!

Q: Did the Catholic guilt thing hit you the morning after?

A: I never felt any Catholic guilt. What I did feel was a nervousness about anybody finding out, because I felt that the minute you say that you're gay then that's it: you are forever. You can't take it back. It felt like you're getting out of a lot of possibilities from life — marriage, children… there's no way back once you said it.

Q: You must've felt liberated going over to England to do your MA in Creative Writing?

A: I did because I felt I really wanted to start my life over. I hadn't had a great time in Trinity — no fault of Trinity's. It was because I was quite shy and quite closeted. I got to the end of that experience and regretted not making more of the time there. So, when I went to UEA (University of East Anglia) I went with the idea that you can reinvent yourself. And that's when I really came to terms with everything and started being able to tell people I was gay. Maybe because I was out of Ireland, it felt like a safe place where I could be myself.

Q: How old were you when you came out to your parents?

A: I was 23. They were cool with it. I remember when I told them I was very much like, "I don't want to turn this into a drama. I don't have the energy for it." They've always been terrific. I told them, they were fine, and we moved on.

Q: Was it a case of them saying, "Oh, we half-guessed?"

A: I don't think anybody was falling off the seat in surprise. There was a lot of Jason Donovan posters on my bedroom wall!

Q: Was he your big crush?

A: (*Laughs*) He was one of them.

Q: What type of music were you into growing up?

A: I was always a pop kid, following the charts. My favorite was always Kate Bush. I'm a Kate Bush obsessive. I was lucky enough that I got tickets to the opening night last year when she was doing those concerts in London, which was incredible. She was always like a mythological figure to me. I was in the second row: I couldn't believe it.

Q: You once did an interview where you refused to talk about being gay. I'm guessing you didn't want to be pigeonholed as a gay writer, right?

A: Yeah. I think when it would come up, I'd feel: if I was talking about a book, if it had nothing to do with the book, I couldn't quite see the point of discussing it. I'm not really personally that interested in the lives of writers. I'm only interested in their books. I don't care what they do outside of that. This phrase "openly gay" is one that always irritates the hell out of me.

Q: You don't see hetero writers being referred to as openly straight!

A: I don't think a person's sexuality has got anything to do with their work. But the problem is: if you pull back from it and if you're not willing to talk about it, it almost seems as if you're ashamed, or closeted in some way. But sexuality is a very personal thing and it's not necessarily something that everybody wants to be talking about. Now, when it comes to this book, sure, because that's what the book is about: it would seem disingenuous of me not to talk about it. If I were talking about Mutiny on the Bounty, it'd seem completely irrelevant to the subject.

Q: Last year I interviewed the Primate of All-Ireland, Archbishop Eamon Martin, and he said that the act of homosexuality was a sin but being gay wasn't a sin. Isn't that medieval nonsense?

A: Yeah. That sort of hate the sin but love the sinner type of thing...

Q: There was an awful lot of insulting things said during the heated same-sex marriage debate.

A: In advance of the referendum happening, I wasn't much looking forward to it because I knew it would bring all the bigots out of their closets and that you'd have to be listening to it on the radio and on TV. I hated that. I don't like that kind of violence in society, you know?

Q: It was even more hostile on social media...

A: A mistake I made during that time was engaging on Twitter with crazies. You can't argue with stupid. But I would go onto Twitter and hashtag the referendum result and see what the latest comments were and then you'd start into some debate with some crazy person — and what always bugged me was like, "Why did anybody care? Why would a married man or a married woman care what somebody else does?" It baffled me.

Q: Did it upset you?

A: I found it an upsetting experience. I didn't like hearing people talking nonsense. We know they made up so many lies and tried to connect homosexuality to the adoption thing, to pedophilia. They would say anything. And you think,

"Why do you care? What does it matter to you what somebody down the street does?"I find those people quite tragic. It's fantastic that it passed.

Q: It was extra special because Ireland passed the first referendum on it in the world.

A: I think that referendum was the closing chapter of all the Church scandals — because, at the end of all the Church scandals, a referendum happened where people could say, "We are no longer tolerating this repression, this bigotry. And this just happens to be the subject that's on the table now and we're going to use this to tell you what we think."

Q: And now we've got another emotive issue coming up with the Eighth Amendment. I presume you're pro-choice?

A: I definitely am. I would be 100 per cent pro-choice, but I can also see that it's a more complicated issue in a way, because where equal rights marriage doesn't affect anybody else, the Eighth Amendment does. This will be another nightmare to go through. I wouldn't be as confident as I would've been with the equal marriage referendum. But I absolutely believe in a woman's right to choose. No question.

Q: In an *Irish Times* article a few years ago, you briefly mentioned that you had unhealthy and troubling relationships growing up. Can you expand on that?

A: As I started trying to date or form relationships with guys, there was a lot of subterfuge involved. There was a lot of lying to people. A lot of deceit. Sex was something that was often conducted in darkened places and outdoors — and that made you feel that there was something wrong with what you were doing. And that's what I meant by it being unhealthy.

Q: What about when you returned to Ireland after finishing your MA?

A: See, even when I got back to Ireland, a lot of people who I would've had a fling with would've been people who were not 'out'. It wasn't like you were going to go on dates, like a guy and a girl would. You wouldn't go out to dinner and a movie. It was built around sex. And while that's fine and perfectly enjoyable, looking back there's an unhealthiness to it because there was no personal intimacy. And even when I was first out and was reasonably comfortable telling people I was gay, I still struggled with the idea of dating.

Q: Why?

A: It still seemed almost embarrassing. I wasn't completely comfortable with it. It's hard now to look back 20 years and understand why. Now, I wouldn't give a shit. I couldn't care less. But I did back then. People were much more defined by their sexuality. When I first started working in Waterstone's I was 25. Anybody there that was gay, you almost defined them by that fact. It wasn't like, "Oh, that's the person who works in the poetry department, or the cinema department." It was an all-encompassing thing.

When I left the shop, I left quite dramatically, shall we say! I got to the point where I felt everybody was always complaining about their lives and work and the shop, and nobody was doing anything to fix it. I was just as guilty of that as anybody.

One night I just saw red and thought, "I don't want to spend my life complaining." So I threw the keys down on the table, resigned on the spot and never set foot in the place again. I went home and I emailed my area manager and I said: "I'm done. I'm not coming back."

When I left the shop, I lost a lot of friends. I think there was not a lot of empathy for the clear pain I was in.

Q: You had your first couple of books published while working in Waterstone's.

A: My first couple of books didn't do particularly well and my editor at the time left the publishing house. I was out on a limb. It was touch and go really for a little bit, whether I was going to be able to sustain a career. I think a lot of people have this with their first couple of books — the publishing industry can be quite unforgiving and if you don't have immediate hits then the possibility of that career surviving is slim.

Q: Was it a tough time emotionally?

A: It was a rough couple of years. Things weren't going well. I got hit by a car. I was on a scooter and I broke my leg. It wasn't life threatening, but I had just got out of what was my first real relationship — a falling in love relationship. And I had been pretty bruised and battered by it. And my career didn't seem like it was going well. I was struggling with that. I was not enjoying my job and I was drinking too much. It was one of those periods in life where nothing was going right and I needed to make a change.

Q: Did you become depressed?

A: I did because I felt very much like a failure. I felt like my literary career was over before it began. The person I had fallen in love with didn't love me anymore. It was the first time I was trying to process those kind of emotions and I wasn't very good at it. I'm still not very good at it. There had been this brief moment where everything was going well — and then suddenly everything was going terrible. I felt like everything was over before it had even begun. I did sink into a bit of depression. I've suffered from that on and off over the years. I still do. I think that was the first time where I was really struggling. I started taking anti-depressants, too — I was on them for about two years. Everything was going wrong in my life and I was deeply unhappy.

Q: Did it get so bad that you had suicidal thoughts?

A: Definitely. At that point, it did. I moved down to Wexford for a year. And while I was there, in some ways, I felt very isolated. There were days when that isolation was really good for me, where I was feeling, "I can walk on the beach. I can read. I can write." And it felt good to be removed from the world for a while. There were also days when that was an absolute nightmare. And you never knew, waking up, how it was going to be. I don't think it's unusual — but the actual process of suicide is a much more terrifying and painful thing. I don't think I would ever act on it. But I think most people have those thoughts.

Q: Mental health is less of a taboo subject today.

A: One of the things now about it — everybody being more free with their emotions and liberated in that way — is that we do tend to express these things and think about them. We are more in touch with our feelings than we all were 20 years ago. Although that's a good thing, it also brings some negatives, in that we're prone to extremes of happiness or unhappiness, depression or alienation.

Q: You once told me that you weaned yourself off anti-depressants at the time…

A: I did. I was wrong in a way too, because what I thought was — when I started taking anti-depressants first, in some way it felt like it was a failure of character, and I wanted to get to a place where I wasn't on them anymore. And then, of course, your mood goes up and down, and up and down. What I eventually recognized is that a lot of this is just a chemical thing.

Q: The serotonin level, right?

A: Yeah. You just need it.

Q: Are you taking medication now?

A: I have to take an anti-depressant every morning, which is fine. It keeps me balanced. So, when I went back on them a few years ago I realized, "Actually

I need to be on these for life." It's one tablet every morning. It's no big deal. But I don't need to use them thinking, "Eventually I'll be able to get off them." Instead, I'll use them thinking, "No, I'll stay on them. It keeps me balanced." I'd be nervous of not being on them, to be honest.

Q: Do you think your depression is simply a chemical imbalance or is it rooted in something like the beatings?

A: Honestly, I think it's just chemical. I handle it fine by taking a tablet every day. I don't think it's rooted in anything.

Q: But you have to be careful with drinking when you're taking pills like that.

A: Yeah. I must admit I like a pint, but I think I've got that on a good balance. Back in those days, yeah, I was completely doing it wrong.

Q: Have you gone to therapy?

A: I tried it once and it wasn't really for me: mostly because I'm actually quite an open person with my friends, my family. If I've got an issue, I can talk about it. I don't think I'm somebody who's got something hidden inside that needs to come out. I think I'm increasingly open. So, I didn't feel I was getting anything from therapy that I couldn't get from talking to my sister.

Q: You wrote on your Facebook page recently that 2016 was a bad year for you.

A: Yeah, it was. I've been in a relationship for the last 11 years and we entered into a civil partnership, but, unfortunately, that fell apart this year.

Q: I'm sorry to hear that.

A: It's been really difficult. We remain good friends. In fact, I just replied to an email from him. It was just one of those things where the relationship somehow comes to an end, but obviously for both of us it's been really, really sad. It's one of the reasons I'm in Sydney now. I just wanted to take a six/seven weeks break. I was feeling naturally down over it, but not in an insane way — just the sadness of it all. I've got the book coming out in February and I wanted to get through Christmas and the New Year. I can come back to start over, in a way.

Q: Why did you split?

A: I don't know. I'm still trying to figure it out: why it went wrong or what happened? We had a very happy relationship. There was no other person involved or anything like that. He felt he needed some space and some distance to figure out some things in his life. I think what's important to me now is that we try and maintain some sort of friendship — because 11 years is a long time to spend with somebody. We've gone through so much together and so it's quite sad really. It wasn't entirely my choice, put it that way *(nervous laughter)*.

Q: It's lovely that you're still talking. There are loads of ex-couples who refuse to speak to each other.

A: That's what I'm trying to avoid. And one thing I've realized — because I'm trying to figure it all out in my head — is that, no matter what the pain or anger, the notion of not being in each other's lives when nobody has done anything to specifically hurt the other person is pointless. We've got to find a way to be friends, rather than losing each other. Because he's too important to me and I hope that I'm important to him.

Q: It sounds like you still very much love him?

A: I do, yeah, very much.

84

Q: It must be difficult being over in Australia on your own.

A: I love Australia. I love coming here. Even though it's so far from Ireland, it's a home-away-from-home. It's my tenth trip here in ten years. I know it very well. I've got friends here. I'm doing a lot of walks here. It's sunshine all day. It's actually very therapeutic to be here and just be able to read, to write, to walk, soak up some vitamin D. I just knew I couldn't have done Christmas and New Year's at home this year. I needed a break from that.

Q: *In A History of Loneliness*, you wrote: "I did not become ashamed of being Irish until I was well into my middle years of life." Was that your experience?

A: No, I don't think so. Actually — for all the problems and all the faults — I'm really proud of being Irish and I love being Irish. I love living in Ireland. I mentioned that I keep coming to Australia every year. My friends and family often say to me, "God! Are you going to move to Australia at some point?" I'm always like, "No. I couldn't live outside Ireland." I'm very much a home-body. I live about ten minutes from the house that I grew up in. I feel very settled there. That line was very much the character's line.

Q: Would you describe yourself as a workaholic?

A: I don't think I would because, in a way, that word implies an obsessive nature. I love writing. I'm passionate about it and I really enjoy it. I work all the time, yes — but because I enjoy it. I love the act of creating novels, of writing fiction, of creating characters, of publishing books. It's given me the happiest and most stable thing in my life. I'm definitely a very hard worker. But a workaholic almost seems like it's a bad thing, you know?

Q: But you're very productive.

A: I am productive. Unlike a lot of my writer friends, I'm fortunate enough that I don't have another job: I'm able to write full-time. I get up in the morning and I go to work (*laughs*).

Q: How many hours of writing would you do in a day?

A: About three or four, I would say. Mostly in the morning.

Q: Would you have any advice for would-be writers?

A: Read more than you write. Write every day. And stay as far away from writing 'collectives' as you possibly can. Writers should work alone, not as part of a group associated with a magazine or publisher. This is particularly true in Ireland where new writers tend to band together, endorse each other's books in some kind of literary circle-jerk, and show up together at every book launch or party where there might be a press photographer present. That kind of thing has nothing to do with writing. It's concerned only with basking in the reflected light of others and making sure that people know that you're a "Writer" with a capital W. The words are all that matter. If you're aiming for celebrity, pick a different profession.

Q: Growing up, what type of books or authors did you admire?

A: When I was about 15 or 16, that's when I really seriously started getting into literature — and moving from the younger stuff or classics to trying to discover what was going on in the world. John Irving was the first person who I really became crazy about as a writer.

Q: You've dedicated the new book to him.

A: When I published my first book in 2000, I sent him a copy and a letter. It's about the only fan letter I've ever written, saying how much he's influenced me over the years. We became friends subsequently and see each other, whenever I'm in Canada or when he's over here. I wanted to dedicate this one to him, because in a way I feel it's almost like my most Irving-esque novel. Most of my novels are quite sad, but this one is funny. At least, I hope it's funny.

Q: There's a lot of black humor in it.

A: If there's anybody who's influenced this book, it's John.

Q: Has he read it?

A: He has a copy of it. I sent it to him. I haven't heard if he's read it yet, but he emailed me to say that it had arrived safely.

Q: I remember at 15, staying up until 6am reading *The World According to Garp*. And then I binge-read all of his books that I could get my hands on in the local library.

A: I think a lot of people who like his books have that experience. If you start reading them as a teenager, you just have to keep going, you have to keep reading them all because they're so funny. But they're so deep and thoughtful, and provocative in ways. He's a great writer.

Q: It must be cool to be friends with someone like John Irving...

A: Yeah, whenever I'm with him, I still feel quite star-struck. You know, just sitting across the table and hearing him talk. I still think he's a great writer. But one of the great things that can happen with writing is that, along the way, you'll get to meet or become friends with some of your heroes.

Q: He pushed boundaries when it came to openly addressing sexuality, in a very honest way...

A: He is somebody who has spent so much of his life writing about sexuality and what he calls sexual misfits and he was writing about transgender people in novels way before everybody was suddenly transgender (*laughs*), you know? That was a subject that was not talked about at the time of Garp, for example, and he was writing about that. He was writing about abortion in *The Cider House Rules*, a very political subject to be writing about in the early 1980s America. About Vietnam, in *(A Prayer for) Owen Meany*. So, he's somebody I respect very much.

Q: The main character in your new novel struggles with his sexuality. Your writing is getting closer to your own experiences, the older you get.

A: Yeah. If you were to follow through from my first book to this book, I almost kept myself at such a distance from stories and just wanted to be missing on the radar, not bring myself in at all. I think it's only now — I'm older, I'm more experienced as a writer, I'm more confident as a person — that I feel I can write things like this. Some people do that when they're younger, some people never do it. But certainly in the last five or six years I've wanted to bring myself into the stories much more. I've wanted to write about my own experiences. And then each one has made me more confident. *The History of Loneliness* was very important to me for that — and this one now as well. I'm glad I'm changing like that as a writer. I feel like I'm developing in some way.

Q: What initially attracted you to writing this new novel?

A: I liked the idea to start with the hypocrisy in the opening sentence: somebody who himself has fathered children, who is going to belittle and abuse and demean a young girl who's got pregnant. We all know in those days that was the worst thing that could happen to anybody. It was terrible. So, I'm starting at the place where I finished with the last one in a different story but then moving on.

Q: Was it a conscious decision to make this novel a black comedy?

A: I don't plan these books out very much. I let them develop. I didn't realize I was going to move down the humorous road. It just comes through the voice of the character, particularly when he's a little kid — that's just the way it went. But then I was really happy that it did, because I have written a lot of books which are sad and deal with tragic issues and unhappy people. It's refreshing for me to write about somebody who — for all his personal problems — is essentially cheerful.

Q: Will you do more black comedy?

A: I don't know. I wouldn't think the next one would be comic. I sometimes feel that every book is almost a reaction to the one before — that you need to change. I'm working on something at the moment and it's not funny; it's not morose, but it's more straight; it's more serious.

Q: Are you nervous about how your new book will be perceived?

A: I'm always a bit nervous. Because one of the things with books — and we're all guilty of this; I'm guilty of this as a reader as well — is that a perceived opinion can form very quickly. You know the way we say, "Have you read such-and-such?" And you go, "No. I heard it was terrible." A few reviews can make or break something. So, I'm always a bit nervous.

Q: A bad review can kill you…

A: It can be very hard. John Banville says, "If you get a bad review in the paper you can rely on your best friend to call up and make sure you've seen it!" You know that all your friends, all your colleagues will see it. Everybody gets nervous because you put so much into the book and you care about it and you believe in it: you hope people will like it. But ask me a week before it comes out — I'll probably be trembling (*laughs*).

Q: I was wondering about the protagonist in the new novel being adopted.

The last time we spoke, you said to me you'd love to have kids but felt you were "too long in the tooth."

A: If I have a big regret in life, it would be that I didn't have kids. I would've been a good dad. I love kids. I love being around kids. But I'm 45 now. If I was a 25-year-old guy, I think it's the same as being a straight person: you think, "Well, I'll have kids eventually." Where obviously it was much more difficult for me then — and I'm too old now.

Q: You're not too old!

A: It would take years to get one (*laughs*) and by the time I actually got one I would be! I mean, if I can have one in nine months I wouldn't be too old. But adoption would take years. I think for a lot of gay people it's a sadness that's there inside — that you're deprived of something that's really an inherent part of human nature. It's not something that weighs me down, but it's probably the biggest regret in my life.

Q: Is this where your passion for writing for children comes from?

A: Yeah, a little bit. I love writing about children. I really enjoy all those events I do with kids. I like interacting with them. And that wasn't something I had planned. I never really expected to be writing for or about children. It came about through *The Boy in the Striped Pajamas* and where that led me. But it's something that I've valued over the years and it's turned into a big part of my life.

Q: *The Boy in the Striped Pajamas* did come in for some criticism.

A: I've always found that the criticism is from not Jewish people, actually. My experience with the Jewish community with this book was not critical at all. I would say it was 99 per cent positive. Anybody who's vehemently opposed to it or any terrible, nasty letters I've got have been from people who didn't have a personal relationship with the Holocaust. I've been in many Holocaust museums talking about the book, in many Jewish community centers in the States and other countries, and many Jewish festivals, and I've never actually had a negative [reaction].

Q: One confrontation over the book did, however, get rather heated during a talk after a screening of the film in the US.

A: Somebody in the audience who hated the book and film said. "How can you write this for children because it's so violent?" And I said, "The thing about the book and the movie, there is no violence in it; it's all left to the imagination of the reader. I deliberately set out writing the book that there was not going to be violence on the page." He said: "That's not true — the book is full of violence." I think we were at cross purposes and whatever happened he suddenly jumped up, leapt on the stage and punched me and knocked me off my chair!' (*In the ensuing melee, actor David Thewlis had to drag the man off a clearly shaken Boyne — JOT.*)

Q: *The Boy in the Striped Pajamas* was a phenomenon. Do you feel under any pressure to repeat that success?

A: No. I've never felt under pressure about that because I know it's impossible. A book like that for a writer — if you're lucky — comes along once in a lifetime. Something that just sells so much and becomes a phenomenon. I could write a book that's a million times better, but it will never sell anything like that. What it did for me was give me the freedom to keep writing books and have an audience. So, I've never allowed it to become a weight on my shoulders. It was a Godsend.

— 2017

Chapter Seven: Emma Donoghue

Emma Donoghue first came to prominence with her confessional semi-autobiographical novel about a torrid romance between two convent schoolgirls, which was published in 1994.

However, in the Noughties it appeared as if she was fading into obscurity because most of her subsequent lesbian fiction and historical novels failed — despite some critical acclaim — to resonate with mainstream readers.

But, at the time of our meeting, that was all about to dramatically change — as the lesbian mother of two young children had just received a staggering €1million advance for her latest novel, which was inspired by the horrific Fritzel child abuse case.

And not having written a commercially successful book in a decade, Emma was stunned when her novel *Room* was the subject of a bidding war with publishers.

"I never had a bidding war of any kind before. All my previous contracts put together wouldn't add up to this. I feel extraordinary lucky," she said when we met in 2009.

"I mean, all my previous contracts put together wouldn't add up to this. I was extremely shocked.

"I feel extraordinary lucky. I didn't set out to write something that would get me a huge contract, but it just so happens that the book I was inspired to write seems to be touching people. From the number of publishers who've wanted to buy it, it just seems to affect people strongly."

The then 40-year-old said the idea for the novel, which is told from the perspective of a five-year-old boy held captive with his mother in a garden shed, literally came to her in a vision.

"I've never felt so sure about a book. I got the plot all at once in my head as I was driving along the road and I'm a very poor driver, so I was in danger of crashing! I don't usually have these visionary experiences, but my whole body was shaking with inspiration.

"And I was thinking, 'Should I pull over to the side?' But no, they say you shouldn't go over to the side of a highway unless you're actually crashing. So, I thought, 'Keep driving.' But my concentration was very divided."

But the Canadian-based author's success has already started to bring out the begrudgery at home, with one Irish broadsheet snottily claiming that Emma was cashing in with "lurid sensationalism" by writing a novel inspired by the grotesque story of the Austrian rapist.

However, Emma dismissed such criticism. "If what you wrote was a very trashy book of which the only possible merit was that it comments on the headlines then you might call it cashing-in. But it's a literary novel. It was a novel that was just suggested to me by this case," she explained.

"I'm not trying to publicize it on the basis of its connection with real cases. It's not that I'm saying, 'Buy this book because it's about the Fritzels.' Because it's not at all, it's a very different storyline. I just thought I might as well be clear up front about which one started me thinking about such a case.

"I think anyone who reads the book will realize I'm not cashing-in. It's not at all exploitative. The scenario in my book is far less scary and hideous than many of these cases that I've researched. It's really not a book about child abuse. The mother in my book really manages to protect the child to a remarkable degree, so he's living a pretty good childhood."

Despite receiving an advance that is the literary world's equivalent of winning the Lotto, Emma insisted that becoming a millionaire would not change her lifestyle.

"I just consider myself so fortunate to never have to do anything but writing. I feel rich, but it's never made me a huge living. So, some years I was earning a lot and some years very little and it kind of averages out," she said.

"And, in a way, with this new money it's not going to change my lifestyle. It's more that I will salt it all away and I will use it to pay myself a salary over the next, maybe, 15 years.

"So, in a way, what it's buying me is the freedom to carry on writing what I love, which is superb because in the middle of a recession you often have anxieties and you think, 'Oh, my God! What if I don't sell the next book, how will I keep earning?'"

Emma first came to attention when, at the young age of 23, her debut novel *Stir fry* was published by Penguin. The backbone of this book was a semi-autobiographical account of two convent schoolgirls falling in love.

One of eight children, Emma says her homosexuality was a "slight embarrassment" to her siblings because "I was so much in the media talking about being a lesbian."

Emma first discovered she was gay when she fell head over heels in love with one her classmates at Muckross Park Convent in Dooneybrook. "I realized I was a lesbian at 14. It really wasn't even a matter of questioning my sexuality, it was just clear to me. But I just fell madly in love with a girl in my class. Bang! At 14. I thought, 'Oh, no!'" she recalled.

"From 14 to 16 I was pining away for my friend, thinking, 'I'm a lonely lesbian and nobody will ever love me!'"

However, Emma had her first love affair with another classmate when she was 16.

It lasted two-and-a-half-years. "I think it was 16 to 18. You're just terrified of anyone finding out. Luckily, I've always been fairly girly, so nobody was looking at me and thinking, 'Oh, she's on the tomboyish side!' Nobody ever guessed about me at school. Only my mother had the insight to spot it," she said.

"I really did feel I'm a stranger in their midst. I had plenty of friends and a very loving family and so on, but I did often think, 'Oh, if they knew I was a lesbian they'd cast me out!'

"And I had friends who were either expelled from school or kicked out of home when they were students just because their families found out they were gay. It's not that I really thought my parents would, but I was very, very nervous of how I could possibly fit in to Ireland, you know.

"I was just terrified that my friends would hate me. By the time I started coming out to friends in my last year of school and then in UCD everything was fine, you know.

"But I was very lucky, really. Nothing bad ever happened to me for being a lesbian — accept I think I was spat at in a park once by an old lady. It shouldn't happen, but — compared with being kicked out by your parents or something — it was nothing. Why should I care about strangers?"

Considering her convent school background, did Emma feel guilty about being a lesbian?

"It wasn't guilty. It wasn't moral guilt. I never lost my sense of a belief and a love in God. I never felt that the form of love I was experiencing was in anyway evil. So, no, I didn't feel guilt," she said.

"I just felt sort of social shame — fear of what people might think. The kind of Catholicism that I was raised on was kind of Post Vatican II: Jesus loves you kind of Catholicism. There was very little hellfire and brimstone — even though the nuns would not have approved!

"I felt the basic principles of Catholicism that I had in my head were very much 'love someone, look after them as well as you can, and don't mess them around', you know."

Did she ever have a relationship with a man?

"No, no. A few snogs, that's about it. Felt up in a field once. That was it. The novelty of it was appealing, you know. During my teenage years I kept expecting that sooner or later I would fall in love with a man. I sort of assumed, 'Oh, we schoolgirls hardly ever see boys. It's a single sex environment; so, surely when I go to college I'll fall in love with a wonderful man,'" she admitted.

"I had lots of male friends at college. It was a wonderful novelty meeting lots of guys and I got really close to some men and I used to look at them and think, 'Is it going to happen?' And it just never did.

"At a gut level, it just never happened. No boyfriends. No, not at all. It's funny, I very often write about relationship between men and women and I never feel that there's a mental block there. Love works the same way, no matter who it's for, so you can very easily put yourself in the mindset of a man who's looking at a woman or a woman who's looking at a man and you can imagine how it works. I don't find it a block in my writing."

Emma has now been with her Anglo-French partner Christine Roulston for the past 15 years. Together they live with their two children in London Ontereo, which is two-hours west of Toronto. Emma admits that she had initially resigned herself to fact that because she was a lesbian that she would never experience motherhood.

"When I first realised that I was gay, I just assumed that I wouldn't have children. I wasn't even aware that there might be ways to have children when I was a teenager, I just thought, 'Oh, I'm gay, I won't have children but that's OK,'" she said.

"But then from about my early twenties — and I met Chris at about 23 — and as soon as I met her I started to think, 'Oh, I can just imagine having kids with her.' She's very, very loving and I could just see it. She couldn't really see it; she was quite surprised at the notion, but I could really imagine it happening within the context of a very stable relationship.

"As soon as I was in Canada, I thought, 'This is do-able. I can manage this. And my kids might be safe from homophobia.' It's one thing for me to have strangers being nasty or spit at me in a park, but I did not want my kids encountering any of that. I would probably have kids anyway but in Ireland I would have had some reservations about it, whereas in Canada I felt very safe to."

Unselfconscious, Emma explained that she used the very same anonymous sperm donor to get herself pregnant with her son Finn and then daughter Una.

"It's funny, I've had people sometimes in a playground say to me, 'Where did you get them?' I'm tempted to say, 'Actually, they were under a raspberry bush!' Or the stork brought them!" she said.

"There's a couple of fertility clinics in our city in Canada and not only is it absolutely fine for them to deal with lesbian couples, but it's all paid for by the state. It's just seen as fertility treatment. Anybody who needs fertility treatment — it's not a special fund for just getting lesbians pregnant, no. Ha ha… trying to boast its population. It's for anybody; it's just seen as fertility treatment.

"They check out sperm donors so much that they have to be pretty much perfect; so, any imperfections come from my side."

She paused to laugh.

"They get paid the most minimal amount. It's something students often do because it pretty much just covers expenses — and they have to go through such elaborate testing. So, I think a lot of them do it more or less in an altruistic spirit. Like blood donation because the amount they're paid is tiny. Actually, now in Canada, they've changed the law so you can't pay them anything at all.

'It was all a very easy process. We were lucky enough that each time it would happen first time, so I didn't… I think my mother must be very fertile if she had eight of us."

"Could you imagine if you have a boyfriend?" I joked.

"Ha! You're right, you're right! It would have been a constant worry to me."

I added, "Never mind ten books, you'd probably have eight children by now!"

"I would, I would! And I think two are enough. I found the whole experience in Canada of dealing with midwives and hospitals and so on was absolutely fine — fully welcoming of us as a pair," she said.

"Luckily, there was no argument between us — because Chris never wanted to become (pregnant). There was no squabbling over this. In fact, she would really not have liked to be pregnant at all. It was very easy that way to make the decision."

The affable Emma becomes momentarily irate when she reflected on how lesbian couples are affectively discriminated against by fertility clinics back in Ireland. She described the situation as "disgraceful."

She continued: "It was all fairly easy, as again in Ireland it would have been all very difficult. Most fertility clinics in Ireland will not touch a lesbian couple. They say, 'No, no.' I've known Irish women who fly to England or who fly to Denmark to try to get very ordinary insemination procedures, nothing elaborate, not even IVF.

"I think fertility clinics in Ireland are just nervous of anything controversial because of the whole abortion background."

But how is that controversial?

'I know," she sighed. "It shouldn't be. But it is."

The conversation moved onto the difficulties of lesbian motherhood. Emma insisted that there really aren't any. "Where we live in Canada there doesn't feel like there are any difficulties. It's so different from here. Chris is their parent legally with exactly the same status as me. When our daughter Una was born the birth cert said 'Mother' and then it said 'Father or Other Parent.' So, we just wrote her name straight into that box. Full rights from the word go," she explained.

"Whereas, if two women are parenting here in Ireland, if one of them gave birth to the child she's the only one with a legal relationship; with the other one there's no legal connection — you can't even authorize an injection at the doctor's.

"So, we not only legally have the same rights, but socially, like at school. My son is six now and nobody has ever said a mean word to him about having two mothers. Dublin is probably getting better, but I still think you would come up against some thick and ignorant people who would attack you for having two mothers; or would say something stupid like, 'You must be gay if you have two mothers!'

"They call me Mum and Chris Maman like in French because She's speaks French. Most of the time they call us Emma and Chris — they've no respect!"

"I think our neighbors they were always perfectly friendly to us, but as soon as we had kids our neighbors really embraced us. It was like, 'Oh, now you're one of us. Now you have children.'

"Finn's friends occasionally have been a little bit surprised: 'Oh! Are they both your mothers?' I remember one of them at a birthday party was like, 'Oh, is she your mother too?!' But kids are very accepting at that age.

"He's the only kid in his school who's got two mothers. We talked to them on day one and they said, 'Yeah, he's the only one but it'll be fine.' I think if the school is good on issues of diversity in general then whatever your particular storyline is you'll be alright.

"They're very good. On Mother's Day he'll make two mother's cards and comes home with them. On Father's Day, they'll say to me, 'What should he make?' And I'll say, 'Oh, he can make cards for his two grandfathers.' There's a lot of men in his life. He even seeks out the men in his life. He'll run up to our male friends and say, 'Come play trains with me.'"

How does she plan to explain the situation to the children?

"The story of it has been so open from the beginning, there's never been any secrets. He just takes it for granted. Crucially, he has quite a few friends who have two mothers," she said.

"It's more you tell them gradually because I'm starting to kind of tell him the facts of life. He saw me being pregnant with his sister. He's seen the birth photos, close up and all, and he and she are both fascinated by the idea of them living in my tummy. And they both love the storyline.

"Now I'm starting to take the story a bit further back and say, 'We didn't have any sperm and we went to the nice doctor and said, 'We need some sperm.' And he said, 'Look, a kind man gave us some sperm.' It's happening very naturally. It's all part of a storyline; it's not like sitting down on a birthday and say, 'I have to tell you something.' So, the donor is just a part of the story line.

"And I think kids really pick up the vibes from you; if you are comfortable with something, if you're not ashamed of how you conceived them then there's no fear, there's no shame about it. It's just how they came to be. And they know they were wanted. That's one nice thing — they know you have to plan for that."

Emma explained that her children will have the option of contacting their biological father when they turn 18.

"We deliberately chose a sperm donor who is willing to be contacted when the kids get to 18 — if they want it," she said. "Once they're 18, it's not going to be a parental relationship.

"I feel better saying to them, 'Look, this is the storyline, this is where you come from. So, I don't know who he is but you can go find him later if you want to. There's no secrets, there's no mystery. I'm not trying to hide anything from you.'

"A lot of teenagers have a burning curiosity to know where they come from, in every sense. All sort of things can have a genetic link, so if they're really curious or eager to meet the guy who contributed half of their genetic make-up, I'm thrilled for them to meet him.

"And yet he's not like a lost father because he was never a father. But it's half of where your face comes from and half of where your health comes from, and all that."

She concluded: "I really don't mind, if people want to know about my family life it's because it's not that usual in Ireland. Publicizing a family like mine takes the terror out of it for the readers who might think, 'Oh, my God! Unnatural lifestyles!' Because you realize, God we're exactly the same as everybody else. We've got the mortgage and the school and the homework to do."

— 2009

Chapter Eight: Joseph O'Connor

When Joseph O'Connor's *Star Of The Sea* was selected as a Richard & Judy Book Club choice in the UK, it propelled the writer to the literary A-list

Joseph O'Connor has achieved the kind of literary success most Irish writers can only dream about. His last two novels, *Star Of The Sea* and *Redemption Falls*, have not only been best-sellers but have also received widespread literary acclaim. But his success was far from being an overnight one.

In fact, the 44-year-old author had written almost a dozen books before, as he puts it himself, his "lotto numbers came up" when *Star Of The Sea* was selected as a title for the Richard & Judy book club on Channel 4. The exposure brought O'Connor's work to a much wider audience and propelled his historical novel to the top of the best-seller lists, as it went on to shift over a million copies.

Before this big break, O'Connor's books just weren't getting the breaks — despite the fact that he was producing highly rated page-turners like *The Salesman* and *Inishowen*. At one stage, he was probably better known in his home country as being the big brother of Sinéad O'Connor.

But after the disappointing sales of the aforementioned tomes, O'Connor decided to take a calculated gamble. He opted to write *Star Of The Sea* as the final installment of his three-book deal with Random House, simply because he felt he mightn't get the opportunity again.

"I wrote *Star Of The Sea* because I thought no publisher would allow me to write it," he admitted.

"I'd been signed to Random on the basis that my early books had been funny, short, contemporary books about young people in London. I think that was the deal. That's what they wanted. But the books became progressively darker, and then finally I have this 450-page novel about the Irish famine and there's no jokes and people die at the end of every chapter.

"I thought the reviews would be good. I thought that it would sell okay, but it certainly wouldn't be a best-seller. It was a nice thing to have a huge best-seller — selling 30 or 40,000 copies a week at one point. I've had novels that wouldn't have sold that throughout their entire life."

O'Connor said he learned a valuable lesson: always try to write the book you want to write. "You should never dream of writing down to the audience," he declared. "Never try to write a best-seller because it's not going to work — and the readers can sniff that out. They know when they're being patronized. But if you discover the book you want to read yourself, and if you write that, and if you give it your best shot, the book will find an audience. People will go on the journey with you. That was a good lesson because I had tried to write very self-conscious, commercial books before and they hadn't really worked. So now I just do what I want to do."

O'Connor has followed through on this vow with his latest opus, *Redemption Falls*, a sequel to *Star Of The Sea*, but even more ambitious in its composition. He described it as "effectively being a scrapbook" of different voices — with one sequence even being told entirely in Irish and American ballads. It has cemented his reputation as one of the most exciting voices not just in Irish but international literature.

Q: *Star Of The Sea* was a phenomenal success. Do you think a large part of this can be attributed to the sheer good luck of being selected for the Richard & Judy Book Club?

A: There's no doubt about it — it was when the Lotto numbers came up. *Star*

Of The Sea ended up having this life that I'd never imagined for it. It was the first year of the Richard & Judy Book Club and my book was very early on — mine was the second or third — and there was a lot of media interest in whether the book club would have the kind of Oprah effect.

I wasn't convinced that *Star Of The Sea* would be the type of book that would do well in Britain, but it ended up selling a million copies. I think it was the third highest selling novel of the year, which was the same year as *The Da Vinci Code*. It just went totally mad. Everybody in Britain seemed to read it.

I remember my father-in-law — a lovely man who died last year — telling me that he was driving along through Slough in the south of England and his car broke down. He went into the garage and the guy in greasy overalls came out with this oily, thumbed copy of *Star Of The Sea*. So, mechanics in Slough were reading it! So, yeah, it had a lot of luck.

Q: Was it a having to pinch yourself type of thing?

A: Yeah, it was. Bob Geldof was one of the reviewers (on Richard & Judy). He raved about it. If I'd known when I was 16 that Geldof would ever be aware of my fucking miserable, pimply existence — never mind be recommending a book of mine — that would have been enough! So, it was great fun. There was a kind of sweetness about that time. Our second child was born around those months and it was just a lovely, warm, glowing, happy time. You've got to enjoy all that and then the day comes when you switch on your computer and start again.

Q: Your latest book *Redemption Falls* is far more experimental in terms of structure, which could easily have been a commercial risk.

A: I was conscious that it's a book that takes a risk. It would have been easier to do *Star Of The Sea Returns* (*laughs*). I always try to go forward or to do something new. And also the subject matter dictated that — it's a book set at the end of a war; it's a very confused America; it's very divided; the president is very unpopular — a bit like the world we live in now. I tried to come up with a structure that would do justice to the world of the book, but also that would be playful. I knew it would be another big, long book, and I have a horror, as a reader, of 400-page books narrated by one voice. You need variety and texture and juice. I tried to construct the book in that way.

I had an image of the readers in a circle around the action — rather than in a theatre or a church waiting for troops to come down from up high — and as the circle revolves, you see the action again from different points of view. Or like a piece of music — that it has different movements and some chapters are told in a minor key. There's a lot of music in the book, as you know. I had to trust the reader to do it in that way. It's a big, noisy, jangling, rattlebag of a book. You take your chances doing that. I'm very pleased that the book has had any sort of life because it's a very challenging book.

Q: Obviously, a lot of research goes into writing these historical books?

A: Yeah, but there's always a lot of research — if you write something contemporary it has to be researched.

Q: But isn't it easier to write a contemporary novel?

A: People love you to get the facts right. I had a book come out a few years ago called *Inishowen*, which is largely set in the *Inishowen* peninsula and I had a scene where the two characters are walking down the streets of the town — it might be Green Castle — and they pass by the church and turn left and come to O'Donoghue's pub. This woman wrote to me: "I used to really like your books! I was so thrilled reading *Inishowen*, but halfway through it I came to this scene and everybody knows if you walk down that street and turn left you don't come to O'Donohue's, you come to Murphy's! And it completely destroyed my faith in the book. I had believed everything in the book up until then and the whole book fell to bits." So, people like you to get the background right.

Q: Did you have any such nightmare scenarios with your recent historical books?

A: I had one at the beginning of *Star Of The Sea* where a character named Pius Mulvey is on the deck of the ship and it's leaving Ireland for the last time. It's a very, very sad scene. And just to kind of sophisticate the scene a bit I wanted to give him one pleasant, bittersweet memory of Ireland. So, I decided that when Pius was a little lad going to school in Connemara, the headmaster taught them a little device to remember the sequence of the planets from the sun. He's on the ship, looking up at the stars and he remembers this thing, which was: "Mary's Violet Eyes Make Joe Sit Up Nights Praying." And the initial letters of each is the initial letter of a planet.

So, the book comes out and a guy writes to me from the Irish Astrological Society, saying, "We have a problem here. P in 'praying' is for Pluto — and Pluto wasn't discovered until 1920!" I took out "praying" when it was reprinted. The same guy writes again — very cruelly, not having told me the first time — that "nights" is for Neptune but it was only discovered in 1847 — the year in which the book is set! So, you have this poor, illiterate guy going to America — is he reading the fucking scientific journals?! It seemed every time the book was reprinted that the solar system was getting smaller.

Q: You have two sisters. One is a painter and the other is a famous singer. Where does all this creativity come from?

A: My parents got us interested in art and culture, but not in any kind of pushy way. My dad, who was from Francis Street in Dublin — from a big family with not much money to spare — left school at the age of 13 and was working to support his family. But I think he got from them, as my mother got from hers, some notion that to be an authentic person, to be a whole person, that you should have some interest in the arts. You know, you should be able to sing a song; you should have read a poem by Yeats.

When they married it was important to them — because they had little formal education — just to open the doors of that world to us. They would feel kind of sorry for people who had no music at all in them, or had no love of poetry. They would take us to the theatre the odd time; there were books in the house. I can remember books by James Joyce; that great novel *Strumpet City*, John McGahern, and Lee Dunne's books being around as well.

Q: The latter authors would have had some of their books banned in Ireland when you were growing up.

A: My parents liked banned books. They'd inherited the notion from somewhere that a banned book was worth reading and books shouldn't be banned. I can remember them saying they admired McGahern because he had suffered because of his work — he'd lost his job and so on. So, there was some kind of pleasurable notion that literature was worth banning, so therefore worth reading, you know? I owe my parents a lot. I owe them that much anyway and I'm very grateful for it.

So, books would be just lying around the house and I think they felt that it was as important as doing your geography or mathematics homework. I think it's an Irish thing too. I now have conversations with English or American friends who talk about the horror story of the day they went home and told mum and dad they wanted to be a novelist — and the fucking smelling salts had to be called for and the vicar had to come round! There wasn't that in my family. They thought that's a good way to want to spend your time. Give it a go, you know?

Q: How did your parents' break-up affect you?

A: It was kind of a turbulent home — my parents' marriage wasn't happy and it ended when I was 13 — and I think for a teenager who's bookish or into music or interested in the arts, the world of the imagination becomes a kind of safe place, a retreat. All kids have this to some extent or another. I can see in my own eldest son now, who's about to turn eight, that for him the world of Harry Potter and the world of story is very real. I feel that's what happened to me. I just never came out of the other side of it. I loved reading and I was one of those kids who'd read anything.

I can remember having a go at a story when I was about 17, after my first girlfriend — a wonderful person called Sarah Maher — gave me a copy of a novel that her father loved, which was Salinger's *Catcher In The Rye*. That was a book that I can remember thinking, "I'd love to do that. It's not enough just to read." I remember after finishing it having a little go at short stories and daring to hope that you might one day be able to do that. That's the book that made me want to write. I still love the book and I still read it every three or four years. In fact, the older I get the more I love it in a way.

Q: Why did it have such an impact on you?

A: When you're young you are so taken by that central character — he's so fucking cheeky. The opening paragraph in the book, which I'll paraphrase: "I suppose you want to know who I am and where my parents are from and all that Charles Dickens crap." At that age, the only novels you're reading in school are the Charles Dickens crap. But here's this snotty nosed little fucker coming along and demolishing the 200-year long tradition of the English novel with the opening paragraph of the book. You are absolutely hooked. It's so funny, but when you're older you see the darkness of the book. Every book I've written has been an attempt to do something as pure and as effective as *Catcher In The Rye*.

Q: Charles Dickens gets a mention in *Redemption Falls*, which most readers would presume is a kind of homage to the author?

A: I have a love/hate relationship with Dickens. I've always hoped that when I die, Dickens will be there in heaven so I can embrace him and then headbutt him! He's such a fantastic writer, but he believed in the story at the expense of the characters. He's the greatest storyteller — ever. People who don't read at all know who Dickens' characters are. We know who Scrooge, Fagan and Oliver Twist are. The great flaw in Dickens is there isn't a psychologically real character in his entire body of work. He illustrates the classic problem of the storyteller, which is the more weight you give to the story, the less complexity you can give to the characters.

As a way of illustrating it, if you think about Oliver Twist: here is this child who's born in a workhouse and has the classic abusive childhood. He runs off to London where he's fostered by prostitutes and thieves. He has this awful life and is turned into a burglar and all the way through the book he never swears or blasphemes or has an ungallant thought. And he talks like a little member of the British Royal Family and you're wondering, "How can this be? How could this incredibly damaged child be like Little Lord Fauntleroy?" You realize the reason for this at the end of the book when it's revealed that Oliver is secretly the child of an aristocrat — and Dickens just can't bear that a child of an aristocrat would talk like the fucking plebs talk. The book embodies the very snobbery that it's constantly railing against.

Q: You went to UCD. Did you start taking writing more seriously then?

A: In a way I did, yes. I didn't have any sort of realistic hopes of writing fiction because nobody ever believes me when I say this, but there wasn't any notion in Ireland during the early 1980s that you could be a novelist as your profession. There weren't any novelists. Neil Jordan had become a filmmaker. There were very few other people around. There weren't readings or festivals of literature like there are now in every little town in Ireland. There really was no notion of even Ireland's literary past being anything other than the face of Yeats on a bank note. So, I became interested in journalism because I liked writing and I wanted to make a living that in some way involved writing. So, in the summer holidays when my mates where going off to Germany to earn big money in the car factories, most summers I had a job with the magazines or newspapers in Dublin.

Q: What was your first big break?

A: With my first summer job, I wrote to every single publication in the country — including the trades like *Shoemaker's Weekly* — and nobody wrote back except Vincent Browne, who had just taken over running the *Sunday Tribune*. He said come in and have a chat. I wrote a piece of about 1,000 words defaming and libeling President Hillary, saying that he wasn't any good and that was very much the *Magill* style — holding politicians to account. I thought Vincent would love this.

So, I get this irate phone call from Vincent: "Come in here and discuss this fucking piece!" So, I go in and he goes, "What makes you think anybody gives a fuck about your opinions? Nobody gives a shit about you. If it was Conor Cruise O'Brien, they might. But this is just absolutely fucking useless. Now go and rewrite it and take all the opinions out and just give me the facts." I did that and the following Sunday morning he rang me up to say the piece was in the paper. He had harassed me and then encouraged me (*laughs*).

Q: Did you feel overshadowed by having a sister with such a huge international profile while you were trying to make your own name in the writing world? Or did her success in any way help you?

A: It was probably both, to be honest. It could sometimes be a pain being asked about Sinéad all the time. But it probably helped in other ways. It's just the way the media works — the way Irish people work generally, anyway. I mean, if I was to ask somebody about you — who you are — and it would be, "He's the brother of that guy or he's married to that woman." You know, we make connections. So, it probably evens itself out. I understood it because I had worked in the media myself. And I wouldn't blame them being curious because it's a strange thing, you know? But I never said that much about it in public.

Q: Growing up, did you know Sinéad would be such a success?

A: Yeah, when there's somebody like that in the family you realise that's a very special person. This isn't somebody who wants to be a pop star — this is somebody who wants to sing. And if it all ended tomorrow she'd be back singing again in The Purty Kitchen. Sinéad always sang. I can remember going to see Sinéad singing in the pubs in Dun Laoghaire to 20 people. I think what's great about Sinéad is that on some level that's the same to her as singing in a stadium to 20,000 people. She's a musician first. She was an artist first and she's one of those people who needs to sing. She needs to express herself that way. I don't think success is genuinely important to her. If nobody ever bought another record she'd keep going. People like that are rare.

Q: Staying on the theme of music, what type of stuff do you like yourself?

A: I can't imagine a day without music. I like Stephin Merritt's band a lot, The 6ths. They had a very unpronounceable album title, Hyacinths And Thistles. I like Duke Spirit, Morrissey, Dylan, Marc Bolan, Arcade Fire, Kings Of Leon and Nick Cave, to mention a few names. I'm thinking of writing something about Rory Gallagher, so I've been listening to a lot of him. I like a pretty wide variety. I like music with a bit of dirt under its fingernails. I love great pop music too. I think Girls Aloud are the best band since The Monkees!

Q: Music has played its part in *Star Of The Sea* and *Redemption Falls*. Will music play a significant role in the third part of the trilogy?

A: The last two books are so kind of operatic and symphonic that I thought rather than finish with a really explosive third one that it should be a little coda, like an Irish ballad — a Connemara ballad. That's actually the way to finish. So, that's what I'm working on now. The third book is going to be very different; extremely short and very chronological; very pure; narrated by one voice. And it's loosely based on a real life story about the great Irish playwright, Synge. In the last few years of his life, Synge had a very passionate, tempestuous but secret love affair with a much younger woman who was an actress at the Abbey. They went to extraordinary lengths to keep their love affair secret.

Q: Which of your books are you most satisfied with and do you actually dislike any of them?

A: I worked really hard on my last two books. I put everything I had into them. There's a drop of my blood in *Star Of The Sea* and *Redemption Falls*. They're the books I'd like to be around in a few years. I don't dislike any of my books, although I have to say that some of them I love in the same way we have to love our children. When I read *Cowboys And Indians* now, which I did recently because somebody was interested in making a film of it, I did slightly want to read parts of it through the grid of my fingers, just thinking, "Oh, fuck!" It's so much the work of a young writer and it has an innocence and a charm. I don't think it's a great book but I have an affection for it.

On the other hand, it is the book of a 27-year-old person. It's absolutely not the way I would write it now. It's so fucking lurid and full of this funny desire to tell everybody: "I've had sex!" You're kind of secretly hoping that your granny might read it and that your girlfriend who dumped you might read it. The whole purpose of the book is to say, "Look! Fuck you all!"

Q: How do you put your books together?

A: They start usually from an image or an idea of a person. With *Star Of The Sea* I was trying to write a much more modern book — a cop thriller set in Celtic Tiger Dublin — and I would find late at night, when I was taking a rest from that book, that I had this image that just came into my head of this man walking up and down the decks of a 19th Century ship. It often happens when you're beginning a novel that you get ideas for other books, because your mind is very open and your imagination is crawling around in the depths. But I found as time went on, this fella in my head just wouldn't go away. I started scribbling down ideas about him and pictures of him, trying to see if I could get him more clearly.

After I had 20 or 30 pages of that I stopped, as I usually do when I have the beginning, and I then try to think of my way all the way down to the end of the story. I think my way down to the destination and then I build a kind of architecture for it. With *Star Of The Sea* and *Redemption Falls*, which are both quite complicated books, it took a long time to do that and to find a shape that would allow all of the voices and all of the music and textures to come in.

Q: How do you approach the actual writing itself?

A: The moment I have a plan, I'll write it fairly quickly. Both of those books were written in very intense bursts of nine months. I work every day. I work office hours. Before I had kids, I worked whenever I felt like it and I would think nothing of sitting up all night writing if I wanted to, but when you have kids your life changes and so I've had to adjust to office hours. Civil Service office hours! Kind of 10am to 4pm! And there's flexi-time. Essentially, by nature I'm a very lazy person, so the only way I can get anything done is to work all the time. If I genuinely only wrote when inspiration struck me, I think I'd write about twice a year and I'd spend the rest of the time in bed with a bottle of gin! It has to become a habit.

Q: What advice would you give novice writers?

A: If you want to write you should just write! That's the most important thing. Don't worry so much about going to writers' courses and workshops and all of that wonderful stuff that you can these days. Sometimes it's the modern equivalent of sitting in McDaid's in the 1950s talking about the novel you would be writing if you weren't sitting in a pub, you know?

You've got to make writing a part of your life. Writing is very demanding. It's far more like being married than it is like falling in love. There will be good days and bad days. And there will be moments when you're fucking sick of the sight of writing, but you have to make a long-term commitment and hope it'll be worth it over that extended period.

Everybody has got a regular time that they can write — like for most of us, it isn't full-time; everybody has got two hours on a Saturday afternoon or four hours on a Sunday morning. You've got to make that time and say to your loved ones,

"Don't come near me when I'm doing that. The door is closed and that's the time that I write." And you have to do it. Whether you've won the Booker Prize or are just starting out, the hardest thing is facing the blank page, and having the balls to face it and see what comes out.

— 2008

Chapter Nine: Donal Ryan

Donal Ryan may be one of Ireland's most successful contemporary authors, but he's also one of the most down-to-earth guys I've happened upon, too.

He didn't know me from Adam, but he swiftly replied to my WhatsApp message telling me to buzz him in ten minutes when I was up against the clock and urgently needed an interview with him for a magazine profile back in Christmas 2018.

It's hard to believe it's less than a decade ago when Donal first burst into the literary limelight with his sublime debut novel, *The Spinning Heart*, because it really does seem like he's been around forever. Perhaps that's because he's been far more prolific than most established authors. Over a seven-year period, he released six critically acclaimed books.

For such a laidback guy, the quality of his work hasn't faltered once. Donal is a master storyteller with a unique voice and his use of language is powerful, with every word carefully and superbly chosen.

In his then latest offering, *From A Low And Quiet Sea*, Donal turned his gaze outwards from rural Ireland towards the Syrian crisis. Arguably his most poignant work, it comprised three stories that eventually intertwined in the most heart-breaking and compelling way.

Donal is now employed full-time as a creative writing lecturer at the University of Limerick (UL). A few years back, he had taken a sabbatical from his day job in the civil service to focus on writing, but ended up needing to go back to work to food on the table. It made front-page news in 2017 when Donal mentioned he couldn't survive on the earnings from his creative writing alone — despite the fact he's fast on his way to becoming an iconic Irish author on the scale of Iris Murdoch, John McGahern, Edna O'Brien and John Banville.

"To be honest, it got blown out of proportion. It was no big deal at all. I was never not going back. I was on a three-year sabbatical from my job at the time. I always was planning to go back. But somebody asked me, why was I going back? And I said, 'To pay the mortgage.' It's a kind of euphemism for life in general, for just day-to-day things. But it turned into a big fucking thing that I was broke or whatever. I was embarrassed really," he said.

"I mean, there's no way you can make enough money to live, raise two kids, and pay a mortgage from literary fiction — unless you're very lucky. You need to win the literary lottery to be able to go full-time, I think. Unless you wanted to scrape around and eat free food at book launches and be hungry a lot, to be honest."

When that furor settled, Donal was offered a lecturing gig at UL. "I'll be here until they drag me out of my office," he joked "In my eighties, hopefully."

As a result, Donal now enjoys the best of both worlds. Donal relished the fact that his new day job involved thinking about literature and he was able to juggle his schedule in such a way to find the time to write. He always recommends to his students to try to put-in two or three hours of hard graft a day.

"I don't think I've ever done more than three hours at the very max. It's enough for anyone. I was always pretty disciplined, when it came to writing. I wrote at night between nine and midnight," he revealed.

"If you can find any three-hour block at all in the day — whether it's six am to nine am, or in the evening, or for me now in the middle of the day when I've no lectures — I can get my five-hundred to a thousand words written and feel great."

Increasingly, Donal finds himself going into a transcendent state when writing.

"It's funny," he ruminated, "I remember Mike McCormack saying when he wrote *Solar Bones*: 'I've no memory of writing the book at all!' I was thinking, 'How's that possible to have no memory of writing a book?' It's a big thing to write a book.

"But, to be honest, the last few books I've written, I've no clear memory of any one day of writing them! They all took around a year really, but that's including a couple of months of lead-in thinking time, you know. And then maybe eight or nine months of writing 1,000 words a day, or whatever. If I've written 500 words, I feel I've a done a good day's work."

In *From A Low And Quiet Sea*, Donal took on the theme of Syrian refugees, which was the first time he had written about anything other than rural Ireland.

"I came across a lot of them in my work as a labor inspector," he explained. "In life as well, I met some Syrian families settled here. There's so many wars around the world, but it got very close, and it became very real, because the coverage of the war in Syria was unremitting and very intense."

Speaking to people from Syria, Donal heard about the welcoming attitude that they'd always had towards refugees.

"In Syria, they would accept refugees from wars in countries around them," he said, "and they'd re-name streets in towns to make their visitors/newcomers feel at home. They had this lovely way of looking at the world."

That background shaped their expectations when — in the most appalling and tragic circumstances — their turn finally came.

"They had the expectation," he elaborated, "that when they left Syria, because of the war, there would be no problem — that they'd be welcomed wherever they went, I suppose, because of the history they had of welcoming people."

Sadly, it was not so.

It was a newspaper story that sparked the idea for the novel.

"I read an article about somebody very like the doctor in my story," he stated, "who paid all the money he had, to get his wife and child into a trafficker's boat. And it turns out that, halfway across, they realized it wasn't manned! Imagine doing that? Imagine sending loads of your fellow humans off in a boat, where they're locked into a hold, off into the sea with no crew on the boat! And you take all the money off them, knowing the chances are that they're going to die!

"Jesus Christ! It's unbelievable," he said, shaking his head at the utter madness of it.

"I got upset with the idea of the UN. What the hell is the UN for, if the UN can't be a huge, mobilizing force, who can actually go to Syria and stop this slaughter going on?

"I had thought that was what the UN was for," he continued. "But it seems everybody's got a veto: Putin's got a veto and the US has a veto — and so nothing gets done. My contribution to it is puny and ridiculous, just to write a story about it — but maybe it'll do something."

Donal was working on a new novel, which has since been published, when I caught up him that December afternoon as he sat in his office taking a break between lectures.

"I haven't started the hard slog of editing yet," he revealed, "but it's looming very close now. It's called *Strange Flowers*."

Just don't try to get him to tell you what it's all about.

"No, I'll say nothing, Jason, because I've gotten in deep shit with the publishers before for shooting my mouth off!" he concluded, laughing. "The publishers have given out to me in the past, even for revealing titles too soon. Maybe it's no harm to actually have it out there. It's down to come out next September."

— 2018

Chapter Ten: Leland Bardwell

I was out for a drink one night in a rural pub in Sligo with the late Dermot Healy and he introduced me to Leland Bardwell. She was 89-years-old at the time and, despite suffering a recent stroke, still possessed a sharp mind and was well able to hold her own in conversation.

She graciously agreed to be interviewed the next day and Dermot dropped me off at her little cottage, which was only a few minutes drive away from his own home with its picturesque view of the Atlantic Ocean.

Born in India in 1922, Leland was considered an important poet by many of her contemporaries, but she was, as is sadly the case with many great talents, underappreciated by the public.

Her little modest cottage was a far cry from her own upbringing in the fine surrounding of the grand Leixlip House, which later became a hotel, but Leland was, at one point, quite literally a starving artist in Paris and would stand outside restaurants and cafés to catch a glimpse of her literary heroes, such as John-Paul Sarte and Simone de Beauvoir. Years later, she would allow the great Patrick Kavanagh, who was in penury, to sleep on her sofa and feed him.

Alongside the film director Neil Jordan, Leland helped to establish the Irish Writers' Co-op that was set-up to publish and promote local scribblers. The Co-op published some of her own novels. Eight years before she passed away, Leland published a memoir entitled *A Restless Life*.

She passed away at the grand old age of 94 in June 2016. I'm glad this interview, which I only transcribed for this book, is finally seeing the light of day because, as the academic and poet Eiléan Ní Chuilleanáin said, she "should be more widely known."

Q: Your Wikipedia entry states you where born in India of all places!

A: I wish to Christ you wouldn't put that in because everyone assumes my father was in the army, which he wasn't. He worked on the railways. These are things that drive me absolutely crazy when people say, "I suppose he was in the army." No. And my father was a Sinn Féin-er, you see. And very pro- Sinn Féin. Everybody thinks because he was a protestant: "Oh, he must've been pro English." But if anybody said to him, "Are you Anglo Irish?" he'd really go mad! "I'm Irish," he say. It's true because the family had come over not from England but actually they'd come over from Spain originally. But that was two or three centuries ago.

Q: Do you feel a connection to India?

A: No, why would I? I was only born there. Oh, I remember bits of it very, very clearly. I remember things like my father going off to shoot some wild animals — although he never shot anything because he hated it! But things like that, crazy daft things like that. I remember dreams I had about being chased by wild animals and I would always run to my nurse in my dreams. I loved her, I just adored her. I remember all that. But I don't feel any connection at all.

Q: Did you ever go back?

A: No, I never wanted to. Funny, people always ask me that. I've no interest whatsoever. But I love travelling. I've been to Russia and places like that. But I just had no desire to visit in India, it's funny, isn't it?

Q: You come from an artistic background.

A: Yes. They were painters and writers. There was a whole bevy of them, both my mother's side and my father's side actually. My father's side they were Hone's, who were well known. There's a Hone painting. (*She points to frame on the wall — JOT.*) Well, it's a copy actually. They're very expensive. I wouldn't be able to afford them (*laughs*).

Q: How old were you when you first came to Ireland?

A: The first time I was two and then I went back out. I had a brother and sister and they were born here in Ireland. But my father couldn't get a job here in Ireland, so the only job he could get was in India on the railways. He was a scholar. He'd studied. He'd been in Trinity in Dublin. So, he was an engineer. So, he got a job in India. It was the only place he could get a job because they were the British Empire and they were building railways, you see. Although just before, or after, or during the First World War, he'd worked in America on the big railway.

Q: So how old were you when you moved permanently back to Ireland?

A: I was about four when we settled here back in Ireland. I remember well being on the boat and the various places we stopped on the boat and the people would get off because they were tired of being seasick (*laughs*).

Q: Did people look at you differently because you were born in India and had a different accent?

A: Yes, they do. I got a lot of this and it really pisses me off, because they immediately assume my father was in the Indian army, which he wasn't.

Q: You grew up in the Leixlip House, which is now a luxury manor hotel.

A: I loved it there. It was everything. The house was burnt down and it was rebuilt because it was a listed building.

Q: How did you first get into writing?

A: Well, I wrote from being a child, actually. I assumed everybody wrote so I thought nothing of it really. But I was very musical and I learnt the piano and I wanted to be a pianist. I thought, "Everybody's a writer. Sure, that's nothing!" (*Laughs*) I really did think like that; I was a bit crazy as a child.

Q: Did you go to university?

A: No, you see my parents wouldn't let me. My brother and sister were older than I. They went and my mother wouldn't pay anymore. "I'm not going to pay any more for your education," she said. And that was it. After I was married, I tried to do one of these awful degrees on paper (*a long distance education course — JOT*) and I had babies at the time, it was very hard. I didn't go to school until I was quite old. I was about 11. My mother wouldn't pay. She just hated me and I was just nonsense. Anybody who had what in those days what was called a governance — and I was thrown in with them. And actually I was very smart and I used to write stories all the time, and poems. I just wrote all the time. And then my brother burnt all my work, all my juvenilia. He hated me. (*Laughs*) A nice boy!

Q: How old were you when you met your husband?

A: I went to work in Scotland and I met him there. I was 22.

Q: Was it love at first sight?

A: No, not at all. I didn't love him — ever! But I liked him; he was okay (*laughs*). Actually, he came from quite an interesting family, strangely enough, but they were all into some kind of arts as well.

Q: You had six children together?

A: I had six children. They weren't all his. I had twins and they were his. And they were born here because we came back here at the time.

Q: Did you have a child with your husband's brother?

A: It's starts to get very complicated! Then there would have been a gap of nine years and then I met another man named Fintan McLoughlin and had three boys.

Q: Why did you decide to keep the name Bardwell?

A: I'll tell you why: because Hone was at the time, when I started to write, my maiden name was a very well known name — some of my uncles, none of them were poets or that, but they were good at writing about famous people. Joseph Hone would've written biographies. He wrote a biography of Yeats. He would've been well-known. You had all the painters. The reason I hung onto Bardwell was because I first published under that name. And the reason I didn't want to publish under Hone was because I wanted to be famous in my own right and not because of my family. And my family never really forgave me. They always said, "Why don't you use your name?" I said, "Because I'm myself. I'm not just one of the family." I was very proud.

Q: You would've been involved in the literary circles in Dublin, I suppose.

A: Well, not really, no. I was the wrong generation, actually. I didn't know any writers in Dublin really. The first writers I really met, apart from my relations, were writers I met in London.

Q: Weren't you on Patrick Kavanagh's trustee committee?

A: No, you wouldn't call it a trustee. What happened was this: when Katherine Kavanagh, who was Kavanagh's wife for about five minutes before he

The Celtic Hemingway, Dermot Healy.

(Left to right) Emma Donoghue who won the literary world's equivalent of the Lottery won she was paid a seven-figures sum for her novel Room; *bestselling fantasy author of the* Skulduggery Pleasant *series, Derek Landy; and Deirdre Purchell, who has enjoyed a varied career as a newscaster, print journalist and best-selling author.*

Donal Ryan, who is often hailed as the heir to the throne of the late John McGahern.

The world according to John Boyne, who is pictured here with the literary icon John Irving.

Ian Gibson, hailed by The Irish Times *as "the creator of modern biography in Spain" thanks to his authoritative tomes on Lorca and Salvador Dalí.*

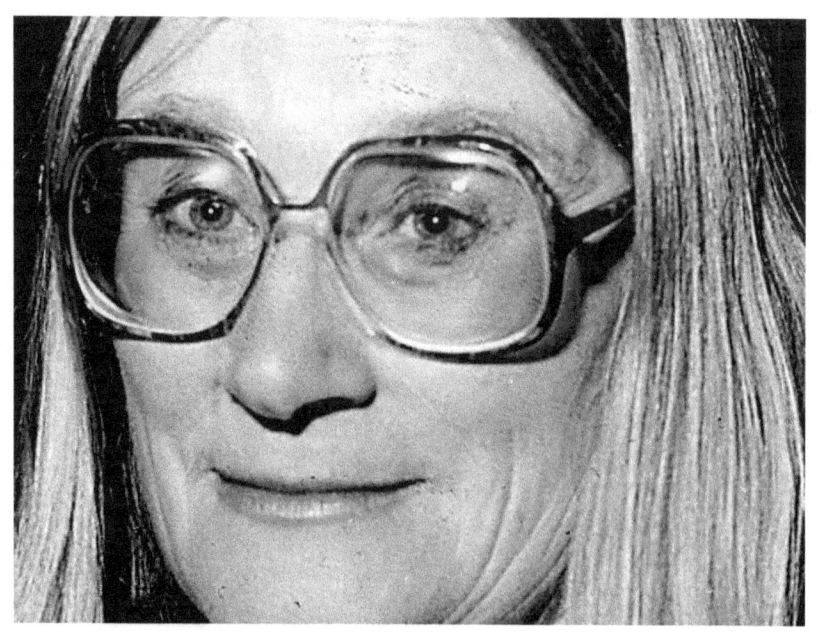

The grand of dame of Irish letters, Jennifer Johnston, and (below) the late poet Leland Bardwell who was considered one of Ireland's greatest poets and a fine novelist too, but sadly underappreciated.

Joseph O'Connor, best known for his 2004 novel Star of the Sea.

JP Donleavy pictured (below) enjoying a pint of Guinness as hellraiser Brendan Behan looks on. Above, JP in later years at his library at the massive 180-acre estate, Levington Park, which is adjacent to the picturesque Lough Owel on the outskirts of Mullingar, County Westmeath. JP's book The Ginger Man *was selected 99th out of the Modern Library's Best 100 Novels of the 20th Century. As the great man himself quipped to the author, "I guess that's better than a kick in the arse!"*

The late author Lee Dunne reveled in his dubious title of being Ireland's most banned author with a total of seven books. Here's the jacket cover for Lee's memoir,
My Middle Name Is Lucky, *which was published by Jason O'Toole's own imprint Killynon House Books in 2006. It was to be Lee's last published work. Lee died in 2021.*

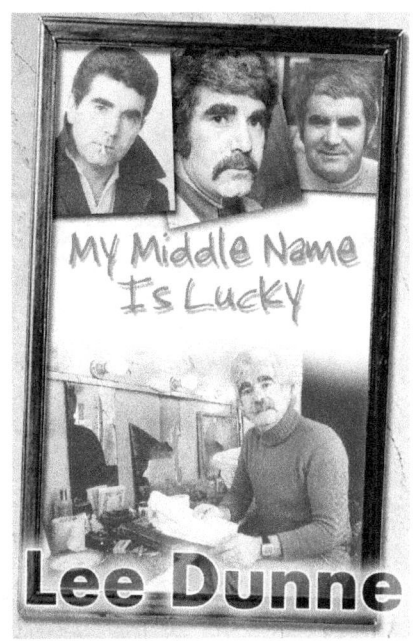

The two-term, sitting Irish President Michael D. Higgins is pictured at an awards ceremony with Ian Gibson. And below, Patrick McCabe, the critically acclaimed author of The Butcher Boy.

Playwright and memoirist Peter Sheridan, whose older brother Jim directed the Oscar–winning film My Left Foot.

Sebastian Barry was the first author to win the prestigious Costa Book of the Year award on two occasions. Below, Brendan Behan's biographer Ulick O'Connor.

died — literally she was only his wife for only a few months — and I remember her saying, "Lucky I married him!" It meant that she inherited his literary estate, which was very good because it held it to be used for poverty-stricken writers, which was very, very fine of her.

Q: You were good friends with Kavanagh?

A: Sort of, yeah. Everybody makes a huge thing about that, but it's quite untrue.

Q: But he used to stay in your house!

A: Yeah, because he had nowhere else. I couldn't put him out on the streets. He was an awful nuisance (*laughs*). I mean, I had to buy whiskey for him before he went to bed. I had to go down the road to the pub. And he never had cash and it always had to be put down on the bill, and the owner of the pub used to go crazy. I should get him a small bottle of whiskey, which he would then put under his pillow. It was a very small flat and he slept in the sitting room on the sofa. He'd put it (the whiskey) down his pillow and in the morning he had to have the whiskey in the tea first thing, otherwise he couldn't get up and get going. You see, he was very ill by the time I knew him. And it was very sad really because nobody would have him, he was an awful nuisance in the flats and he never had any money and he was groaning and moaning. And I felt very sorry for him. I felt, "I can't put this man out on the streets." People make a huge thing (out of it). Because I knew Kavanagh you must've been sleeping with him night and day! Which was untrue (*laughs*).

Q: Did Kavanagh and Katherine get together through you?

A: That was very funny. That happened in England. This is very interesting, I had this flat in London and like all places I ever lived it was crammed with Irish people. And Katherine, whom I'd met in London, I took a great liking to

135

her, she was a great woman, she always had a job. She was probably very good for Kavanagh because she was good-natured, humorous and she had a few bob. So, she had everything really. And I put them into bed together!

He said, "Get into the bed there." He was lying on the floor in a kind of a bad thing in the sitting room. And he said to her, "Get into the bed there." And she was very nervous, she was very shy. I said, "Ah, come on! He's very nice He wouldn't do you any harm." (*Laughs*) A famous speech! And then they were always together holding hands for weeks. It was lovely. And then eventually he used to go over to London and stay with her.

She came from a very interesting IRA family. Her mother was very strong during the Troubles, did an awful lot for women's rights and things, getting the vote for women. She fitted in very well into Kavanagh's idea of an Irishwoman, which was very good.

In a way, I was responsible for their meeting and then finally her marrying him, which was very nice because then she was able to leave her money through Kavanagh's wish that somebody in their middle years should get some money because that was the worst time of life, to be broke if you were a poet or a writer.

Q: Why did you pick Sligo to live in?

A: It was entirely chance. I'd won a prize and I'd happen to be here minding the dogs for Dermot (Healy). They were going to the continent for a month and they had dogs and cats and things like that. And I was sort of wandering around at the time and came over here to mind them. And I was staying in Dermot's house, which was then with no electricity, no running water, no nothing. And it was desperate. It was candlelit. And it was winter, so it was dark at four o'clock.

But I'd won this ridiculous price from the Arts Council for my writing and he said to me, "Don't drink that money or whatever." I wasn't drinking here in the day or anything like that. He said, "Buy something with it. Buy some property." And it was just before the Celtic Tiger and places like this were very cheap. I said, "God! I'd never thought about buying a house. That's the last thing on my mind."

I heard this (cottage) was owned by a man in The Bronx and I had to write to him because he had ownership to it. I wrote to this man in The Bronx and I said, "Can I buy the house?" It was 12,000, which was for nothing, even then in the '90s. But I didn't have 12,000; I had 7,000 when I got the prize. I used that and then I borrowed money from two sons, but I did pay it back.

I had to send the money by post to The Bronx! He said, "You better send me the money." I consulted a lawyer who said, "Well, that would be a very foolish thing to do. You might as well throw your money in the sea and trust the postal service, or trust a man you never met in The Bronx!" I'd talked to him on the phone. He got the money — and I sent it to him by post! And he said that that was fine. We built up a relationship on the phone and by writing to him, so he very much wanted to sell the house to me. He was an Irishman.

Q: You had a stint in Paris during your formative years.

A: I always wanted to live in Paris, actually. And I managed to screw about six months in Paris at one stage. I was starving, literally. It was after the war. There was no money. You used to queue every morning at six o'clock for translations because my French was excellent. And you always missed it, a decent job. And I used to sell newspapers to survive. I was starving. I was literally hungry.

Q: Did you get to meet any famous writers in Paris?

A: Not at all. I just gazed at them.

Q: Whom did you gaze at?

A: John-Paul Sarte. Simone de Beauvoir. I knew the pub they used to go to, you see, and I'd stand outside the door and look at them (*laughs*). It's ridiculous.

Q: The Shakespeare bookshop as well, I suppose.

A: No, I didn't know that 'til much later actually. I didn't know anything about that sort of thing at all. I only really learnt about that after. It's funny, I was all the wrong generation.

Q: You were literally a starving artist?

A: My God! The hunger. I really was hungry, yeah. A terrible hunger. It's awful, there's nothing worse.

Q: What did you eat?

A: Literally, anything I could get. There was a very cheap cake, which cost about a shilling, which was very dear. And I used to eat that and it would do me for half the day. And then, if I was lucky, I would get something else during the day, somehow or other.

Q: You mentioned donkey mince in one of you poems.

A: That's right. This man told me about donkey meat, which was very cheap. And to eat the potato and drink the water that was used to cook the potatoes because there was vitamins in them. And to survive on that. So, I got potatoes and donkey meat. And that would be your one meal of the day, but very little because you could barely afford it, even that was very expensive. And I was very, very hungry. I suffered from malnutrition very badly.

Q: How long were you in Paris for?

A: Only about seven months. I had to go back (to London) because I did suffer from real hunger in Paris.

Q: Which works are you most proud of — there's been five novels and countless volumes of poetry?

A: Well, in a way, they always say *The House* is a classic. It's a classic because it deals with the situation of the Protestant and Catholic situation. I've got reviews where it's the best books written in such and such a year and that kind of thing, because it tiptoed into that situation. "You're only a Protestant! What would ye know about it!" I got a lot of that, which was very, very hurtful and nasty actually. Well, that's the way they talked. I had some pretty tough, nasty things said to me over my life about that actually. Oh, very, very nasty, actually. It's very hurtful. But that's more or less stopped. The generations have more or less evened out and the Protestants are forgotten really as having Anglo attached.

Q: What other works would you be most proud of?

A: I don't really know. The critics, as I said, liked *The House* very much.

Q: What about the poetry?

A: It's very hard, poetry changes all the time with the decades. I get hate mail from Leixlip, this crazy man he writes to me and says I'm a disgusting writer! I keep the letters because they're really quite funny. I'm bringing him out because this is the thing about poetry that people still think about poetry rhyme; there's a generation that can't get away from that, that poetry (is supposed) to be that. This guy always says, 'There's not one single rhyme in your poem!' Although I used to love writing rhyme poetry, mind you. I loved it, yeah.

So, in a way, poetry is the most difficult of one's skills, I think because you never know where you are with the times that are in on it. How far are you getting into what is poetry? In the olden days when it just rhymed it was so easy because you wrote a good poem and it rhymed. And the subject matter — when poetry was written about love, or hate or beauty, or beautiful places. The arts change all the time, don't they? Look at the change of painting in the 19th Century — Picasso and all that — (is) the same way that writing suddenly came out of the rhymes and that makes it very difficult to write, and you don't know how far you're hitting.

I enjoy writing, or trying to write poetry most, I think. But, at the moment, because of my stroke — I had a very unfortunate stroke, it took my reading and writing, which is very rare. I can just about write. Very slowly. So, I'm only writing poetry now. I had finished a novel, which is sitting there in a drawer, which needs work and it's difficult for me now to do that. Which is terrible and I find it awful.

Q: Do you find it a bit depressing?

A: Very.

Q: You're a prolific writer. It must've been very difficult to write such a huge body of work and raise six children?

A: Yeah. The first time I was published I was quite old. I was pushing 40, which is now days old because kids of 19 are publishing.

Q: I was 35 before I had my first book published.

A: (*Laughs*) That's old! I was old when I published, I was 40-something.

Q: Was it emotionally difficult for you to write your autobiography?

A: Not in the slightest — I just wrote it.

Q: Did you find it therapeutic?

A: Not really, no.

Q: Did it make you nostalgic?

A: No. I was just interested to put it down and once you start you go zooming off. You do enjoy writing about your past because it's so easy (*laughs*). Because you where there (*laughs*).

Q: You were involved in setting up the Irish Writers Co-operative, which was an important time in Irish publishing.

A: That's true. That was very important, actually. The film director Neil Jordan came to me one day. We met in the street; he was walking up and I was walking down Leeson Street. And he said to me, "Have you ever written any prose?" Because he was then trying to get money from the English government, because he couldn't get any from the Irish government, because we couldn't publish anything, there was no publishers in Ireland, and (he wanted) to get money for publishing. And he didn't get it from the English because eventually the Irish Arts Council gave him some money and he started a publishing thing.

So, then he said, "Have you ever written any prose?" Because I had already started publishing poetry. I said, "Yeah, I have an old novel there in the drawer, which nobody seemed to like or want to publish." So, he said, "Will you give us it?" So, I showed it to him and four or five days later I met him in Grogans pub and he said, "I'm going to publish that novel. It's brilliant." So, he started the Irish Writers Co-Op from getting money from the Irish Arts Council. And anybody who got published by the co-op then became a member of the co-op. So, I then started to work with the co-op and I loved that because we had a lot of books coming in from people who couldn't get published in Ireland. I loved doing it. I used to cycle all around Dublin and seeing all these writers.

Q: Then you had the magazine *Cyphers* as well.

A: We were always doing things. We were always starting writing and reading, getting people to come and give readings. I was very energetic; I loved doing that kind. I loved working with the Co-op and working on people's books. *Girl on a Bicycle* was my first novel and that was published by the Co-op. I gave that to Neil

Jordan. And that was the beginning and that had a huge effect because it's had such good reviews in *The Irish Times* and things like that.

Q: You had five books of fiction published in total.

A: I had one more novel with the Co-op. The next one was published in the North, Blackstaff Press. They published *Mother to a Stranger* and that did very well. I was very lucky because that was the first time I made any money because of the translations. A lot of my work has been translated into French and German. *Mother to a Stranger* was translated into German and they loved it. It came out in '91 or '92. It hit a kind of a vein in Germany and it sold probably more copies of that novel in Germany than any other titles. I had a collection of short stories before and they'd been translated and published by the Germans.

Q: You've been married twice, is that right?

A: No, I've only been married once. We reared the twins first of all in Ireland. They were born in Ireland and we sort of fizzled out when the kids were about — they very, very young — two/three. No, more, four, I think. It was sad for them. It was hard for them.

Q: But you obviously felt it was the best decision for you to end the marriage?

A: Well, you see, when I when I got married to Dave Bardwell I was in love with this guy, he was Irish, he was a cousin of mine and we were always to get married and that kind of thing. But then he kind of fizzled away and I was very sort of heartbroken, as one is at that age. And I was working in a free school. I had a very good job in London because it was easy to get good jobs. All I did was typing for God sake, nothing! But I was working in embassies and things, which sounded very grand.

I saw an advertisement in *The New Statesman* about somebody wanted in this school in Scotland, it was a free school. And I was interested in that because I wanted to learn. I felt I wasn't learning anything, I wasn't doing anything about life or anything. So, I wrote this man and I said I'd like to work there and he wrote back immediately. I must've written a very good letter and he said, "Come tomorrow."

So, I chucked up everything and went to Scotland. And that's where I met Mick Bardwell. He was teaching there, in that school. It was a very interesting place because a lot of people who had been consciousness objectors during the war ended up in places like that. They were very fucked up by the situation and they were treated badly — there were some awful stories like a man being out into water for days at a time. You know, things like that. Unbelievable cruelty from the British, which they deny. And a lot of them were very neurotic as a result of being very badly treated and hurt.

Q: After you broke up with your husband Mick then you met his brother?

A: Well, I'd met his brother before when I went to Paris. That's all I'd ever wanted to be was in Paris and gazing at the writers. I'd go into the bars where the writers would be and I used to gaze at them and think, "Oh, I wish I knew them and could talk to them now." I felt I belonged with those kind of people.

Q: It's very strange coincidence that you met Mick's brother.

A: Not very strange because it was so much the same (*laughs*).

Q: But you had a relationship, which was unusual.

A: Well, yes. And it didn't please anybody. It was very wrong of me I suppose in the sense of breaking up family.

Q: How long were you with Brian?

A: I suppose for about five, six, seven, eight years. We came back to London then and we lived in London and that where's Jackie was born. Jackie was the only child I had that was born in England; all the rest were born here.

Q: Why did you break up with Brian?

A: I was that kind of person — I was hopeless when it comes to relationships. I was always wandering. I was a wanderer and I wanted to wander all the time. I wanted to live in France and then I wanted to live elsewhere. My mother had damaged me, good and proper really. I didn't know how to deal with human relationships at all. She hated me. And she wouldn't let me be educated, and all that. She really treated me very badly. I was pretty fucked up me in my head really. I was looking for something very hard and I always either writing or painting or off playing music, or doing something, but never getting anywhere with it. Do you know what I mean?

Q: Where you able to reconcile with your mother before she died?

A: God no. I minded her for a year-and-a-bit, literally slept in her room and that and looked after her and gave her injections of morphine every four hours. I was 19 going on 20 when my mother died.

Q: Why do you think she hated you?

A: Well, she told me. She made it quite clear. She was a strange woman. She was very talented herself. That's one of her paintings there. It's very good. When artists come in they always ask me who did that. It's one of her best one actually, which I managed to steal!

Q: Did you get on well with your father?

A: My poor dad! Actually, I talk to him all the time now that he is dead! He apparently, I'm told, was very proud of me, that I was such an extraordinary strength, that I could survive in appalling situations. But he didn't know how to be a father. He'd been in the war. He belonged to that generation (of when) parents didn't really like their children particularly. They probably loved their children but didn't show it. My mother would be furious if I used the word love. "You know nothing about love! Don't use that word." Like (it was) a bad word, you know. She might have been exceptional like that, possibly. She was very nervous about that kind of thing, terrified of sex, terrified of everything, coming from that generation. And it's sad really because she was a very brilliant woman, but never given a real chance to show how brilliant she was…

Q: But your father never said he hated you, did he?

A: No, I was afraid of him. When I went to England first I was convinced that all children hated their parents, that that was the norm. I really did think that and that's why I think I was a bad mother because I assumed that children didn't want to be with their mother. Because I only liked it when I was away from my parents. My whole ambition was to get away from them and I thought everybody was the same.

Q: How did you meet your third partner Fintan?

A: In London. I met him in a pub in Soho (*laughs*). The only money he ever earned… the rest of the time he just stole money from me… was (when) he had a taxi for three-and-a-bit years. And he gave me a pound a day (*laughs*). Eventually, we actually threw him out of the house. He was impossible. He was breaking the place up. He was mad. Fintan was a manic drinker. He was manic really. He was schizophrenic, totally, totally. He always had this impression I had money because I was a Hone and there was money in the family. And of course I didn't have any money. I was absolutely broke. I was living on nothing and I was three jobs in one day. I was actually with Fintan for quite a long time, about 15 years. But for a large portion of that last period we weren't living together as such; we where only living together because we had to live in the same house.

145

Q: It must've been very sad for you?

A: You see, I'm not like other people. People think that's awful. But that is just part of life really to me. Tough going, well tough cookie, you know what I mean, that's it, that's the way life is and you accept it, and that's it. People think I'm crazy.

Q: I don't think you are.

A: You don't? Oh, good (*laughs*).

Q: Did you ever have a problem with drink yourself?

A: No, I never had a drink problem. But I like drink. And I would drink a lot, if I had a chance, if I had money. I like parties and things like that. But I can't drink now since I had the stroke, unfortunately.

Q: Do you have any big regrets in life?

A: That I wasn't educated, but then that's not my fault. So, I can't blame myself for that. I didn't finish my degree when I started to study after I was married. Well, of course, I do have regrets about treating my children badly. I feel very bad about that, very guilty. I know that parents suffer from a lot of guilt anyway — even if they're absolutely spotless in every way, mentally and physically. But I do wish I'd been a better mother. That I regret. I regret that I didn't show much love to them and, you know, that kind of thing. Because I believed literally, it was so drummed into me that parents hate their children and children hate their parents. And I really believed that the first thing children wanted was to go away from their parents. I was very badly hurt and actually a bit crazy really. I should've been psychoanalyzed or something done about me (*laughs*) when I was much younger.

146

Q: Did you suffer from depression?

A: No, I didn't suffer from anything like that. No, I was very lucky. I was very, very strong mentally and good physically. I was good physically. I was very good at games. I was very good rider. Horses were very important for me. Still are. I went riding not long ago! Myself and the writer now who's making his name, Sebastian Barry, he used to come out riding with me. I was supposed to be looking after the horses, but he used to come out and give me a hand to ride one of them and I'd ride the other one, and we'd go galloping in the park (*laughs*).

Q: Were you ever religious?

A: I was terrified of religion, literally terrified. When I saw the clergy I would walk across the streets in Leixlip and hide. He was horrible man anyway (*laughs*).

Q: Are you a spiritual person?

A: Unfortunately, no. I can't say I was really. I'd like to think that I was, but I wasn't. I was terrified of religion. What I think is, for what it's worth, the God you have is inside you is something of you and use that during your life to try and.... but not sort of consciously — not sort of telling, "Listen God, what am I supposed to do now?" That doesn't enter what I think about it. But I think, "Give us a break." I feel sometimes that my own mistakes have made my life trebly hard and I feel that, in a way, I translate that into a kind of a being — not a being exactly, not exactly a spirit; it's very hard to describe, but something there inside you that is beyond my control. And that has made my life doubly hard. I can't really describe it.

Q: So, you don't believe in heaven and hell?

A: I have a kind of a sort of a hope that you'd be conscious of, say, the family. I often talk to my father, for example. And I feel I'm talking to him because we never talked to each other when he was alive. I talk to him a lot. But I can't really say whatever that's something inside me, or whether I'm bringing him from another (place). I like to think that I'm doing that, but that's sort of wishful thinking in a way, I suppose.

Q: So, you'd be hopeful there's an afterlife?

A: I don't really think of it as an afterlife. I think of it as a kind of a spirit. This is very arrogant of me, but I always feel that I have very strong spirits — and my spirits will be strong enough to hang around. But it's sort of arrogance really. I like to believe it, but I can't say I'm absolutely sure.

— 2011

Chapter Eleven: Peter Sheridan

Peter Sheridan was playing in the garden with his four-year-old grandson in the summer of 2012 when he found himself flabbergasted and at a loss for words when asked, "Grandad, what did you do in the old days?"

It suddenly made the then 60-year-old feel like he was from the Stone Age, but it also inspired him to reflect on his past by writing a candid memoir—which was released in 2013—that was addressed directly to his grandson to comprehensively answer the question for him when he's old enough to understand.

Perhaps Peter, who has already written two best-selling memoirs dealing with his childhood and his father's complex love affair with another woman, subconsciously also wanted to outline all his achievements in theatre because his career has been overshadowed by the phenomenal success of his Oscar-winning older brother Jim, who directed *My Left Foot*, *The Field* and In *The Name of the Father*.

"It's weird—people you don't know go, 'You're the movie director's brother?' It's kind of like, 'Actually, we're equals', you know," he told me.

The two brothers originally started out together when they established The Project Arts Theatre. But while Jim used this as a steppingstone to launch himself in Hollywood, Peter's own career trajectory has taken many dramatic twists and turns during the past 30-odd years.

Peter and Jim were first introduced to the stage as teenagers by their distraught father following the death of their younger brother Frankie from a brain hemorrhage.

"He didn't go to work for months after Frankie died. He always had a dream to be an amateur actor. He took that opportunity in the wake of Frankie's death and started a drama group," Peter explained.

Eventually, the two brothers took over the running of the amateur theatre group and toured the country with a production of *Waiting for Godot* in 1971. It brought them to the attention of Colm O'Brian who asked them if they were interested in using his Project Arts Centre to stage plays.

This ultimately led Peter and Jim to founding the Project Theatre Company in 1976, which quickly established them as the L'enfants terribles of the Dublin theatre scene with their many controversial shows. "It was absolutely insanity for five years," he said. "It never stopped."

It certainly sounds like it from listening to Peter reminisce about their times in charge. Perhaps the biggest controversy was when they caused outrage getting the Gay Sweatshop Theatre Group from London over to stage a play about homosexuality—over a decade before it was eventually decriminalized.

"The idea of gay men and gay women onstage caused an absolute furor. It's the only show I was ever involved in that got a standing ovation before the show started," he said. "It was such a feat to actually get the play on because we all had to get our way through these protestors who were outside with placards. We had protestors outside and inside the theatre.

"It caused an argument with Dublin Corporation because a lot of the councillors were very conservative and very Catholic. They put a proposal to suspend the Project's grant and that was carried. We finally got it reinstated but there was a whole campaign involved in doing that. I tell the story at some length in the book."

They also hit the headlines when Jim got into a fight with ex-Sex Pistol singer John Lydon (A.K.A. Johnny Rotten) when he pulled out of a planned concert at the last minute.

"Jim went over to London to confront him because he said he'd headline that gig and then he said he wasn't coming. There was a row in a house in London. The papers picked it up. It was headlines back in Dublin," Peter recalled.

Who won the fight?

"I say Jimmy did actually."

They got U2 in as a last minute replacement and this lead to the future superstar band being offered to play at the Project every Saturday night for a six-month residency. But this too caused un-foreseen problems when an anti-U2 gang of thugs stormed into the venue in an effort to disrupt their concert.

"One of them produced a knife and Mannix Flynn wrestled the knife off the guy and ran up the stairs and hid the knife," Peter said. "But somebody had phoned the police and the cops arrived saying, 'We heard there was a knife produced. We want the knife.'

"And we were all like, 'We didn't see any knife!' And Mannix looking at me looking at U2 looking at the cops! And the cops went off then and left us alone. That was a classic incident. I actually don't tell that in the book."

Peter remembered Phil Lynott on another occasion grappling Bono "in a headlock and wrestling him down onto the floor" in the Project's foyer back in 1982.

"My two boys were in the audience and they were so impressed that Phil Lynott and Bono were at a play that their dad had written. At the interval, we were messing around the foyer and Phil was saying to my son, 'What football team do you support?' I said to Bono, 'You're not interested in football, sure you're not?' Which he wasn't," Peter said.

"Phil then caught Bono in a headlock and started wrestling him down onto the floor, saying to him, 'Northside boys against the Southside!' My kids thought this was the best thing ever—two rock stars fighting over what football team they supported and where they came from."

The Sheridan brothers finally left the Project behind in 1980, with Jim then immigrating to New York to direct at off-Broadway theatres. But Peter shocked everyone by opting to take a year break from theatre to go on and run a market stall selling radio and stereo equipment in the Liberties. "I learnt one thing in the markets, I'm not a salesman," he quipped.

For Peter working in the market was simply a means to an end to put food on the table for his family. Peter had met his wife Sheila when he was 16-years-old at a dance, but she rejected him because he was "too small" and also happened to be two years younger than her.

He recalled, "It was such a put down—I got mouldy drunk as a result of that. I got very drunk and felt sorry for myself."

But three years later Sheila, who was by then involved in the theatre group herself, was won over by Peter's charm. "I never thought she had any interest in me after that first encounter, but she asked me out to her house to help with an essay—but I didn't know it was actually a come on!" he said, laughing.

"It was a total whirlwind. Once we had that first kiss we were never out of each other's company; we lived in each other's world completely."

Within three months Sheila had fallen pregnant with their first of four children and Peter proposed. But her father was infuriated that his daughter was going to marry someone from the wrong side of the tracks.

"Her family didn't think that I was a good match," he confessed. "No. Her father was very against it."

The couple spent their first three-and-a-half-years living in a mobile home in the back garden of a council house in Crumlin, Dublin. "We'd absolutely no money. It was a huge struggle to try and make a few shillings in Ireland at that time," he said.

They eventually moved into a house when Peter found himself taking over The Project Theatre, but even then they were still watching every penny. "In The Project, me and Jim split a salary; it was £57 a week split between the two of us," he said. "That's so we survived. It was always like living by your wits."

After the self-imposed sabbatical from the stage to work in the market, Peter then formed an amateur theatre group in his old neighborhood aimed at inspiring novices to get involved in acting. He directed them in a sell-out show at The Project, which prompted the future Oscar- winning director Danny Boyle of *Slumdog Millionaire* (2008) fame to invite the cast to stage the play at the Royal Court theatre in London.

"It probably was, in my ways, the highlight of my theatre career at that time because it was so unusual to take a group of people with no background in theatre and do plays with them that became really successful," he said.

Peter next headed over to LA in 1987 for three months to direct Colm Meaney in a play he'd written about the contentious H-block hunger strikes of 1981 by IRA members.

"The show was the show that got Colm the gig on *Star Trek*," he explained. " They were saying to me, 'You're crazy to be living in Ireland. You should be here. You'd have a huge career here if you came over.' My plan was to direct that show, come back to Ireland and take that family out. That's where the book ends."

At the time of talking to him, Peter was planning to write a sequel to explain why his shot at a glittering Hollywood career failed to materialize.

It certainly didn't help matters that he was battling with demons in his personal life and was fast on his way to turning into a full-blown alcoholic. But the sojourn to LA turned into a nightmare for Peter when he found himself getting hooked on cocaine.

"I'm just at the coke problem when the book ends because my coke problem really kicked-in when I went to the States and directed *Diary of A Hunger Striker*," he said.

"I was living in downtown LA, which is a really dangerous place. I was drinking in bars that I shouldn't have been in, really dangerous places. I got on great because I could play pool. If you can play pool in America they love you. And I'm a pretty mean pool player. So, I could play and the Mexicans and Salvadorians loved me—the only white guy in the bar!

"I got very close to a guy, Cuban Mike, who was the main coke dealer in downtown LA. He took me under his wing, loved me—so I had a steady supply of coke for three months every night.

"I had occasionally dabbled, a line of coke here, a line of coke there before going to LA, but it wouldn't be anything. It was like a permanent supply where I didn't have to pay for it and it was a guy giving me as much coke as I wanted on any given occasion and I really got into it and I loved it. I got very partial to it. It's a great ego booster.

"And I came back from America knowing that I really had to do something about it. It was a very important juncture in my life because I realized that coke could become a huge problem very quickly so I cut it out. I came back to Dublin and I cut it out. The alcohol was still there, but I knew I had to do something about it."

Peter eventually faced up to his alcoholism two years later in 1989 when he was in Edinburgh doing a play and suffered a terrifying panic attack, which prompted him to attend AA meetings. "The show opened and I went on a little bender. I was walking down the street and I had a panic attack at 11 o'clock in the morning. I was consumed with fear. I didn't know where I was. I didn't know what fucking city I was in. The streets were crowding in on top of me, terrified. Petrified. It shook me to my core," he confessed.

"And it was the panic attacks really that got me in the end—not the falling down drunk or not being able to get out of bed in the morning. I decided to come home and really give it a chance to stop."

Peter's drinking came close to destroying his marriage. "There would've been issues in the marriage. A lot of rows around drink," he said. "Sheila used to write letters to me about my behavior on drink and leave them on the table. I kept all the letters. They will feature very strongly in the next part of my memoir. Wonderful, brilliant, fantastic letters. They are the letters of someone really pleading with somebody to do something about their drinking." Peter wrote candidly in his critically acclaimed memoir *Number 44* — a title derived from the number of the family home — about the tragic death of his younger brother and about how he himself was sexually abused by a lodger staying at the family home.

Did he believe that grappling with these traumatic events was at the root of his addictions?

"You can analyze yourself and think, 'Oh, that's the reason why.' But there are other people who would have those experiences and not end up as alcoholics. So, in a way it doesn't matter. It doesn't matter what the cause or what you think the cause had kick started something," he said. "The actually truth is I was using and abusing alcohol to cope with my everyday reality. All that matters is maintaining that sobriety."

Peter, who has been clean and sober for more than a quarter of a century years, said he would never been tempted to hit the bottle again.

"But I'd have to walk away if somebody took coke out of their pocket. I wouldn't want to sit around and watch somebody snort coke up their nose," he admitted.

"But the funny thing is I have never been in that situation in 23 years. I've never been sitting at a table where somebody took out a wad of coke and started putting it on a mirror."

In the same year that Peter was wrestling with his drinking, his brother Jim directed *My Left Foot*, which was based on Christy Browne's autobiography *Down All The Days*. Was it frustrating that he wasn't working on the film?

"It was a bit because the story was one we had done on stage together. I wrote the adaptation of *Down All The Days* in 1981 and we put it on in the Oscar theatre. And I knew Christy better than Jim knew him. I was closer to Christy," he explained.

"So, there was this odd thing in my head of like, 'Oh my God! He's doing it. He's doing a movie about a guy I know better than he knows on a story that I've written for the stage — and now here he is.' There was a kind of uneasiness around at that time, but we did try to work together on stuff after that."

Why didn't they work together at the time?

"When *My Left Foot* happened I think a lot of people were saying to Jim it might be better for him if he made a break on his own. 'Get away from your brother. Use this as a vehicle to establish your own career as a movie director.'

"A lot of people were advising him to steer clear of a relationship with me on it because it might diminish his status within the project. And so he did. I don't think it was a rejection of me, but it was just an acceptance that that reality was the one that he bought into.

"And I suppose because it was a new experience for him. The Coen Brothers hadn't happened, so the director/auteur thing at that time was very much an individual thing. A director would be a director, whereas when the Coen Brothers and the Farrelly Brothers came along they showed that two people can actually do this job together. So, I think we missed the boat at the beginning when he did *My Left Foot*."

How did he feel on Oscar night?

"That's a bit strange alright. It is weird," he said. "Suddenly people are describing you as being somebody's younger brother who is much, much less successful. But I kind of don't see it that way. But that's the perception because movies and Oscar nominations matter so much that it catapulted him right up there in that world. I have no ungood feelings about that."

Peter's shot at a Hollywood career was then derailed when Sean Penn walked out on his film about Brendan Behan only days before the cameras were to roll back in 1996. What were the mysterious "personal reasons" for Penn's decision to quit so suddenly?

"I don't think he was ready in his head to play Brendan, but he couldn't bring himself to say, 'Look, I'm not ready.' So what it became was he said to me, 'If I go to Dublin to take on this role, Robin is going to move state with the kids and I'll never see them again, so I can't come,'" Peter explained.

"I couldn't in my heart say, 'I still want you to come here.' How could I say to a guy, 'My film is more important than your family?'"

It was a shock for Peter who had bonded with Penn over a four-year period as they worked on putting the film together.

"It's so difficult. You spend four years trying to put a movie together and if it doesn't happen, it's soul destroying," he said. "You think, 'I put all that energy into something and it has disappeared in front of my eyes.'"

Peter ended up only ever directing one film based on Brendan Behan's experience of being incarcerated in a borstal as an IRA volunteer during World War II.

"The budget was based on Sean being in it. So, then when we got to do *Borstal Boy* (2000) —which is a much smaller version of that story — the budget shrank from being a $10 million picture to being a $1.5 million. I never got paid. I never got my director's fee," he pointed out.

At the time of this interview, Jim was talking about directing *Sheriff Street Stories,* a film based on their childhood, which still hasn't been made yet. Jim spoke about wanting to get Brendan Gleeson to play their father. But Peter admitted to having mixed feelings about the project.

"It's kind of awkward because his memory and his view of growing up is so different to mine. It's amazing that within the same family two people can have different experiences," he said.

"I was close to my dad and he would've been much closer to my mother emotionally. He fought with my dad, whereas I would've been more my dad's favorite. The film is kind of a conflict with the father that I don't quite get because it wasn't my experience of him. My experience of him was much warmer, much more paly.

"I found it hard to get inside Jim's story. It doesn't resonate for me in the same way that *44* resonated for me. It is my version of the story. And in order to make the lm Jim bought the rights to 44 because he really didn't want me making a film."

But despite such differences of opinion, Peter insists they won't fall out.

"Jim and I don't quarrel in that way. He's dead sound," Peter concluded.

— 2013

Chapter Twelve: Derek Landy

As these type of rags to riches success stories go, Derek Landy's is hard to beat. After being kicked out of college, the Dubliner spent his days toiling on the family farm and his nights working on his fiction as he dreamt of one day becoming an internationally renowned author.

After ten years as a struggling part-time farmer and part-time writer, Derek then miraculously became a proverbial "overnight success" when his children's story about a skeleton detective became the centre of a bidding war amongst publishers — with Harper Collins paying a staggering €2 million-plus advance for the rights to the Skullduggery series.

At the time of this interview it was four years on — and five books into the series — since the 35-year-old won the literary world's equivalent of the Lotto, but this affable writer confessed that he still had to literally pinch himself when he reflects on the phenomenal success of his Skullduggery books.

Q: How many books are you planning for the Skulduggery Pleasant series

A: The plan was always to do nine books; I always call them three sets of trilogies. (*He would eventually do 12 books in the series with three spin-offs - JOT.*) As for if there's going to be any after that, when it's done it will have taken up ten years of my life. And, at the same time, I'm really not looking forward to when it's over because I'm absolutely adoring it. The fact of the matter is I don't know yet how it ends. That isn't how I write. I write with (the knowledge) a specific thing will happen in each book, but I don't know the details. So, I don't know if the final book has a happy or a sad ending, or if they all live or they all die. It will be as much a surprise to me as to any reader.

Q: You've been writing them at a phenomenal rate too.

A: Technically, it's one a year, but yet in three years I managed to have five out. I'm not sure how that works! There is a certain amount of pressure for the deadline. It's a struggle.

Q: But it sounds like you're very much enjoying the process?

A: It's a love of the horror genre. Skullduggery is my indulgence and because it is an on-going series I can throw in practically every idea I've ever had; every scene that I've always wanted to talk about and explore. In these books you are getting a lifetime worth of ideas that all stem from the horror genre — the mystery, the action, you know. It's all in here.

Before Skullduggery, I had written two small Irish movies that didn't get me any money or really do a whole lot for my career, as it was. So, Skullduggery has completely changed everything. It's changed my life and my career. And it's fun. I can only write when I'm having a blast. I really love writing these books. So, that is a spur in and of its self. With every book I write, I am advancing the ideas. It generates enthusiasm to go onto the next one. I am lucky.

Q: You were struggling financially before HarperCollins paid a seven figures advance for the publishing right.

A: I was living at home with my parents. I was working on the family farm. Technically, I was working part-time on the farm, especially for the second movie. But actually it was more like I was working part-time on the writing.

I was brought up on the farm and I promised myself from an early age that I would never work on the farm, apart from holidays or whatever else. But it turned out that I was destined to spend ten years, after I got kicked out of college, working on the farm.

It was that really stark reality and the possibility that I might never break out or make it, that really helped me focus on writing. I taught myself how to write screenplays and once I had two of them under my belt the idea for Skullduggery just popped into my head as a book.

The name Skullduggery Pleasant came to me and it told me who he was and what he was and what he was like. Usually ideas for writers don't usually come in such perfect packages. You'd get an inkling of a hint of an idea and you have to extrapolate and draw it out. But when Skullduggery appeared he appeared fully formed. It was staggering that something like that (occurred), an idea like that doesn't occur very often.

Q: Even Oprah has endorsed your books.

A: It hasn't really taking off in America though. For reasons that I really can't understand because it's so, so good. It has won a few awards over there. From my point of view, I have realized that whenever it is successful in a certain territory I have to go and tour there, so I'm quite happy to let it shimmer away in the States because going on tour for weeks at a time is not my idea of fun.

Q: Which is your favorite so far of the five books that are out?

A: The latest one is always the best written because you learn so much with every new book. You learn more with every new book and hopefully you're becoming a better writer. The best writing is always in the latest book.

But my favorite is probably the first one because I hadn't a clue what I was doing. I didn't know how to write a book. I had taught myself how to write screenplays. I sincerely hadn't a clue how to go about this, so I decided early on to pack it full of everything that I adore. Every kind of genre and every subgenre and just pack it in there in order to keep the interest up because I have a notoriously short attention span. So, I just make it fun.

It was six months of me working on the family farm, with my mind a million miles away, and then coming in and writing it all down and having a blast for six months. It was just funny. I hadn't a clue if anyone would read it, let alone buy it. None of that entered my mind. There comes a certain point when you just become obsessed with the book you're writing.

Q: It certainly was a whopper of an advance for your first book deal too…

A: Because of the script I already had an agent. She had been at me for years to write a book. I sent her the first 30 pages and she sent back a reply saying, "This is fantastic."

I think February or maybe March of 2006, she sent it out. I was fully expecting if it does well you'd get a very small advance, forget all about the big advances you read about as it's not going to happen to you.

We sent it out and for three weeks it was pretty quite and then my agent started call me every day for a week, saying that this publisher is interested, and that publisher. And Harper were the first. And then it was a week of fantastic news. And the slow realization that this could actually become a book. It wasn't instant, I was still quite weary. We had practically every publisher interested and we hadn't opened the bidding yet.

I was going to go over to London the following week to meet all of them and then Harper just made a pre-emptive offer. And, yeah, it was the kind of thing you don't actually expect to happen to you. Because if you do expect it you're an idiot! I'm really glad it did happen.

The thing with big advances like that a lot of it is a publicity stunt; it garners headlines before the book is even out. It sets it in the minds of the trade papers and the critics. They are aware of this book before they've even read a word of it.

Q: I presumed you were totally shocked?

A: I was stunned. From the phone call from an agent telling me about this offer from that moment my life was completely changed. Apart from (the fact that) I actually had money (now) it was, "Oh, my God! I now don't have to struggle and my parents can stop worrying about me. I am not going to be a burden on them anymore." Pretty much, my life has been sorted out. It basically changed my life. So, it took a while for that to really register. Skullduggery has absolutely changed my life.

I was probably one of the big last signings before the world just spun into recession. So, after me there hasn't really been a big headline grabbing advance, payout. I'm really glad I got in there. It is an advance — you earn it back before you actually see any royalties. You'd get a few people going, "Is he worth it? Is the book worth it?"

There is nobody who writes to get famous. You don't sit at home going, "Oh, I'd really like to be famous. I know! I'll become a writer!" It doesn't happen.

Q: How did you celebrate such a mega deal?

A: Actually, it was so low key. When Harper paid that pre-emptive offer, it was my family and we all went down to our local pub, which was dead quite. It was practically empty and we sat at the bar and it was the weirdest night because everyone was struggling to contain their enthusiasm, because we didn't want to announce it yet. It was very low key. I think I had a glass of coke or something.

Q: Was there anything in specific that spurred on your desire to become a writer?

A: I had a stammer and obviously I still do, but when I was a kid there were periods when it got worse and got better on its own. The thing about a stammer is that you do come across as shy because what's the point in telling a joke or having a witty comment if you are going to be spending half an hour trying to get it out? I wasn't shy, I was self-obsessed. I was a happy kid. Always reading and always with my head in the clouds. As I got older, I really started to appreciate words a lot more. The stammer was a way to really appreciate the written word, a lot more than I probably would've done otherwise.

Q: Did you encounter any snide remarks about your stutter?

A: You'd get the odd comment from people who really didn't understand it, but the thing is as soon as they realized it wasn't just me making a mistake, it was actually a stammer, then they would be, "Oh, okay." And it would stop. I never really had any problems with anyone bullying me or making fun of me because of the stammer. I assume that's pretty unique. It never became an issue. You kind of would expect it to be a bigger deal or lead to embarrassments, or trauma, or schoolyard taunts — but no, it actually hasn't. Really, I've just been hanging out with the nicest people.

Q: What was your college experience like?

A: I went to art college. I was always going to either be a writer or an artist. As it turned out, I wasn't really cut out to be an artist because I went to animation college and I was kind of expelled from that after the first year!

Q: Why?

A: For being absolutely rubbish at it and for not actually doing anything. I just had like a year of fun. I had such a good year in college. I had a good time in school. I made friends. I had a laugh. I wasn't too keen on the whole work aspect of it all. But I managed to get by. I had a taste of college, found out I liked it a little bit too much and then spent ten years working on the farm because of it.

I'm stunned that I actually got in, in the first place; I didn't really last that long, but it made me focus. I had messed up (secondary) school so I didn't have the best exam results at all.

So, when I was kicked out and I realized that, "Oh, my God! I might spend the rest of my life working on this farm because I'm incapable of working at anything that I don't absolutely love." — so, I decided to really focus and to concentrate on the only thing I had left and that was writing.

Q: What else comes to mind when you reflect back on that time?

A: I think I was always the problem child. I wasn't a problem in terms of attitude, in terms of getting into trouble or whatever else, but I was just a problem child in the way that I did not work at anything. I was the always the one that they had worries about. I have two sisters and a brother who are all extremely capable of studying, of knuckling down and doing the work that they had to do…

After I got kicked out, I was now the issue. I was a problem because how could my father ever think about retirement if I was working on the farm? I had no intention of taking over because by then I had started writing and I'd found this dream that rarely comes true. My mother absolutely knew this. My father had the thing where he actually believes that if anyone can do it then I can. So, he was always quietly confident that I would make it; my mother was much more practical and realistic.

Yeah, for ten years, even as the scripts were made into movies, it was still the problem that I was living at home. I was working part-time on the farm now, but I was still the problem, still the burden — and then suddenly overnight I stopped being the problem child and I became the golden child. I suddenly was the kid everything had happened for. All my dreams were coming true. And I was the one that they could stop worrying about. And it was such a nice change.

Q: Let's look at the two movies you wrote during this period, *Dead Bodies* and *Boy Eats Girl*.

A: The main thing about *Dead Bodies* is that it proves that I was a writer. This is wasn't like a dream that was completely unrealistic. I have met people who will never be writers and yet they view themselves as writers. You just know that they don't have it. And it's such a common occurrence. The danger is that you are one of those people.

Dead Bodies was a fantastic boost of confidence. Suddenly, it made me a 'professional writer' even if I couldn't afford to do it full-time. But that really is the thing about writing. If I continued liked that, especially in the climate of Ireland right now, I would be struggling to get anything made. I would be this guy of a dream of being a writer really petered out. I would have these delusions of being a writer and I'd be following this dream ignoring reality. I'd be this sad little guy who it never quite worked out for.

And then Skulduggery came and because everything did work out. Suddenly I was lauded for staying true to my dream and not giving up and fighting against insurmountable odds to actually succeed. It's a fine line. It really is.

With *Boy Eats Girl*, the story stopped being mine before he (the director) even started shooting!

Q: You seem to have some an eclectic fan base judging by your book signing events.

A: I get the best readers. I was signing for this huge 40-year-old biker guy and he was hairy, he had a huge gut, he had a beard, tattoos and he was like, "Hello. Will you sign my book for me? I love these books."

We're having a great chat and then he moves out of the way and standing behind him is the cutest little nine-year-old girl who isn't even big enough to reach the table. She's an abnormally small, cute little nine-year-old girl. It was the much glaring example of the diversity of the readership. They are both proud to be there; they don't feel at all self-conscious that a biker is standing in a queue with a nine-year-old.

In certain areas of Dublin, there are about six girls who tend to follow me around to every event I do. And they are hilarious. They are hysterically funny. The thing is they know all of my jokes and (when) I'm on stage doing an event, I tell the same stories again and again and they know all my jokes. You can hear them occasionally when halfway through, they're going, "Tell the cat story! We want to hear the cat story again." Oh, bloody hell!

Q: Jokingly, I'm guessing, it's easier now to meet women following all your success?

A: Yes, it is (*laughs*). It's a good opening line. At the start, I was warned by practically everyone to watch out for the gold diggers! "You can't trust them! They'll only be after the money." So, for ages I was waiting for the gold diggers so I could have some fun! But they actually haven't (arrived). Everyone so far has been — No, wait! How to I say this in a family, friendly way? It's been really good so far. But I'm unmarried, I don't have any kids, I'm not engaged and I don't think I'm in a long-term relationship. I should meet someone soon and settle down because my mother and every single one of my aunties would love if I'd settle down soon!

Q: I heard you've got a black belt in karate.

A: I stopped training actually about a year or two before I started writing the Skullduggery books. I hadn't trained in years, but I've finally gone back to that kind of thing. But now I'm doing Krav Maga, which is an Israeli form of fighting.
It's really good. It's so odd, but it's really good to be punched! It's really good to wake up in the morning and feel the swelling on your face, or the bruise, or all the muscles that are strained. It's the feeling of something of, "Okay, I was doing something extraordinary yesterday." So, yeah, I am back in the combat art. Technically, not a martial art but it's a combat art.

Q: I'm presume you're no longer living on the farm

A: I have my own pad. Far enough, I don't have my own pad a huge difference away — I'm about seven minutes away from my parents. I'm now out in Rush. I'm surrounded by fields and meadows and horses. Even though I thought I hated the country when I was a kid because you had to get a bus everywhere and it was such a drag — now I absolutely adore it. It's the peace and the quite and the solitude that you need. By their very nature writers are solitary creatures. I am quite happy sitting alone and writing alone for months on end. I do not need anyone. It's filled with toys and memorabilia and dogs and cats. But, again, it's close to a town and my parents. But, no, I'm a grown up, I have my own house.

Skullduggery changed my life; without it I would still be working on screenplays, which would mean that I would be living at home. I'd be a 35-year-old guy living with his parents, working on the farm, writing in his spare time. Meaning that his father could never contemplate retirement because he had his son to support. Absolutely everything that has happened since February 2006 has just been amazing. I'm waiting for the other shoe to drop, but so far no sign of it.

— *2010*

Chapter Thirteen: Ian Gibson

If you were to ask your average well-read Spaniard to name the most famous contemporary Irish writer you'd probably be surprised by the answer. Nine times out of ten, along with the usual suspects from the Irish literary world that are translated and revered in Spain — namely John Banville and Colm Tóibín — the name cited would be that of Ian Gibson.

Gibson accepts he's an obscure figure back in his beloved homeland. However, in the Spanish-speaking world, Gibson is a serious player thanks to his award-winning books — most notably about the poet and playwright Frederic García Lorca, who Leonard Cohen credited as being the "greatest influence" on his own haunting lyrics.

The 77-year-old Dubliner originally started off teaching at Queens University and then at London University, before deciding to make a new life for himself in Spain. He broke through when his debut book about the murder of Lorca was banned by Franco, forcing Spaniards to smuggle copies in from France.

Gibson has other strings to his bow apart from biographies: he's written novels and narrated documentaries, including the BBC's two-part show *The Great Famine*. Another subject clearly close to his heart is sex. Gibson has written a book about the erotica collector Henry Spencer Ashbee, and is also the author of *English Vice: Beating, Sex and Shame in Victorian England and After*. The latter is a study of flogging and flagellation, widely credited with the outright banning of corporal punishment in British schools.

These days, Gibson is considered the chief authority on Lorca, and has also written the definitive biography on Salvador Dalí, even interviewing the eccentric genius for his 700-page tome.

He has written biographies of the leading poet Antonio Machado, and another on film director Luis Buñuel. One critic in *The Irish Times* hailed Gibson back in 2014 as "the creator of modern biography in Spain" when reviewing his book on Buñuel. No wonder the author was swamped for autographs and selfies the moment we stepped into the café in the splendid surroundings of the Círculo de Bellas Artes in Madrid. In fact, at one point, it was hard to get a word in edgeways: it appeared as if the entire café wanted a meet and greet with the man himself.

Q: Ernest Hemingway once stated that the best training for a writer was an unhappy childhood. Was this the case for you?

A: It wasn't perfect — put it that way! I'm from a tiny minority within a minority. If you're going to be a Southern Irish Protestant be an Anglican, because there you get a little bit of stained glass, the liturgy and a feeling for culture. But I came into the world in a tiny Methodist community — and that is not to be recommended in Dublin circa 1939, because you haven't been born into a social group with any feeling for the arts or literature. They were very isolated.

Q: Did you feel alienated?

A: I felt I didn't belong to the mainstream. I wanted to escape from the family environment. It was very restricting. Also, it had got inside me: it was part of me and I wanted a change. But I was on the road to salvation — my version of salvation — when they sent me to a Quaker boarding school, which was coeducational. It helped a lot. The Quakers are far more broadminded than Methodists. So, I begin to run away very early. I've been running away all my life (*laughs*).

Q: Did you feel a calling to be a Methodist preacher?

A: I did think maybe I was being called and that's terrifying, because there is this business in the Bible about how if you are called and you don't respond you're damned forever. I was imbued with the New Testament and Bible class and Sunday school. I got out of that when I discovered French literature, and then when I went to Trinity, that really saved me. And then there was the difficulty of not being able to get hold of Ulysses, the censorship, the sinister John McQuaid and all the ghastly business with Protestants and Catholics. It was a woeful island in those days. So, I'd no sooner graduated that I wanted to move away.

Q: You once said in an interview with a Spanish publication that Guinness liberated you during your formative years!

A: There's no question about that. After our matches, when I was playing for Old Wesley First 15, everybody would hive off to the local and have a few pints. It was a ritual. So, I started to savor the joys of Guinness around the age of 17 or 18 — and it was a liberation. The moment you've had a few drinks you feel better and you feel free from shame. And that was a great problem for me: the feeling of being ashamed about sex and myself in general. You have a few drinks and everything is temporarily relieved. But my father was a teetotaler, and that posed another problem.

Q: Did you feel guilty about masturbation?

A: Not pathologically. At my Quaker school masturbation was known as 'revving' — what a fantastically apt word! The dormitories reverberated every night with creaking beds. I was initiated by a future Dublin dentist who said, "You must try it — it's time." I will withhold his name! Nobody felt too guilty about "revving" — it was a sort of communal frenzy! My problem, more than guilt, was a generalized sense of shame about sex, love and tenderness. My father was terribly timid, and timidity is catching; he had a peculiar way of looking at me, of noticing my blushes when anything touching on the subject arose.

Q: How old were you when you lost your virginity?

A: I was 16. I had a fantastic and very passionate relationship at that school I mentioned. They say the first love is the only love — and, in my case, there's truth to that.

Q: It was very unusual for someone from your generation to lose their virginity at 16.

A: It's all set up for you, isn't it? You're in a co-educational school and almost the only thing you weren't doing together was having a shower together or sleeping together. The girls were there all the time. The Quakers were incredibly advanced. They really do believe the thing exists — so let them be together and get to know each other. And reduce the tension a bit. But they didn't want you to go out on weekends into the fields and "practice sex," as they nowadays say.

Q: There were no condoms either.

A: I was an expert at coitus interruptus!

Q: Did you ever question your own sexuality as a kid?

A: I never had the slightest homosexual inclination. Sadomasochistic, yes. So, that was always something that excited me as a child, when I was seven or so: I was fascinated reading Knock-Out comics with those beatings and canings. I had no language to describe it. I didn't even know what a turn-on was, nor what sex was. All I knew was that already at the age of seven those stories fascinated me.

Q: You wrote a book about Victorian sex, shame and flagellation…

A: One of the reasons I wrote the book was because I consider that corporal punishment — as it was then practiced in Britain and Ireland — was a disgusting, disgraceful procedure. The French knew way back in the 19th century that it could be a sexual turn-on and that it was dangerous to beat children. The Brits never faced up to that, miserable hypocrites. Nobody writes a book about such a subject unless he can understand what he is writing about. So, I could explore that fantasy and also make a contribution. I remember being warned, "You can't do it." But I'm glad I did it because it documented the illness. The critic Auberon Waugh said, "This book has made me be ashamed to be English."

Q: Your book played a major role in the banning of corporal punishment in the UK...

A: When I published it in 1978, the British were still beating away merrily. Soon afterwards there was a parliamentary debate and the practice was abolished, under pressure from Europe. And even when they abolished it, there was not a single person to my knowledge — even in the House of Commons — who acknowledged that my book played a role in the abolition, although I know that it did. Nobody had the courage to stand up and say, "One of the reasons we're abolishing it is because beatings are a sexual turn-on, or can be." And that has been recognised as such in European psychology, by Freud and others. And that's the reason why it should be banned — not just because it's cruel, but because it's sexually dangerous and it can turn somebody into a life-long addict. The proof is there, oceanically, in Victorian pornography.

Q: You also wrote a book about Henry Spencer Ashbee, the erotic collector.

A: The possibility that he might have been the anonymous author of *My Secret Life* was fascinating. I went to the British Museum's Private Case — now 'Private' no more — to see the parallels between Ashbee's prose style and that of *My Secret Life*, and I think I found some tics that make it likely that he was the author, but I wasn't able to prove it. If I could've proved he wrote *My Secret*

Life that would've been news in the 1960s and '70s — but nobody gives a damn nowadays. So far as I am aware, nobody has clinched who wrote the book.

Q: Is it true that you were inspired to write your biography about Lorca because your brother was gay?

A: Not exactly, although it may have played a part. The book is dedicated to him because his sufferings helped me to understand Lorca's. You know, in the 1950s it was bad enough being heterosexual in Ireland but to be gay was atrocious. Can you imagine what it was like for my poor timid father to have a gay son? And not only gay but manic-depressive. When he went high he was terrifying. He died in a clinic in Bristol.

Q: I'm very sorry to hear that…

A: It was terrible. He was in his fifties. Quite young. He was a fantastic person, very charismatic and very funny. He could've had a big career in television. In fact, he did begin to have a career in television, in RTÉ, but a manic-depressive presenter or stage-manger didn't fill the bill, understandably, and he lost the job, after which he went from bad to worse. Knowing all this, having been in on it, helped me to understand Lorca.

Q: It must've been horrible to witness your brother sink into despair?

A: It was absolutely shattering. He was in-and-out of Saint Patrick's Hospital. I'll never forget the time I had to take him back on the plane to Dublin because he had a breakdown in London. He was on lithium and then he stopped taking it. He was completely manic, mad, crazy. And in St Patrick's he began to cry when we got inside and he realised he was back there again. I've never seen anything like it: the tears literally spurted from his eyes in two jets. Can you imagine? In two jets!

Q: Leonard Cohen said Lorca was the biggest influence on his lyrics…

A: I was invited to go with him to Lorca's village in Granada, Fuente Vaqueros. Because Sony did a CD that included one of his songs and I wrote the text on the back. They invited me to go with him, but they weren't prepared to pay me a fee. I thought it was unfair. I mean, why should I give up two days work on what I was writing at the time to go, even if it was with the great Leonard Cohen?

Q: Did anybody think you were mad to turn down the offer?

A: My son Dominic said to me, "You have to be a fucking eejit! I would've paid for myself!" (*Laughs*) My son was probably right. If I had gone I would obviously have had a long conversation with Leonard Cohen about Lorca and I'd be able to answer your question more adequately. It is a fact, of course, that Cohen was deeply affected by Lorca's poetry.

Q: You wrote that Lorca was like a rockstar when he went to Argentina for the performance of his play Blood Wedding —that he couldn't go anywhere without being mobbed.

A: I don't think any Spanish writer had ever equalled Lorca's success in Buenos Aires in 1933-34. He really was the talk of the town. He filled the theatre day and night for a month with Blood Wedding. It's a vast theatre: it holds 2,000 people. That is when he sent his father a big cheque for 30,000 quid or so and said, "I'm not just this poor poet. Please take Mum out for dinner on me." So, he was a fantastic one-man show. He was an incredible performer. It's not normal for anybody to have so many amazing gifts, because they weren't just talents: they were gifts, you might say, given by the gods. The gift of poetry. The gift of theatre. The gift of music. The gift of conversation. The gift of drawing. And the gift that Spaniards praise very highly: *el don de la simpatía* — the gift of the personal touch, the gift of empathy.

Q: Was his murder politically motivated?

A: It was basically political in that he had aligned himself with the Republic. By 1936, he was the most famous young writer in the country. In Granada there was great jealousy as well. There was a mixture of political motives and personal motives of rancour and jealousy, including somebody in his own family, a distant cousin who was a fascist. *The House of Bernarda Alba* is based on a real family in the second of Lorca's villages. It hadn't been staged yet, but news had seeped out about the theme of the play. The family found out a few weeks before the Civil War that it was based on one of their members, Francisca Alba, the village and its sexual mores. They were outraged, particularly that distant cousin, with his ultra-right-wing tendencies.

Q: It's also been suggested that his death was down to the fact that he was a homosexual.

A: No, although the fact that he was gay didn't help. The main thing is that he was a left-wing republican, plus somebody who was earning a lot of money, somebody with incredible personal charisma, all of these things coming together in your own town — as if this had happened, let's say, in Greystones, or in Bray (County Wicklow) or a little bit bigger. That's it. A few months later it mightn't have happened. Somebody could've said, "For Christ sake — don't touch him because he's famous. It's going to do us a lot of damage." As it did when the news broke that September.

Q: You met Salvador Dali when researching your biography about him.

A: I got to meet him because I had published my biography of Lorca. And Dali's closest friend had read parts of it to him because he himself was in very bad shape physically, the eyes and so on. He read him some passages from the book about his friendship with Lorca and he wanted to add some more details.

So, I was summoned to his throne in Figueres, which was a remarkable thing for me. I was in Madrid and the phone call came, saying, "If you don't come today the master may not receive you, because he kicked somebody out yesterday. He's like that. He wants to see you today and if you don't come today he may never want to meet you." So, I was on a plane in a jiffy. I hired the fastest car I could find in Barcelona and roared up the motorway to Figueres. So, I was there within a few hours.

Q: What was he like?

A: It was a fantastic experience. He was all dressed in white silk with a red Catalan cap on his head. He was full of tubes. It was terrible. He began to tell me all about his friendship with Lorca. And I hardly understood a word because he was talking in a mixture of Catalan, French and Spanish, but terribly badly articulated because his mouth was full of tubes and the hand was going bang bang on the chair, from Parkinson's.

Q: Did he talk about the rumours of a sexual relationship with Lorca?

A: He told me that it wasn't possible, much as he would have wished. Because he wasn't homosexual. And because it would've been painful. You couldn't believe a word Dali said, really. But he insisted that had it been possible, he would have been only too happy "to make his arsehole available to such a great poet" — those were his words — who, moreover, he loved dearly.

Q: Did he say anything else really about it?

A: He told me about a fantastic girl, Margarita Manso, who was a companion of his at the School of Fine Arts in Madrid. He recounted a scene that took place at the Students' Hall where he and Lorca lived. The three of them were together, I think, in Lorca's bedroom. Lorca was sexually excited and about to grab Dali and bugger him. And Dali was screaming, "I can't! I can't!" And the girl was watching this. And Lorca switched his erection to the girl, who was fascinated with both of them. And it was the first — and only time — in his life that he had made love to a woman because Dali had got him going, you know?

Q: Do you think Dali was in denial about his sexuality?

A: I knew a very close gay friend of his and he said to me, "Dali wasn't really anything sexually, but he was certainly more gay in potential than hetero!" He really just wanted to see people doing it. Dali organised parties in his house in Cadaqués and used to sit masturbating in a corner, watching people screwing. He never took part. I don't think he had much sex with anybody. He was terrified of physical contact.

Q: He would've loved online porn!

A: He would've been sitting at the screen a lot of the time, yes! It's an amazing thing — isn't it? — to have such explicitly erotic material generally available online, any variation you want. I suppose in the monasteries and holy places around the world, beginning in the Vatican, everybody has access to a screen and sees these images — it must be a tremendous temptation.

Q: Do you think Dali was fucked-up sexually?

A: Well, yes. But what does that mean? Sex is a complicated matter. The drive is there and — depending on the circumstances of your childhood and inherited traits — it can go one way or another. The variations and pitfalls are endless! It's a miracle that anybody can actually get it up, it seems to me!

Q: The Irish Taoiseach Enda Kenny said that he wants to have a national conversation in Ireland about porn!

A: Do they still call it porn in Holy Ireland? "Porn" basically is only just like coming in when your parents are at it! It was forbidden to see — and now you can see it. To see? In my day it wasn't even discussed. So, I don't know whether I would call it porn or not. I mean, it's certainly very invasive: you just can't get away from it. The obsession with sex is everywhere. It makes it more and more difficult to grow old!

Q: Shouldn't the Taoiseach have better things to be talking about?

A: Yes, of course. The outrages committed by the Catholic Church in Ireland, for example. You're not going to be able to repress sexuality, it always returns. It's better to face up to the fact that people do this and that it's there — and it's not going to go away.

Q: In her biography of Franco, Pilar Eyre wrote: "He wasn't interested in sex, he silenced his desires with his hunger for power and was therefore able to remain celibate almost all his life. Ambition replaced orgasms…"

A: Paul Preston is the authority on Franco. I don't know that much about him and his orgasms, or lack of them! What I do know is that he was the greatest assassin ever produced by Spain, and there must have been some very deep reason for that. Resentment, perhaps.

Q: I'm sure you are familiar with the story that Franco's father was in a whorehouse the day he was born.

A: Yes. I think his father was a very liberated man sexually and very promiscuous. And not only that — unlike my father, who never touched a drop in his life — he enjoyed his drink. He was a handsome man, swaggering, and a great success with women. And he didn't like his son Francisco very much! Clearly he constituted a major problem for Franco, as did Franco's brother Ramón, a famous airman and also a great man for the ladies. Franco had to be Number One and one way was to become the all-powerful dictator of Spain.

Q: Do you think the same could be said about Eamon de Valera, who so happened to have a Spanish father — that he replaced sex with power?

A: (*Laughs*) I don't know that much about De Valera. He never struck me as very sexy!

Q: A lot of Spanish men regularly visit brothels.

A: They did until recently, certainly. The traditional system wouldn't have worked without prostitution. That has been the case for centuries. It was considered normal that fathers would introduce their sons to sex in a brothel and take them along to be initiated. Because obviously you couldn't do it with a decent girl from next door! So prostitution formed a very useful function in Catholic Spain.

Q: You've no objection to sex between consenting adults, even if it's paid for?

A: No, not at all. I just hate the idea of paying for sex. I've never been with a prostitute in my life. I don't like the idea. There'd be some women who enjoy being prostitutes, in which case there isn't any great problem. But I wouldn't like to think men are using women who are brought here under duress from other countries. Sexual slaves, in a word.

Q: Spaniards appear to be more sexually liberated than we Irish?

A: Surely Ireland has changed in this respect! I mean, do men still drink too much in order not to be forced to perform and perhaps fail?

Q: Well, it's still illegal to have an abortion in Ireland.

A: I'm appalled by that. I couldn't live in a country that didn't have abortion.

Q: Did you realise that it still takes five years in Ireland before you can get a divorce?

A: (*Laughs*) Five years? Really? Who are the Irish boyos who pushed through this legislation?! Well, what can I say? Old attitudes die hard.

Q: On the positive side, Ireland was the first country in the world to pass a referendum on same sex marriage.

A: Thank God the people voted in favour. That's a huge step forward — after centuries of oppression. But from what you're telling me, it appears that the place isn't progressing as quickly as I imagined.

Q: Have you ever tried Viagra?

A: I tried it once, then I got prostate cancer, had an operation and it no longer works. You can inject yourself, if you feel the need to do that. And there are probably new techniques. But Viagra doesn't work. A great pity.

Q: Prostate cancer is topical in Ireland, because the broadcaster Gay Byrne recently revealed he'd been diagnosed with it.

A: You are assuming that I know who Gay Byrne is. Actually I do; he has been around for a long time now. I sympathize. All these issues should be out in the open. One isn't to blame for having this. One isn't to blame for this thing called sexuality. Why can't we get it out in the open?

Q: Did you suffer from depression after your operation?

A: Of course. I had a normal sex life. It would be nice still to be potent so maybe I'll do something about it some day should the need arise — pun intended!

Q: What are your thoughts about euthanasia?

A: I want euthanasia! I think people should be able to have it. I've just done my will: I don't want any machines. When it happens, I want to be left alone and to go as quickly as possible.

Q: If you were diagnosed with a terminal illness, would you go to Dignitas in Switzerland to end your life?

A: No, I'd rather do it myself. I'm beginning to ask my medical friends, what is their view (*laughs*)?

Q: Do you still consider yourself Irish?

A: Well, I come from there and I think about Dublin the whole time — it's inside me. I never felt fully Irish, though, because of my family being from an English background and Protestant and so on. I never felt Irish in the way a Catholic would. But I feel fantastically Irish here in Spain. Spain has been a great liberation. I don't have to explain all the tiny nuances of where I come from: I'm Irish and that's it. I suppose I use the Celtic thing excessively. Because people expect that from you — so why not let them have it? I play it up a bit.

Q: Are you religious now?

A: Christianity has terrified people for 2,000 years. I can no longer go for the personal God and the pie in the sky. That's completely gone. You know, the thought of a great giant figure up there somewhere — that has gone completely. That was the God we were taught.

Q: Do you feel Gerry Adams and Martin McGuinness are heroes or terrorists?

A: I suppose there's a bit of everything. Coming from where I come from — part of a minority, and my fear of being swamped by the other religion — I understand how the Catholics in Northern Ireland would feel about the Protestant majority. I was almost a fanatic myself. I felt that there were evil elements in Catholicism: the Virgin Mary and the Saints, Papal infallibility, indulgences, confession and all the rest of it.

I was taught to believe that Catholicism was an evil version of Christianity. It filled me with terror. When I was teaching at Queens I could see that in the North as well. You've got two communities who theoretically believe in the same religion, at least in the basics, yet there are major differences. I was, myself, on the brink of anti-Catholic fanaticism, so I can understand the anti-British hatred felt by some Irish Catholics. It doesn't mean I would condone it. But I can understand that mindset.

Q: Would you like to see a united Ireland?

A: Yes, I really would. It could be fantastic. Because the Protestants have a strong work ethic and many other positive values. Why wouldn't they be able to work alongside Catholics? Where is the magnanimity? Why isn't it possible to bring the two together? I'd like to see it, but I wouldn't want to force it upon anybody.

Q: If Spain left the EU, the country would probably implode...

A: I feel that very strongly. This country has been so insecure for so long — bouncing in one direction, changing in another direction, civil wars, God knows how many. There's been no sense of the country moving forward with some sort of agreement on the basics: there's always been a tendency to undo what the previous government has done. Rather like Red Hugh O'Neill and Red Hugh O'Donnell in Kinsale: they're so busy fighting among themselves that they fail to coordinate their efforts in order to defeat the British.

Spain's a bit like that. "You are more responsible than I am. You're to blame

— I'm not to blame." They're constantly squabbling among themselves. So, to be in Europe is a sort of framework within which all this dispersed energy can be channelled. Nobody here talks about getting out. It would be absolutely crazy: people have lost their inferiority complex, they've overcome their shyness about learning other languages. I think it's meant a very positive change in Spain.

Q: You once said that the right wing in Spain is the most extremist in the EU.

A: There is no ultra-right wing party here as such: it is within the conservative party, the Partido Popular. I meant that those attitudes persist within the party. And there are tics — Franco tics — which survive. Until recently they had an overall majority. In the current situation they're more docile because they have to reach compromise solutions. But, if you ask me, they are wolves in sheep's clothing — not true democrats.

Q: Your body of work has been mainly written in Spanish. But do you feel underrated in your homeland?

A: I don't blame the homeland for not knowing what I've written. How could it? But at least it made me a member of the Royal Irish Academy and gave me an honorary D. Litt., which is nice (*laughs*). Some people are aware of my biography on Lorca. Most of the other books haven't been translated into English. The main thing is that I've done what I've wanted to do.

Someone once said to me, "If you're going to write a book about somebody don't write a book about somebody nobody has ever heard of — find somebody famous to write about." I didn't choose Lorca only because he was famous but because he fascinated me.

Q: Was it a shock when Franco banned your first book?

A: Not at all. The book was published in Paris in 1971 and the subject was Lorca's assassination by the Fascists at the beginning of the Civil War. It had no chance whatsoever of being sold openly in Spain. But it crossed the frontier massively. The moment Franco died, in 1975, it was issued here. It was very timely. No book of mine has done as well as that book. It was hugely successful.

Q: Did you receive any threats or feel intimidated?

A: If you mean when I was researching, I did have nightmares about them coming for me. But they never did. It was a police state. But it wasn't dangerous for me, in that I don't think they could've done anything to me — at least not officially. But the people I was talking to were in some danger. They could've been beaten up because it was a pretty ruthless place then. There was a lot of fear. I had to be very careful not to implicate people and not to give their names in the book. It was dangerous.

Q: The last time we met, you mentioned that you were planning to write your last ever book in Spanish.

A: Did I really say that? Anyway, I've just finished a book in Spanish called *Aventuras ibéricas*, which should be out by the time this interview appears: a hotchpotch about my decades here, with the stress on my rambles around the peninsula. I have a chapter on the Roman roads, one on the Iberians, another on the Goths. Then there are chapters on Lorca, the Catalans, Don Quixote Land, La Mancha... and a final chapter about why I love and despair of Spain at the same time.

Q: You told *The Irish Times* in 2003, "You can't spend years on a biography without in the process discovering something about yourself as well." What have you discovered about yourself?

A: That the circumstances of my childhood turned me into a sort of literary detective, obsessed with getting at the truth. I didn't know what I wanted to do with my life. I didn't want to be in the university, teaching. I didn't have any gift as

184

a poet or as a novelist. And I found my vocation as a researcher. I found that I had an ability for language. A certain flair for talking to people and getting out there and burrowing away and tracking things down. I have an obsessive personality — maybe that's also to do with coming from Ireland.

— 2017

Chapter Fourteen: Ulick O'Connor

Even though our paths only crossed once in person, I was saddened when I heard Ulick O'Connor had shuffled off this mortal coil at the grand old age of 91 in October 2019.

He was one of Ireland's finest nonfiction writers and his lively biography of Brendan Behan left a lasting impression on me when I read it in my teens.

Apart from being a biographer, playwright, poet, legendary raconteur, barrister, and former intervarsity boxing champion, was among other achievements, Ulick was also a columnist with the *Sunday Mirror* for many years. As I wrote the weekend after his death in my own column in the very same paper, "I'd die a happy man if I could achieve even half of what Ulick accomplished during his stellar writing career."

There's no denying he was a giant of the Irish literary world but he was also an eccentric and difficult character at times, to put it mildly. Apparently, Dublin taxi drivers would run a mile when they seen him trying to hail a cab!

Coincidentally, Ulick's death occurred exactly ten years to the date our paths had crossed for the first and only time. A month or so before our meeting, Ulick had rang me up out of the blue one day to introduce himself and told me he enjoyed a book I had out at the time, which is always flattering to hear from one of your esteemed peers.

It was later agreed I could call out to his home in Rathgar, Dublin to interview him and afterwards we could go for a spot of lunch at his local tennis club.

My then editor and mentor Paul Drury, who sadly died in 2015 at the relatively young age of 57, after a lengthy battle with mouth cancer, told me to ask Ulick straight out — no pun intended — if he was really gay. There had been much tittle-tattle about Ulick, a lifelong bachelor, having a penchant for younger men. There had even been some scurrilous talk about him enjoying the company of rent boys. It was a legitimate question to ask seeing how Ulick himself had caused huge controversy when he outed Behan as gay in his book.

When Ulick gave me the grand tour of his splendid home the first thing that struck me was the huge amount of *Playboy* magazines scattered everywhere. There were copies piled up in the corner, on his desk, on bookshelves and in the bathroom. I even remember a big mountain of them on a bed in an upstairs room used as a gym. It honestly felt like he was overcompensating for fears of the rumor about his sexuality.

Naturally enough, Ulick swore blind he bought the smutty magazine for the articles, which I found hard to swallow — this time! I've actually written for *Playboy* myself on occasion and don't remember ever reading it.

Seeing this as the perfect opening to ask about his sexuality, I chanced my arm by telling Ulick: "I believe you because why else would a gay man bother with *Playboy*?"

You should've seen the look of indignation on his face.

"No, I'm not gay," he told me.

"But you've heard the rumors?"

Shaking his head, he insisted he'd never even heard such rumors — although, good-naturedly, he readily expanded on why people might have come to that conclusion.

"I'm not married and I've lived on my own. If you're not married, people always presume (you're gay). I have no feelings about it at all. I'm not against it. It's part of life but it's not my game. I'm not built that way. I was very attracted to women from the very beginning, when I was a kid I had sexual instincts.

Whatever the reason — and I would think it was modesty — but I never flashed the girls that I was living with, like a French girl that was an Olympian," he said.

He then began to regale me with stories about all the notches on his bedpost — including an affair with actress Mary Ure, the then wife of *Jaws* star Robert Shaw, who died from a heart attack at the side of an Irish road in 1978. There's a beautiful memorial in Tourmakeady, County Mayo, near the location where he died. You'll find a picture of it on his Wikipedia entry.

The boast about the dalliance with Mary, others in my office observed, felt like Ulick was overcompensating by wildly exaggerating about his love life. But there was no denying he was a fabulous storyteller.

I remember he even claimed the adulterous affair was brazenly initiated by the beautiful blonde film star while her unsuspecting husband — the Hollywood hard man — actually sat beside her! As the celebrity couple listened entranced to the Irish literary lion's colorful tales of Behan, Kavanagh and Gogarty, Ulick said found himself simultaneously playing footsie under a dining room table with Mary Ure, who was star of *Where Eagles Dare* and *Look Back In Anger*, which is a film I absolutely love.

Her husband, at the time a major international star, looked innocently on as the trio enjoyed a candlelit supper in a picturesque restaurant near Shaw's holiday hideaway in the west of Ireland. And later that night Ure sneaked off to sleep with writer — unbeknownst to Shaw, whose box-office hits included *The Sting* and *The Taking Of Pelham One Two Three*.

"She took a fancy to me and started to tickle my foot," recalled O'Connor, who was 81 at the time of our interview. "Mary passed a note under the table to me, asking what was my address. They dropped me at the hotel and about half an hour later there she was at the door."

It was just one in a string of love affairs, countless one-night stands, visits to prostitutes and even the occasional menage-a-trois that the grand old man of Irish letters openly confessed to in a frank and controversial interview with me that appeared in the *Irish Daily Mail* in 2009.

I was surprised by how Ulick was not exactly bashful to discuss his love life, even admitting to visiting brothels. He recalled having "about eight" great loves in his life and "about 15 affairs." But how many one-night stands had he notched on his bedpost, in between penning acclaimed biographies of Brendan Behan and Oliver St John Gogarty, a standard textbook on the Irish literary revival and a considerable corpus of poetry and plays?

"Oh, well, I don't count them. I haven't counted them. I wouldn't even bother counting them. It either happens or it doesn't. I was lucky that way. But in the life I led they were there and I never pushed. I just let it happen. There were a number of people, titled girls and all that," he said.

But, although unashamedly sexually adventurous, Ulick, as I mention earlier, was adamant about never experimenting with men — but he did recall men hitting on him, including playwright Noel Coward, who refused up to his death in 1973 to publicly discuss his homosexuality.

"I met Noel Coward at lunch. He offered me a lift home, went back to the Shelbourne (Hotel) and then asked me up for a drink. I was chatting away with all my literary chat, trying to extract some literary vintage from the meeting and all that," he told me.

"He said, 'What I want to know is do you like men or women?' I said, 'Women unfortunately.' He said, 'Why do you say unfortunately?' And I said: 'That's the way it is.' There was no more in the conversation about that but I didn't spend all that long afterwards in his presence."

Did he consider such an overture as a compliment?

"I suppose it is, except that somebody like Coward would be looking for someone every day, you know."

Why did Ulick himself never marry?

"I could have settled down. There were one or two people. There was an American millionairess whom I could have married. She had a lot of money, she used to travel on the Queen's yacht, and she wasn't prissy or boring. But certainly with my temperament, or my single-minded attitude towards what I wanted to do, I think it could well have been a mistake," he said.

"The main reason I didn't get married was because I wasn't very good at making money, particularly, and I didn't want to have the responsibility of children and a wife and all that. I could starve myself, but I didn't want to starve other people. That was really basically what it was about. The other thing was, I had girlfriends and I didn't need to get married, basically."

He recalled women practically jumping on him when he was living in the U.S. "Living in the Chelsea Hotel, that was the thing. I mean, you'd get picked up in the Chelsea and dragged up. The episodes there! They would tear you apart sometimes. I still love and am very fond of women. I wouldn't have any permanent sort of girlfriend, but I certainly have no depletion of my interest in women," he said.

Reminiscing about his many sexual conquests, the liberal-minded Dubliner told me how he once enjoyed a menage-a-trois with a millionairess and another one of his many lady friends.

"I didn't sleep a wink! The next morning she left because she had to take her mammy to mass. She was a very rich woman. She lived in the same apartment block as Jackie Kennedy. I used to see her going up and down the stairs occasionally but I never had the nerve to go up and say hello. I was no good at that. I knew Bobby and I met Ted," he said.

With such broad-minded views on sex, it was of little surprise to discover Ulick has some very outspoken opinions on prostitution. He believed it was "preposterous and outrageous" that it is illegal in Ireland for consenting adults to indulge in the so-called oldest profession in the world.

"Yes, I have been with a prostitute. In Paris and Amsterdam there are legalized brothels. It's wrong to make something punishable by law, which is being done by people consentingly. There is no actual reason that you can say it shouldn't be done," he said.

'They are bringing in a law in Sweden now that you can get arrested for paying for sex. It's so sick! That brings the law into disrepute. If you have things that are happening every day and are going to keep happening every day, and it's illegal, then the law goes into disrepute because everybody's doing it. And only the fellas that are caught are..." here he was so overcome with anger that his voice trailed off.

While insisting that he had never experimented with drugs, Ulick "absolutely" believed all types should be legalized too. "Cocaine and heroin do little more damage than drink. There are 30,000 people drunk in Dublin every Saturday night. It's just preposterous. Also, if they took off the ban on drugs — it's just like alcohol in Chicago bred all the gangs — it will deplete the number of criminals," he said.

Ulick himself didn't start drinking until he was well into his thirties.

"The only reason I didn't drink originally was through sport — I had to keep fit. Secondly, Dublin at that time... the two professions I was alleged to be taking part in — writing and the law — were shot through with alcoholics," he said.

"I saw the most brilliant men, like Brendan (Behan) and John O'Sullivan the painter and others, in pubs lying flat on the floor. Misbehaving, literally, not so much in their misbehavior but in the use of their gifts and intellectual. And they didn't seem to be able to control it. It seemed like a form of sickness. And I didn't want to get mixed up in it.

"The civilized thing, I took a glass of wine. In fact, I'll still only drink wine. That's not done out of prejudice. It's the only thing I like and I'll take a glass of wine now and then.

"I never was a writing person, if you know what I mean. I just did that. I was so obsessed with sport really that writing was just as much part of me as the sport."

During the Seventies and Eighties, Ulick was a regular — and never dull — guest on the popular Irish TV chat show *The Late Late Show*. He light-heartedly recalled how his presence prompted teenage schoolgirls to write him, asking him on dates. Some even invited him to their school debs.

"All these letters used to come in from schoolgirls who used to watch me on television late at night in the dormitory and then they'd all write letters. You'd get six or seven on the same day," he recalled.

Though, of course, he never took up any of the offers, Ulick missed his late-night appearances and believed he was being censored by the national broadcaster. "I think I've been boycotted for 20 years. I don't know what it is. I know that there are programs that I'd be obvious for, that I'd be the expert on, and they wouldn't have me on," he claimed.

"The only two programs that would have me on in the last few years were

Mary Kennedy in the afternoon and the Seoige girls recently. And both of them are gone. Both of them are wiped out.

"RTÉ should be closed, like the Seanad. It's outrageous. It's turning on itself. It's a tyranny. It's at the bottom of a lot of our troubles. It's the only station in the world — except for in Finland — where the license fee is collected by a station that, at the same time, is allowed to advertise. Then they're paying about a million euro of our bloody money to Pat Kenny. That's twice the American president's salary. He was appalling on *The Late Late*."

Such flashes of anger revealed that, despite his age, Ulick maintained the fighting spirit that made him a boxing champion as a young man.

Is the urban legend true that he knocked out a twenty-something troublemaker who dared to insult him about his age?

"I would have knocked out a few people. I would certainly have had fights like that if people went for me. I was quite fast," admitted the former pugilist.

"I didn't have that many, but I did have street fights. I can remember people coming up and starting a fight that I wouldn't have a hope — two or three of them. And I'd land one on the guy and, as I landed it, I would be gone. And I would run like the hammers."

Did he ever lose a fight?

"No, I didn't because I'd run if I was losing. I can't remember having to do that, but I was quite fast."

Why would people attack him?

"I never understood why. Maybe I had a habit of saying something that would get to the core of what was going on and would annoy them so much. Secondly, I was well known and known to be controversial. I don't know, but I did have a number of fights, alright," he said.

"These were all fights that I got into because either people picked on me who didn't know me, or people did know me; or if somebody was in trouble. If I found somebody in trouble I'd feel bound to try to help them. All you'd want to do is get them out of trouble and then scarper and leave whatever damage you've done behind you."

Ulick — who counted Mohammad Ali as a close friend — still holds the National Stadium's "quickest knockout in the history" record.

"It took four-and-a-half seconds. Then I won the British Universities' (welterweight) Championship in 1951. I was never beaten as a boxer," he said.

"Also, when I was a schoolboy I won the men's pole vault championships of Ireland and I broke the record for pole vaulting two years later in 1951. At the same time, I was playing rugby for Saint Mary's and London Irish. I also played cricket in the summer."

Ulick even claimed to have knocked out Brendan Behan, who had a fierce reputation for brawling, when they squared up to each other outside Davy Byrne's pub on Duke Street back in 1948. Another writer who also once sent Behan crashing to the ground was JP Donleavy during a drunken argument on London's famous Fleet Street.

"We had an argument inside and we went outside down the laneway. He came at me with his head to butt me, but I hit him a left on the nose, a good hard one, and he went down, and then I floored him with a right. He then got up on his knees and hands and I said to him, 'Do you want to come in for a drink?' And that was the end of it," he said.

It was the second and last time the two men met, but O'Connor went on to write an acclaimed but hugely controversial biography about the hell-raising author. The book, which was an instant international bestseller when it was released in 1970, caused outrage because Ulick exposed Behan as being bisexual.

"There was about a page-and-a-half dealing with his sexuality, which was largely as a result of being in prison. He was very much a woman's man, but he was bisexual," Ulick said.

"My theory at the time was: if you're writing a biography and you're trying to bring a man alive on the page, you've got to mould all the various characteristics and make them blend, so that by the end of the book you know the man inside and outside. And to drop one aspect of it would have been wrong. Morally wrong.

"Dominic (Behan's younger brother) was extremely angry about it. He told the *Sunday Times* that if he got me he'd knock my head off. I had to leave London the week before (the launch). *The Mirror*, whom I wrote a column for myself, had bought the (serialization) rights; so they made me leave London the week before to stop the other papers. But, as I was leaving, I bought a copy of the book at the airport and sent it to Dominic. Then Dominic wrote to a guy who was writing a column the next week in the *Sunday Times* and said, 'It's a good book and I think it's fair,' which it was."

But Ulick ended up taking a libel case against the now defunct Hibernia newspaper after it published a piece by the Official IRA's Chief of Staff Cathal Goulding who lambasted the author for revealing Behan's sexual habits.

"Cathal Goulding was Brendan's friend. He was responsible for a lot of mucking up and I just went for him because what he wrote in *Hibernia* was libelous. I sued him and I won and I got an apology from him. *Hibernia* published my reply and an apology from him. I put it in the article: 'We apologize for this thing and Mr O'Connor has asked for money to be given to the British Legion,'" he said.

He paused to laugh, before concluding: "Remember Cathal at that time was the chief of staff of the Official IRA, so I gave the money to the British Legion. I thought it might be a good idea."

I'll end this chapter as I did in my column in *Irish Sunday Mirror*, which was published the day after his funeral: We'll never see his likes again, as they say. RIP.

— 2020

Chapter Fifteen: Lee Dunne

Lee Dunne went to his grave at the grand old age of 86 in April 2021 with the dubious honor of being the most banned writer in Ireland, perhaps even in Europe. It was a title he relished too, and I can't say I blame him.

During the 1970s, eight of his novels and a movie entitled *Paddy*, which was based on his debut novel *Goodbye to the Hill*, were deemed unsuitable by the Irish censorship board. The film was only officially released in Ireland in the Noughties with, ironically, an age 12 certificate!

"The banning of *Paddy* was a sick joke that was caused by a momentary flash of Maureen Toal's magnificent breasts. I thought the film was about as obscene as the minutes of a Presbyterian Church meeting," Dunne once emailed me.

The majority of Dunne's controversial books were soft porn that were commissioned by the UK paperback publisher Corgi and, by contemporary standards, would probably be classified as light sex farces. But during the repressive 1970s, when even prophylactics were prohibited, or required medical prescriptions in the Republic of Ireland, Dunne was denounced from the pulpit by parish priests, who urged their congregations to burn his "blasphemous" books, including *Goodbye to the Hill*, which is now considered a seminal classic coming-of-age novel.

"In 1964, I sat down one evening with the idea of writing a short story about a 14-year-old office boy who rides down this hill to Ranelagh Road six days a week, for three years, vowing in his own way: 'Someday real soon, I'm going to say goodbye to this fucking place,'" he recalled.

He adapted *Goodbye to the Hill* for the stage and it ran in Dublin for a record-breaking two years and ten months. I'll doubt the record will be broken either.

Lee told me: "It is arguably Ireland's most popular play. And I still light a thank-you-candle to whatever scriptwriter in the sky dictated it to me so that I could pay the back rent and the coal bill and a long line of creditors. Ten years after that main run of the play people are still talking to me about it on a daily basis. Unbelievable, I know, but I swear this is true and I will produce it again when I find an Angel who wants to back a sure thing. I'm happy to record that the book is right now being reassessed and there is a growing opinion among those who decide these things that my novel is seminal to the 1950s."

After the banning of his books, Dunne was so incensed that he even held a demonstration on Grafton Street, with a placard denouncing censorship. "I gave away about a hundred copies of the banned book with the intention of getting arrested and being taken to court where I could have made a test case against censorship. But I couldn't get arrested!" Dunne recalled.

Dunne confessed to having led a hedonistic lifestyle. Apart from being married three times, Dunne candidly admitted to bedding countless women. "I had hundreds of infidelities during my first marriage, which lasted ten years," Dunne proffered, with a tone of remorse that seemed genuine.

He was prone to waking up in strange beds — and even in foreign countries — after heavy drinking sessions. Eventually, he gave up the booze, but, for a short period, he swapped his dependency on drink for drugs, before eventually checking himself into a clinic for treatment. "I had an amazing, cathartic experience at The Rutland Centre," said Dunne, who had been clean and sober for close to 50 years.

Apart from the soft porn paperbacks, Dunne penned a novel about the Dublin slums entitled *Does Your Mother?*, which was highly praised by Jennifer Johnston but is now out of print, which is a shame. Other notable titles include the aforesaid *Goodbye to the Hill* and its sequels *A Bed in the Sticks* and *Paddy Maguire Is Dead*.

The third part of the trilogy was the last book banned in Ireland and only seen the light of day again when I reprinted it with my now defunct publishing company, Killynon House Books. I also brought out a humorous memoir by Dunne about his time in New York trying to get a play staged on Broadway, which was entitled *My Middle Name Is Lucky*. I encouraged him to write it and had a great time working with him as his editor on it.

Dunne also wrote another memoir entitled *No Time For Innocence* and had two thrillers in print, including *Ringleader* published by Simon & Schuster in hardback in 1980, which was later republished in Ireland under the title *Ringmaster*. In later life, he also had three titles published by a leading independent Irish publisher. One of the novels *Barleycorn Blues* was probably his best work of fiction since the 1970 publication by Arrow of *Does Your Mother?* Personally, I am particularly fond of his historical novel *Seasons of Destiny* — but I'm biased because he said nice things about me in the acknowledgments. His novels *Goodbye to the Hill* and *A Bed in the Sticks*, which are about a teenager with aspirations to become a writer were two books that really inspired me in my teens to start writing. So, as you can imagine, it was a real buzz for me to be mentioned in his novels *Seasons of Destiny*, which was the sequel to *Dancers of Fortune*, a book that Dunne had originally written in the 1970s under the title *Jews and Gentiles*, but it was rejected by his then US publisher, despite them giving him an advance for it.

He hasn't had a new title published since 2006, but he has some unpublished manuscripts under the proverbial bed, including the thriller *You Get What You Pay For*. Again, I was thrilled when he gifted me a signed copy of the typed manuscript.

Some of the Q&A here was printed in a special St Valentine's Day edition of *Hot Press* magazine. It was entirely apt because I always found it hard to converse with Lee Dunne without the subject of sex dominating the conversation, seeing as he wrote so many books on his favorite topic!

He once told me, "After 300 women I lost count! Seriously, I gave up counting…"

Lee is only gone a few months at the time of writing but I already miss his great wit.

Q: You are the most banned author in Europe. How do you feel about this dubious title?

A: If they have nothing better to say when you are pushing up daisies, it is better than nothing. I never felt the stuff should have been banned. I won't be defensive about it, I will discuss it, but it was just crap. My mother would be spinning in her grave if she could hear this, but the notoriety of being banned never really bothered me. It bothered me that it cut down my sales of books in Ireland, as seven or eight of my books were banned, and it bothered me that I was tied to a country that was so repressive. It has only been in the last couple of years that one of my books was un-banned, *Paddy Maguire is Dead*, and two of my movies were shown. It just seems so ridiculous, I don't mean to be smart-arsed, it's a joke — that's how I feel about that.

Q: Where did you get your inspiration for what were the soft porn novels? Did you have to do much research!

A: It is fantasy really. The best sex you are going to write about is the girls you are never going to screw. That is why masturbation is so big, because you get the chick you want, you get her doing what you want, and you are being touched and touching at the same time — all those things that make sex so good. Those were quickie books, written for very respectable English publishers. I was offered a lot of money to write some funny, sexy books about London cab drivers. They were fun books, but not really dirty. When you read these titles (*The Cabfather*, *The Virgin Cabbies*, *Midnight Cabbie*) you know they are intended to be funny, with sex running second to the comedy inherent in the very titles. They were seen as soft porn back in the '70s, but now they would be perceived as light comedy!

Q: Starting out as a writer in the 1960s, you also wrote some sex novels under a pen name?

A: I just didn't think it was a good idea to put my name on what would be called a hot book, maybe even a dirty book. So, I used the name Peter O'Neill. I read a piece in the *New Statesman* from a guy called Maurice Girodias — who ran a publishing company called Olympia Press, which was synonymous with pornography — and he was interested in receiving (manuscripts). I was so full of sex — I loved it, I loved thinking about it, and talking about it. I had always enjoyed reading sexy books, and I knew I could write a horny book, no problem. I wrote the first one in ten days.

Q: The opening line of one of your books, *Big Al*, states: "During my teens I wanted to make love to my mother."

A: I didn't remember that, but I will tell you this: that's a great opening line for a book. I am delighted that I had the wit to do that. I probably had a hard-on on the way into the world!

Q: I have heard stories about priests up in the pulpit, during the 1970s, urging their congregation to burn your books?

A: I was surprised because they were funny books. The books that were banned were essentially funny, apart from *Paddy Maguire is Dead*. By definition, pornography can't be funny. Pornography has to be about heavy breathing. If you look at my books, they are funny books about larger than life characters. A lot of the flair in those books came from my admiration for the old black and white movies, film noir and all that, which was serious, but the funny ones were great, great flair, great lines, great one-liners. I grew-up on them — that was my education.

So my number one thing is that I was surprised that the books were banned. When *Paddy Maguire is Dead* was banned I was appalled because it is a good book. I thought that was very sad. I would have been happier to make more money out of the books and I would have done if they had not been banned. It cost me a lot of money. I gave up everything to be a professional writer and I have subsidized that with gigs from time to time, which I am still doing when I get them — personal appearances, after dinners, all that. So I never made the bread I might have made.

Q: Were you always a horny little devil?

A: Absolutely. When I was growing up there was no *Playboy*, there was no top shelf material, there was no television, there was no anything! It was a graveyard with lights! A lot of the kids I grew up with were the same, we were all horny, all we could think about was sex. We'd look at the pictures of nylons or a corset in adverts in the evening paper. Of course, back then, it was taboo to think or talk about sex. When I was ten, I was looking at girls; I was fascinated with boobs. By the time I was 12, I was obsessed with it and when I was 15 or 16, I was involved with a woman. I didn't want a girl, I didn't want young ones, I wanted a woman with breasts and hips — a woman who would put her arms around me.

Q: Why weren't you interested in girls your own age?

A: I had no interest in having sex with them and, besides, there was no chance anyway. I was interested in women.

Q: How old were you when you lost your virginity?

A: I was 13. I felt inadequate. I didn't last as long as I thought I should, but that's OK when you're 14, it's when you're 30 that you'll feel a little bit miffed.

Q: That's very young!

I wasn't the youngest one in my neighborhood. Thank God for the lovely, young Protestant girl, who wasn't all hung up, who parted (her legs). She was older than me, but she thought I was beautiful. I was a very good-looking kid. I can say that without blushing because it has nothing to do with me today. Now I'm just a very good-looking older guy (*laughs*).

Q: How many women have you slept with?

A: Probably 1,000. (*The comedian and TV personality — JOT*) Des Bishop's father, Mike Bishop, was my best friend. We were the champions of Chelsea. It was just fun, but we were working at it full-time for maybe three years. Scoring and keeping tabs like cowboys with notches on their gun. It isn't that many when you think about it. It is like one a week for 20 years. Four a week for five years. It is not that many if you are into sex. I mean there are people who are into sex and who eat, drink and screw sex. I was one of those. Mike Bishop was the same. He was the only guy who could pull better than me. The Bis' [Bishop] could have got laid in a coffin!

Q: Did you ever get an STD?

A: I hardly knew anybody back then that didn't touch for gonorrhea, it was kind of like getting your spurs as a cowboy. Gonorrhea was nothing, which brings me back to what young people face today — Aids makes the mind boggle.

Q: Was it all straight sex, or were there threesomes, or other imaginative options?

A: Of course. No man doesn't want to go to bed with two women. Friends of mine, guys, we had two women in a room together, whatever. I don't think that is any type of big deal. It is perfectly natural. The older I got, the more and more women I found were up for that. And up for another woman. That type of thing. Great, two women, wonderful.

It was a major turn-on. To me, lesbian love is the turn-on of all time. Always has been. I don't know what that means about me. But to watch women doing it and to be part of it was just wonderful. I knew I had a great heart because I was afraid my heart would blow up! To witness such a joyous coming together of two beautiful women, their incredulity and joy in each other, the joys of touching each other's bodies — it was just incredible.

Q: Do you think younger men today have it easier when it comes to seducing women?

A: No. There is no such thing as a free ride, if you will pardon the pun. Young people are facing a daunting life in terms of the availability of everything. They are getting sex easier but, in a way, it takes some of the hit out of the experience because it becomes very commonplace and you get chicks all over men and they don't have to chase. Now you can see a guy and a gal walking along and she's got her hand on his arse. It didn't happen in my day.

Q: What do you think about the sex industry emerging in Ireland, such as lap dancing clubs?

A: My wife and I made a great effort to have a lapdancing club closed in Bray. I disapprove of lap dancing clubs, other than in a restrictive setting.

Q: So how would you restrict it?

A: Have a building the size of Clerys and in there have lap dancing clubs and brothels, run by the State, who ensure that the girls are clean, they have a check every week. If a guy wants to be whipped, he can go in and pay his fucking fee and have respect for his wishes. He can walk out of there without shame, or anything else, and without fear of being blackmailed by the kind of people who blackmail people who are different. You should be able to go in there and buy pornography, watch pornographic movies — whatever you want. But let us be clear: we all know what this is. No guy can say, "I thought I was going in to buy a shirt," and he ends up getting a blowjob! Do you know what I am saying? I am not against any of it, I just think you have to localize it, you can't have it all over the place, and you got to protect kids from this.

Q: What are your thoughts now on porn?

A: My thoughts on porn are the same as my thoughts on alcohol: I don't drink but pubs are OK by me. I don't buy porn. I saw porn in New York that would make your hair stand up. I was in Greece recently and there were porn movie houses in Athens — but in a million years I wouldn't be bothered. I am not judging, I am just saying I don't go to rock concerts either because they are too noisy for me. When I listen to music I want to hear the music and the vocals. It's personal taste. But if others want it, that's OK.

Q: Do you think alcohol helped you to come out of your shell to hit on women?

A: No question. I'll tell you straight, when I was 17, I was 5ft 10 and had blue eyes, black hair, and all my own teeth, and I was regarded as a very good-looking guy. I had taken lessons in how to dance — and yet I couldn't walk five yards across the floor to ask a girl to dance. I still think that any alcoholic is an egomaniac with an inferiority complex. I couldn't walk across the floor to ask a girl to dance because I thought that everybody in that ballroom was going to be looking at me. You see, the ego and the inferiority complex. I went around the corner to the pub and drank a pint of cider with a large whiskey, and I came back and I could walk the length of the ballroom. I was free of any concerns about anybody else, and that was the beginning of my friendship with alcohol. The trouble with alcohol is it becomes more demanding as the years go by and I ended up in really serious trouble.

Q: How long are you off the booze?

A: Since October 1969. I probably tried most drugs — apart from heroin. I was popping amphetamine to give me a hit, to keep me awake when I was writing. I used drugs as a substitute for booze. I went on *The Late Late Show* once and I was very jarred and I had dropped a handful of speed. They didn't care what you did provided you kept people awake. That night I was argumentative and I tore strips off this American clergyman, a sort of benign racist, who finally admitted under my relentless questioning that he had no black members in his congregation. Half the country loved me, the other half hated me over that incident. In fact, the next day somebody approached me on the street and called me a fucking bastard.

But after treatment in the Rutland Center, I never looked back again, thank God! If somebody said to me, "Will you have a drink?" you might as well be asking me if I would like a drink of some petrol. The ridiculous thing is when you are a drinking alcoholic, you think you can't live without it. But I heard the magic words, stay away from drink for one day at a time. And I am smart enough to do that.

I came home from that first AA meeting and my wife Jean said, "Oh you're not pissed tonight!" I told her I'd finally found a way to quit drinking. And she said, "I'm delighted for you, but I just want you to fuck off out of my life. Por favor."

Jean couldn't be blamed for her response. You see, she probably didn't believe me as I had sworn not to drink a hundred times before — on my knees, crying like a baby, saying, "Forgive me. I love you." I was never abusive to her; I never put a hand on her. Thank God. I knew nice guys in AA that came out of a blackout having beaten their wife up. She knew I wasn't a bad guy — I was just a screaming, alcoholic lunatic at times.

Q: It sounds like your first wife suffered a lot from worrying about you when you disappeared on benders.

A: It was tragic. It was sad for her. She was a great woman. She deserved better than being married to what turned into an alcoholic arsehole. I meant well and I never disrespected her, except by my absence. I would say I'm going out for a drink and maybe not come back for a week or ten days. I didn't know where I was half the time, I started having blackouts. The Wernicke-Korsakoff Syndrome — where the brain just starts to become saturated with booze — you can lose your memory for days. I drove a London cab for two days with no memory of it. You don't crash, you don't go through red lights, you're functioning but you're not there.

One day I was really shaken, in a terrible state, really pathetic. You're talking about a man who's like a frightened child. The laughs are gone and the sexy image is gone and you are very scared. And I went to an AA meeting in London. The guy chairing the meeting was someone I'd drank with, but I hadn't seen him for four years. And this guy was so bad on the booze that he used to foul himself in the pub when he'd be talking to you. He would shit in his pants and didn't know it. When he disappeared, I just thought he'd died. And I had a drink for him: "God bless you!" An AA meeting is chaired by an alcoholic who's recovering.

He started to remunerate the symptoms of alcoholism and I ticked off the first 17 in my head. If you have five you've definitely got a problem. That night I heard the magic words: "Stay away from one drink for one day." It was so simple. Not to equate simple with easy. And I never drank again. I did it one day at a time.

Q: You once told me you had to leave your second wife because she wouldn't stop drinking.

A: Again, I have to take a lot of responsibility here, but I could see she clearly had a drink problem. She had written to me asking if I could help her with the drink problem. I took her to an AA meeting. She rang me at two in the morning — as I was in bed with a gorgeous air hostess — and she said, "I need help. I just woke up in bed with a guy that I don't even know. And I should have been home at nine o'clock. Could I say that I was talking to you and some AA friends about giving up booze and the time just went crazy, went away?" I said, "On condition that you come to an AA meeting with me."

The next night I blackmailed her into going to the AA meeting. I started helping her. Six weeks later — bang! It happens. I couldn't see at the time, but we'd transfer our addiction from booze to each other. We became addicted to each other. It was just incredible, wonderful lovemaking, sex, whatever.

Within no time at all, we were living together. It was tough, but it was good for a long time. She would ultimately go back drinking. I had to leave her because she became impossible to live with. She wasn't overtly drinking, but I knew she was. And God knows what else she was doing because when she drank she got naughty.

Q: Infidelity?

A: I'm afraid so. You hear about it afterwards, of course. That's what happened when she drank. I had to leave her for my own head.

Q: You said you were unfaithful yourself during your first marriage?

A: Absolutely. Hundreds of infidelities in a ten-year marriage. When I first got married in 1959 I really thought that I would never look at another woman and that's kind of innocent in a way. Stupid, perhaps, but I really thought, "This is it." After about a year of marriage I was looking at other women. I had this cab driver friend who said, "After you have the first one, come and talk to me." I said it is never going to happen but he insisted, saying he had been down this road because you get a lot of women, especially if you are an attractive person, who want to go to bed with you. I had promised to love, honor and obey — and I am going to work with this.

Eventually, I had to go and talk to him. That was the beginning of the marriage infidelity and then it just became a habit. When I went out of the house, I stopped being a married man in my head. With drink involved, of course. During the cab driving years, I would stop the car, go into the pub and have a few drinks, end up with a chick, and wake up a day later and not even know where I was, who I was with! And I would have to go out looking for the fucking cab.

Q: Did you ever wake up in a foreign country?

A: It's funny. On one occasion, I woke up in a hotel room beside this very attractive blonde and I looked out the window — only to discover that I was in Amsterdam!

Q: Lucky you had your passport with you!

A: After that for a year-and-a-half, I never went out without my passport. I came out of an alcoholic blackout walking along the Champs Elysees with a very beautiful French woman on my arm. I said to her, "What was it about me that first attracted you to me?" And she said it was my red knickers. I said, "What!" How could she see them! I was wearing red silk underpants and she told me that I took my pants off on the plane and danced in the aisle. She thought I was crazy, wonderful, cool, and that was how I pulled her in a blackout. We spent the night together, it was great, and I never saw her again, like hundreds of others.

Q: Were you ever with a prostitute?
A: Only in the very first days in Soho. When I went to London I was 17 or 18 and Soho was like an Aladdin's cave. You had hundreds of beautiful prostitutes standing around, stunning creatures by Irish standards, where so many women dressed down so they looked like miraculous medals with tits. So I went with a pro: it cost a pound. I had a couple more but I never needed it — I just went for the experience. The amateurs always found me!

Q: Were you not afraid of getting a girl pregnant?

A: I never thought about it. In the '60s, the girls didn't ask you your name either. Promiscuous women tend to look after themselves. You are less likely to get one of those ladies pregnant than some innocent girl who just loses the head and succumbs to you and you pop her, and then you make her pregnant, and then you can have problems. I looked after myself — I carried condoms and stuff like that.

Q: What are your thoughts on homosexuality?

A: When I was a young guy, poofs were coming on to me all the time. On the cab, guys would openly say to me, "I would love to go to bed with you." I was in the merchant navy with really raving fags, which we called them in those days. I don't mean any disrespect. That was the terminology used at the time. I think gay people are gay people. I think heteros are heteros. I don't make any judgment on it. It was never my bag, but I am young, I have time — I am only 72! I know that if I was on a desert island with a goat and a beautiful 25-year-old who was gay, I certainly wouldn't be fraternizing with the goat!

Q: You knew Brendan Behan. Did it surprise you that he was bisexual?

A: Brendan admitted to being bi. It was no big deal to Brendan. I remember walking with him behind a young man and a girl, who were both very beautiful, and he said, "Would you like to screw her?" And I said yes, and he said he would screw either one of them, and I said, "Are you serious?" And he said, "Yes. A screw's a screw." It was that casual. He'd been in prison, so, yeah, but I don't think that is any kind of big deal.

Q: You were friends with Charlie Haughey when he was Irish Taoiseach. He himself was a renowned womanizer and must have loved listening to your sex stories?

A: That was what attracted Charlie to me. He read *Paddy Maguire Is Dead*, which is semi-autobiographical, and he wanted to meet this guy who had all these chicks, because Charlie was very interested in sex — and had quite a reputation as a hammer man, a lady's man. So, he was interested in my stories. He wanted to share the color that he couldn't actually have in his role because he was living in a goldfish bowl of public life. Like (the broadcaster) Gay Byrne couldn't have done what I did, because Gay was on television every Saturday night. Like a lot of healthy young men, Charlie was mad about women. He loved the fact that I was sex mad and very successful with the ladies. He was mad to know about all the birds. Charlie loved a laugh and my stories of pulling birds in the cab would have him hooting with laughter. Charlie was fascinated by the "pull," as we called it.

Q: How did you spend the time with Charlie?

A: When I was married to my second wife, Charlie would come down to our house in Wicklow with Terry (Keane). I have never spoken about that to this day. What I am saying here I say with respect — like all men Charlie was good and bad. Overall, he did himself down, and I am sorry about that, but it is nothing to do with me. He loved the women. He nearly fell off the chair listening to my stories. He had a great sense of humor and I would tend to be amusing.

Q: Speaking of the Prime Minister's office, in one of your novels, *Barleycorn Blues*, he writes about a fictitious leader of the land who likes to conduct extramarital affairs in parliament! I presume this character was inspired by your friendship with Haughey?

A: Yes, it is. And yes, Charlie hinted that the desk in the Taoiseach's office had come in handy once or twice, but he never mentioned any names and, of course, he was never restricted to one person. So, anything could have happened! But I didn't know if he was being serious or was pulling my leg.

Q: Do you think he had a problem with alcohol?

A: He got pulled many times by the cops while jarred behind the wheels of a car and stuff like that. He had a drink problem and he knew it. He said to me one day, "The way I'm going, Jesus, Lee, I'll soon be joining your mob," — meaning Alcoholics Anonymous — "but 'I'm not like you; I just can't walk into AA meetings, can I?"

Q: Are you surprised that there haven't been more sex scandals in Ireland?

A: Oh, yeah. There were certainly some very famous people and, of course, you would have to remember that most of them were married, so they would have to keep it quiet too. Terry was the only one wild enough to come out and talk to the media about their relationship. Terry Keane is not the most likeable woman in the world — but I kind of empathize with her. I Like her, but I thought she was unwise to speak publicly about Charlie and I think perhaps she realized that herself.

Q: Did you ever have an affair yourself with someone famous, which you hoped wouldn't be leaked to the tabloid press?

A: I was very careful about my affairs. I never spoke names. In America I had an affair with a woman who was a very famous film star. (*Off the record, Dunne mentions the name of the actress who was married to one of the biggest Hollywood stars in the 1970s — JOT.*) She loved me very much. I have never spoken about those things. I just thought, "No names, no scandal."

Q: Were you ever pursued by a jealous husband?

A: I actually got a jealous husband once when I wasn't even doing anything! I know one guy who tried to get people to beat me up, but he asked a very heavy guy who happened to be one of my biggest fans, and he warned him off. That was the end of that. I was fortunate, but, again, I was innocent. I got out of a couple of windows in my time! You can never trust the fact that the guy is working late. Sometimes I had to quickly get dressed in case I had to fight the guy pounding on the door, and I would be wondering, "What am I doing here? It is too heavy. I don't need this."

Q: What turns you on?

A: Essentially, it was always physical — a sensational body. But then, when I got a bit older, a smile or eyes that twinkle, and somebody with a sense of humor. I would have to confess to the fact that I would have been in my 40s before I stopped seeing the body first. A sensational body still makes my head turn. I have always been in love with breasts.

Q: Did you ever enjoy intercourse in public places?

210

A: I was at a stage with the cab driving where I was doing it in the back of the cab and I began to put the cab in more exposed places — under a street lamp on a main street. Like, I really wanted to be caught, I was like a burglar leaving his fingerprints. I was getting crazier. I did get caught in the back of the cab naked with a woman. I was a bit mad.

Q: How about orgies?

A: Orgies are at best unhygienic! My biggest turn on was — and still is — watching two women together. Not naked women, but two women in the cinema, in the back row, just making out like a couple, getting turned on by touching each other. Fantastic! That would be my big fantasy. But I have seen it in private.

Q: We have talked a lot about sex — but what about your thoughts on love?

A: Being in love can be a lot of fun, exciting and exhilarating, but sex has very little to do with love. Lust is a must, but love is something else again. Being in love to me literally means being insane to some degree, simply because it's all to do with hormones, no matter how we dress it up. It's about wanting to lay somebody, and since people are essentially mindless in this state it creates all kinds of problems. If people "in love" get very lucky they may live to survive the ailment and get to know each other well enough to come to love. And each and every person that ever lived should get to be that lucky, at least once.

Q: You married you third wife, Maura, an Irish-American you met over 30 years ago now while she worked as an editor on your novel *Requiem for Reagan*.

A: She's 18 years younger than me. It's a big gap at any age really. But my age never came into it with Maura because she said, "You're like a leprechaun, you're just amazing." I'm living in married bliss with Maura. I am obviously now very happily married. I am very grateful to have the wife I have. I have a friend who is 80 and he has finally accepted that he can't get any more erections, which I think is sad. "Keep it going, José," is my motto.

Q: Did Maura have any reservations about marrying such a notorious womanizer?

A: No. Maura and I were friends for a good while before we became an item. And she is a very wise lady who knew that I was no longer like the little kid that wanted every toy in the shop. We were great buddies and when she committed it was low key but for keeps. We are still so much in love and even better buddies than we were back in those early days.

Q: Even though you've said "goodbye" long ago to your hell raiser's streak, do you reckon your debauchery lifestyle did hinder your once-promising writing career?

A: I made mistakes. If I was going again — knowing what I know now — I wouldn't have spent so much time being Jack the Lad. Let me put it this way, if I was advising a young guy now, I'd say, "Spend less time in pubs and spend more going to British Counsel meetings about writers and what they're entitled to." In other words, find out what's available to you and your company should be people who are in a position to help you. Go networking. I never did. I was more interested in chicks than I was in meeting the top editor of so-and-so. I'd say, "Fuck 'em."

I didn't make the right moves many a time. I was kind of immature emotionally. My talent was bigger than I realized. I never had any self-esteem in that area. I had to battle this inherent inferiority complex that you are born poor with. It takes a bit of overcoming and it takes a long time before you feel entitled to the success you're getting.

I look at Lee back then and he was never a bad guy. He was wayward but he had a lot of fun. He was blessed that he was good looking, tall enough, the ladies loved him. I'm talking about this now without a hint of embarrassment because it's like talking about somebody else. I didn't make the right moves many a time. I would think, "Yeah, I might get a movie out of this guy, but I couldn't stand working with him!" And I'd leave. I wouldn't do that today.

I had talent, but nobody gets everything. I had to battle this inherent inferiority complex that you come out of the slum dwellings with, especially if you're parents had been poor all their lives. It takes a bit of overcoming and it takes a long time before you feel entitled to the company of this woman, the deal you're getting, the success you're getting, because you're coming from generations of people who think they're coming from a different place.

You come out of the Dublin slums with hang-ups, I don't care who you are. With serious hang-ups. And some people never articulate it like I did through the work. God gave me strong fingernails to hang in. I never thought I would make 35 and I have doubled it. I am amazed to be around still. I feel I can certainly make 80, but I want to make it singing and banging the keyboard. Death holds no terror for me since I see it as a natural part of life. The all important thing is not to die in a bad humor!

— 2007

Chapter Sixteen: Deirdre Purcell

For someone who insists that she's "never had any ambitions really," Deirdre Purcell has been an impressively high achiever in several fields — including acting, broadcasting, and, of course, writing, firstly as a journalist and later a best-selling author.

Deirdre grew up in the working-class suburb of Ballymun, north Dublin. Educated at an inner-city school, she later won a scholarship to Gortnor Abbey — a convent boarding school in Mayo. There, she resolved to become a nun like her teachers.

The Dubliner has enjoyed various career reincarnations during her lifetime — she started off treading the boards in the Abbey Theatre before going on to become the first female news anchor with the national broadcaster RTÉ. Then, just as she was becoming a household name as a newscaster, Deirdre astonished everybody — and "deeply worried" her parents — by turning her back on TV to take up a job as a journalist with the now defunct *Sunday Tribune* newspaper. That, in turn, led to her becoming one of the nation's best-selling authors.

Surprisingly enough perhaps, Deirdre was also on the board of the Central Bank in Ireland when the banking crisis happened. It was a part of her life she was reluctant to specifically get into when I spoke to her. In fairness, there was pending court cases at the time involving the reckless bankers and it has to be pointed out that she probably didn't want to say anything that would unduly influence those sensitive procedures. Besides, she was doing the interview to promote a book and not to justify her role on the board or maybe badmouth others. But here's what I wrote about it in the *Irish Daily Mail* back in 2011:

She was nominated for the position on the Audit and Risk Management Committee by then finance minister Charlie McCreevy, who also appointed her to the board of the Financial Regulator (FSRA).

It irked her when I asked if she was buddies with McCreevy. "That's the cynical way of looking at things! Absolutely not. I never met the man. I got a call out of the blue from him. I don't know where or how he got my name. I didn't know him at all. I'd never met him. I met him subsequently when I was interviewing him…"

If there was no prior personal connection, it begs the question, then, of why a novelist was appointed to the board of the Central Bank?

"I was astonished," Deirdre told me. "It was one of the most interesting things I did. It wasn't that I'd been chosen willy nilly. I'd been on various things to do with finance. For instance, I was on the Abbey Theatre board for 12 years. I was on the board of the Financial Services Ombudsman for 13 years. I was on the Government's Millennium Committee. I didn't go in as a kind of a dolly bird with no financial experience whatsoever."

All these posts, she points out, gave her plenty of fiscal experience. "But I wasn't taken in for my experience in banking, I was taken in for my life experience, independence and as a kind of a public interest or consumer representative. Certainly in the Regulator I was the consumer person on the Board. So, nobody expected me at the beginning to know all about contracts for difference — and most people didn't know about contracts for difference. I learnt on the job," she said.

Deirdre was unwilling, however, to comment on the "life experience" she gained during the collapse of the banking system in 2008 — or the claim that the Central Bank failed to give adequate warnings about reckless lending in the banks.

She left its board in 2010, a few months before an overhaul saw the remaining members replaced.

"I was there for the whole Quinn thing. Not all of it, but I was there when that was starting. Since my expertise wasn't specifically banking I decided to concentrate on the credit unions and on consumer issues," she said.

When pushed, all she would say on the crash was that there was "deep concern" at the height of the crisis "as soon as the board realized what was happening." She also rejects the suggestion that they were all asleep at the wheel leading up to the crash. "I don't agree with that at all," she said. "It was a very good board. I know that's not the conventional wisdom, but that's what I thought."

I ask whether Deirdre found it a stressful period.

"I found the last part of it very stressful," she conceded.

Was she he thinking: "I wish I had never gotten into this?"

"No," she insisted. "I'm the type of person who likes to finish what I start."

Deirdre had just published a new book when we met in the lobby of the Gresham Hotel for a little over an hour in 2013. Before the interview started, I reminded her of how she was one of the first people I ever interviewed when I was working as a cub reporter for a local newspaper called *The Finglas Forum* in 1993. We had met at an event in the library in Ballymun, close to where she grew up, and she graciously agreed to an on-the-spot interview, sitting beside me on the outside window ledge in the glorious sunshine, as her mother chatted nearby with old friends and acquaintances.

I didn't have any questions prepared because my request was spontaneous with the aim of pushing my way to the feature section of the community paper with my "exclusive" interview of a local star. I became a bit flustered when I realized I had no questions to ask, but Deirdre had a wonderful calming effect with her personable and laidback approach. She probably just said it to put me at ease, but I remember Deirdre told me she preferred to do interviews without knowing much about the subject because she felt it helped with the end result. I also remember Deirdre even mentioned she had read an article I'd written for the now defunct *In Dublin* magazine, which made me chuffed no end.

I not only walked away with enough nice quotes to write-up a profile on her, which was subsequently published that weekend, but she offered me a lot of solid advise about writing and I still to this day use many of the techniques she suggested.

I was thankfully able to come a little bit more prepared question-wise for our second interview — even if I needed to dash out to the store next door to buy some batteries for the tape recorder!

Q: You don't like the description Chick-Lit.

A: I don't. I think it's insulting actually. I don't know any writer of any genre who doesn't try to write the best book he or she can. There are some male writers I know who are writing books that if they had been written by a woman would be absolutely desecrated. But the people who are lumped into Chick lit are people like Marian Keyes, Patricia Scanlan. People like that, who are writing about families, about dark things, about dealing with illness, who are dealing with bereavement. Patrica Scanlan books are very spiritual. None of them are Chick Lit but they're all kind of lumped into with: "Oh somebody's going to be vomiting into a urinal in some dive in Dublin!" And they don't do that.

I have a great deal of sympathy for publishers. Publishers need people to be corralled into genres, all of that. And so if you look at all the pink covers, white covers, the blue covers, and all of that, they have to try and stand out in a bookshop. I mean, if you have been in a bookshop lately it's just mindboggling how many books there are, how many new books there are, and new writers, all the time.

So, I have some sympathy for publishers, they have to find some way to differentiate the products they have from somebody's else products. But journalists persist — if there's any woman writer, she's either literally or she's Chick lit. There's a whole mountain writers in between those two genres.

Q: I think if Jennifer Johnston started out now she'd probably be lumped in as Chick lit!

A: She writes about love and families and relationships —

217

Q: These are the same things you'd write about.

A: Yes, but she got her reputation early and she deserves every inch of it.

Q: She's one of Ireland's greatest writers.

A: Absolutely. Jennifer is great. She was on the board of The Abbey when I was there. She's a very, very interesting woman. She really is. So, there were very few Irish women writers in popular fiction around that time. Maeve (Binchy) was the first popular writer and then Patricia (Scanlon) was second, I think, and then I came along third, and there's a whole rake of them now. Some of them are writing about the kind of things that are supposed to be Chick lit, or are said to be Chick lit, but they all have kernels of good stuff in them.

Q: Would you use the word sexism to describe it?

A: No. I would use the word lazy.

Q: You're writing less and less fiction these days…

A: I've only written one novel in the last six year and that was called *Pearl*. I wasn't sure if I was going to write fiction again. I just kind of hit a wall. I became more interested in non-fiction. Non-fiction is so much easier.

But then I went to talk to my publishers around Christmas last year (in 2012) and I said, "I'm not sure if I'm going to produce another novel." And she said, 'Ok." And they were very understanding. She suddenly said, "You love Christmas, why don't you write a novel based around Christmas?" And it was like a light bulb going off in my head. A light bulb moment.

(*She was referring to her novel* The Winter Gathering, *published in 2013. She subsequently wrote another festive novel entitled* The Christmas Voyage, *published in 2017 — JOT.*)

Embarking on a novel is very, very difficult because you know what's facing you. It's 24/7, 365 days of the year. It's neglecting things that you should be doing. I know people do and I've great admiration for them, (but) I can't fit in a novel around other parts of your life. It's virtually impossible. To be any good, you have to have it as your prime endeavor. You use every facility you have and use every emotion that you've ever had. At least I don't do what I did at the beginning, which is what all beginning novelists do, you know, (to) think that every thought you ever had is really profound and you have to get it into the novel. I don't do that anymore — I concentrate on the story.

But embarking on such a heavy load, starting to pick it up is hard. It can be exciting in the middle of it when things are going well and you know it's going well. Sometimes if you find you're laughing at something you've just written — that's fantastic, it's such a bonus.

Q: How many hours would you write a day?

A: It depends entirely on what else is my life. That's what I mean, it's very hard to fit in stuff around other things that you're doing. I mean, I know people do it and I just don't know how they do it and be true to the novel. I don't know how they do it. I need big spades of time, so all going well my way of writing would be to vanish down to Kilcatherine (Cork), which is where our house is. It's a mystical place where we are. It really is. And I spend maybe three solid weeks literally 24 hours a day. Now, I don't be writing 24 hours a day, but I'd be thinking of nothing else 24 hours a day. I wouldn't have clocks, or watches, or anything, and I would just eat, sleep and write around the clock.

Q: That would drive some people mad!

A: It doesn't drive me mad. And I think the quality of the stuff is much better. I know that. The output is five times more prolific because you aren't getting assaults of things coming in; your brain has time to open out and relax into the thing. I find in a situation like that I don't have to struggle for words or the way to describe things. It just flows. But it takes a few days to get into it. And then you have to go back to real life at some stage.

Q: One reviewer pointed out that you've a lower profile these days.

A: I'm not in charge of my profile; I never was. I don't make any efforts to increase my profile. I'm not interested in that really, much to (the chagrin of) anybody who wants to publicize me. I'm not being negative about it; I'll do anything I'm asked — within reason! I've a very, very good friend who is called Patricia Scanlan, who is another author.

Q: She used to work in the Finglas library. She's a lovely woman.

A: She's gorgeous. And she insisted that I get a Facebook page for this book. So, I set it up. I find it absolutely incomprehensible. I'm not untechnical. I'm technical enough, provided it's Apple, the Mac. But I don't know what do to now: I have this Facebook page and people are reacting to it, and I'm just writing as if it's a letter to people. Patricia also said, "You have to be on Twitter." I got on Twitter, but I don't know how long I can manage to keep on it. Adrian, my son, is very big on Twitter. He tweets a lot.

From that point of view, I think my profile has remained quite big in terms of the people who know me and who read my books. Mind you, I still go around the country and people say, "Oh, you're the girl who reads the news!" I'd be in a shop or a restaurant, or café, or something and I see people: "I know I know her! I know I know her! Did she play hockey with my sister, or what?!" And then they come up to you and say, "Don't I know you?" And what am I supposed to say? Am I supposed to say, "Of course you do!' Or am I supposed to say, "No, you don't!" What am I supposed to say? So, what I usually do is: "Well, most people think I played hockey with their sister. Have you a sister? Did I play hockey with your sister?" Anyway, it's faster just to say, "I'm Deirdre Purcell. I'm a writer."

Q: You started off as an actress and then when you were young you went off to America.

A: I was in The Abbey and I got a scholarship to the university in Chicago and I went there. I was 23, I wasn't that young. Here's the timeline: left school in 1962, aged 17, two weeks later I was in the civil service; six months after that I was in Aer Lingus; two-and-a-half-years after that I was in The Abbey; three years after that I was in America.

Q: I heard you hadn't planned to even go to the audition for The Abbey!

A: That's all true. My friend asked me to audition with him, just to play the scenes with him so he didn't have to do monologues. So, I agreed to do that and I got offered the job. Three years after that I was in America. The opportunity to go to America was just irresistible. Then all that other stuff happened — travel agency; cocktail waitress; running a dinner theatre. I worked in the library in the college, all of that stuff.

Q: Is it true your first play was with the late great Donal McCann?

A: Yes, it was. He was young at the time too. He wasn't just starting — the potential was seen. He was becoming quite a star.

Q: I heard one of directors there bullied you?

A: Yes, I was bullied. But I wasn't the only one who was bullied. I mean, I wasn't singled out per se.

Q: He didn't like women, I heard.

A: That's true. Now, there are people who think he was a genius. So, take your pick.

Q: What type of bullying?

A: Just shouting and jumping and losing his temper and being personally vicious, you know, that's all.

Q: Was that one of the reasons why you decided to go to America?

A: I decided to go to America because I had been to America once before with Aer Lingus. I walked in the Aer Lingus' delegation in the Saint Patrick Day's parade. And I thought New York was fantastic. America was fantastic. Everything about America was fantastic. And then when I got the opportunity to go there, I mean, I was still 23, I'd only been really in Ireland and a few Aer Lingus holidays abroad and things like that. So, the opportunity to go to America was just irresistible really.

Q: You met your first husband almost as soon as you stepped off the plane. It sounds like something straight out of a romantic novel with him saying on your first encounter that he was going to marry you …

A: He did.

Q: Were you taken aback?

A: I was.

Q: Was it Love at first sight?

A: For him, yeah. I thought he was just having a laugh really, but he wasn't apparently. I met him on the driveway into university on my very first day there.

Q: How long were you married?

A: Seven years.

Q: How come you broke up?

A: All kind of reasons. Private reasons.

Q: Did you go into it in your memoir?

A: Yes, it's in the memoir, but I hope I haven't let anybody down. But it is in the memoir. There are too many other people involved and there are too many lives that are affected by any break-up. It's none of my business to increase their disturbance or distress.

Q: It was a difficult time to be a single mother with two children...

A: It certainly was. Even having children in those days was difficult.

I was under contract, a kind of a casual contract in RTÉ for my second child and there was no maternity leave. I didn't even have annual leave. So what I did was, coming up to having my second child, I worked right up until the night before he was born and I had worked 11 extra days in the previous couple of months to have days in lieu to take off to have the baby. I was a continuity announcer, but casual. And I only took the 11 days off and I went back to work.

It was extremely difficult — financially, emotionally, every other way. I felt terrible of course, but I managed. But there's an old saying, whether it's religious or cultural or what, is: "The back for the burden." And I don't even believe that one, but what I believe is that you deal with what you're presented with. You don't even know you're dealing with it. When you've children you've no option, you just deal with it, you just do it. It was extremely difficult but with the help of friends and family I got through it. It was an actual learning curve for me; I think if I had stayed in the States it wouldn't have been the same.

Q: You were something of a trailblazer being the first female news anchor on Irish TV.

A: First staff one, yeah. I can never remember her name, but there was somebody else before me — she was one of these casual newsreaders. But I was the first staff (one), yeah. I didn't see it as an achievement at the time. I don't mean to sound weird about this, but I've no life plan. I never had a life plan and I never had any ambitions really — things happened. I just went with them, or I didn't go with them. I tend to jump at challenges or opportunities, but I don't go looking for them. I was nine years altogether in RTÉ. There was about two-and-a-half-years as an announcer and the rest was in the newsroom. People still go, "Oh, you're the girl who reads the news?"

Q: Did you experience any sexism?

A: No, I didn't at all. The only difficulties I had about being a woman was there were no allowances for clothes and I had to wear something different every night. I fought for a clothing allowance and the compromise was that everybody in the newsroom got a clothing allowance, which was taxed. The radio subs got the same money I did! It is funny, but it wasn't funny at the time because I still had to get the clothes. I was very lucky in that I had a friend who was a brilliant, brilliant dressmaker — not just a dressmaker, she was a real stylist — and she made blouses and tops for me and jackets, and things. I just gave her the material and she made them — and she made them extremely well. So from the waist up I looked great every night!

Q: So you could wear the same trousers every night!

A: All the time. Or jeans.

Q: You were obviously under a lot of public scrutiny with being the first female newsreader back in the 1970s.

224

A: It didn't suit me. It does suit some people, but not too many people. What I hated was I didn't like being recognized. The hardest bit was being made answerable for everything that went on in RTÉ. Everything. Being made answerable, being made responsible for RTÉ in public — that was the hardest thing.

And also — I still can't believe this — people would follow you around in supermarkets and look into your trolley! I never made much money because there was no big salaries then. I was getting white sliced pans and cabbage and everything like everybody else in my Finglas supermarket in Superquinn. Maybe I was being paranoid, but I could see people going, "God Almighty! You'd think with her money she'd get decent food!" I was getting decent food for my family, but we were eating an awful lot of mince!

Q: Did you have any weird experiences or stalkers?

A: There was one guy, but I managed to get it stopped. But that's all. The Guards got involved, yeah. It wasn't messy, I just told the management and the management contacted the Guards and it stopped. I don't know how it stopped or what happened but it stopped.

Q: Did you get any weird letters or — ?

A: I don't want to discuss that.

Q: Why did you leave RTÉ?

A: Because Vincent Browne asked me to join the *Sunday Tribune*. That's why. No other reason. It was another opportunity. My ambition is to always be the best I can at what I do.

Q: Did people think you were mad?

A: My parents did. A permanent and pensionable job! Yeah! My parents did. They were very upset. But they encouraged me still because they knew I'd done so many other things and I was going to do this all my life, so they encouraged me. But I know they were deeply worried. Because the first *Tribune* had collapsed.

Q: What did you think of Browne?

A: Put it this way, I worked for him for seven-and-a-half years. But journalists, when I'm interviewed, usually ask one of the clichéd questions, which is: "Who influenced you in your life?" Nobody influenced me in my life. I can say that with certainty — except Vincent Browne. Vincent Browne is the only person who influenced me. He forced me, despite my timidity, he forced me to be better than I would've been if he hadn't pushed me. He forced me into doing better than I thought I could. He was a very influential and a very complex character. I've heard people saying he's cynical — he's not! He's a very rare species — he's skeptical, incredibly skeptical, but he's not cynical at all. He's also one of he brightest people I've ever met in my life anywhere in the world. He really was influencing on me.

Q: Another famous Irish broadcast figure you worked with was Gay Byrne *(The host of one of the world's longest running chat shows,* The Late Late Show, *who passed away in 2019).* The broadcaster Andy O'Mahoney famously put his foot in his mouth on live TV in 1989 and asked you if were "physically attracted" to Gaybo and if you had fallen in love! *(O'Mahoney asked why she "refused to sleep with him" and Deirdre jokingly replied that he didn't ask her! Then O'Mahoney asked, "Were you surprised that he didn't?")*

A: I don't think it was premeditated, I just think it popped out. Strange. Andy's a very serious intellectual. I thing he just got a rush of blood to the head. I actually don't know what possessed him to ask me that question. The interview was to publicize Gay's book. It had to be on *The Late Late Show* obviously, but Gay couldn't interview himself. So, he stepped aside that night and Andy came on to interview me. Gay felt he couldn't be interviewed about a ghostwritten book, so Andy O'Mahoney interviewed me just for that segment.

Q: Were you mortified, seeing as it was on live TV?

A: I was taken aback. But I just got over it. The audience kind of reacted more than I did, in memory; it's a long time ago now, 1989. I've great admiration for Andy actually. His book programs are really good.

Q: But were you annoyed by it? Or was Gay annoyed by it?

A: You'd have to ask Gay that. I'm not sure that annoyed would be the right word. I was kind of bemused. We were all a bit bemused. I'm very unshockable. The only thing that shocks me is deliberate cruelty either to people or animals. That's the only thing that I can't understand how anybody can do it, I just can't. That's the only thing that shocks me.

Q: Why did Gay ask you to do his book?

A: As far as I know, what happened was the publishers drew up a list of people that he could work with and I think he picked me off the list. I think it was as simple as that.

Q: His original publisher told me he tried to get Gay to update the memoir recently, but he wasn't interested. So, I'm surprised he actually did the first book with you.

A: Oh really! I would suspect Gay was too busy. I suspect that's what happened with Gay because he was incredibly busy. I mean, I used to be meeting him in little pokey rooms in RTÉ when he was between the radio and television.

Q: You met your second husband Kevin Healy at RTÉ…

A: He was a journalist.

Q: And then he moved up the ladder... was it eyes across the canteen?

A: Please stop now! Don't do this! There was no "eyes across the canteen!" We met in the newsrooms.

Q: You've been together 30-something year. It's half your life.

A: Yeah, it is a long time. I have huge admiration for Kevin. Because Kevin left RTÉ, he retired — how many years ago now? About 12 or 13 years ago — and like myself he had no qualifications expect the Leaving Cert, and he went down to Kings Inn and he did the diploma for two years, and then did the two years degree course, got an honors degree in law and became a barrister. So, he's now a barrister. So, I've great admiration; I mean, somebody at that age doing that is tough. He had to do 27 exams. I mean, hello! I've great admiration for him from that point of view.

Q: What made you decide to get married in 2001?

A: We were living together for about 24 years. It is a long. We had kind of run out of reasons not to, I think.

Q: Sadly, your mother became very ill shortly before your second marriage...

A: I didn't know she was going to die. But she was very ill, she had been ill for about ten years. And she was in hospital and I knew she wasn't going to come back to that house, so that's one of the reasons we had it (the wedding) in her house. So, she came out to the wedding in one of these taxi-ambulances. They were wonderful.

And they were wonderful in the hospital — they did her nails and they did her hair, and they dressed her beautifully. And she was in a wheelchair and she had lost her speech — most of it anyway. She really enjoyed the day. It was very moving. When we went off on our honeymoon, my husband had to come back for work and I was staying on where we were, but then my brother rang and said, "You have to come home." So, I came home. I was there for her death. She lasted about three weeks after the wedding.

Q: Going back now, did you grew up in the working class area of Ballymun — or its much posher neighbor Glasnevin, in North Dublin?

A: I grew up in Ballymun, off Ballymun Avenue, Willow Park — they now call it Glasnevin. My mother was one of the ones who fought valiantly against the renaming, but she lost out. I still think of it as Ballymun. We did live in Ballymun as well as in Willow Park; we lived on Deanswift Road, which was definitely Ballymun.

Q: You went to boarding school.

A: I did. I adored it.

Q: Many don't like it.

A: I know. And I'm the exception to the rule. And it was nuns. And I absolutely loved the nuns.

Q: Did you want to become a nun when you were a teenager?

A: I did, yeah. We were a very small class of boarders. I think there were only 11 in the class of boarders and, I think, six entered (the nunnery) — now, I'm not sure if they all stayed there, but six entered. Quite a high percentage of the 11 of us entered. I didn't.

Q: Why not?

A: My parents wouldn't let me because they said I was too young and I was, I was only 17. I think it's a great life and I think those nuns, if you look at nuns nowadays in their eighties or nineties, they haven't a wrinkle on their faces and they have actually done great work.

They were very forwarded thinking and wanted us all to go to university in an era when girls weren't generally encouraged, from my generation, from my background, didn't have aspirations to go to college. But we were all channeled to go to university. And these nuns, most of them, could've run multi-national corporations. They were great, they really were. More women than you think have this kind of great admiration for the nuns of that era. Many of them maybe entered because their parents wanted them to — they certainly made the most of it.

And if it hadn't been for the nuns there'd be no Mater Hospital, really, in Dublin. They ran hospitals. There was no MRSA or anything like that when they ran it. Everybody looks at the negative side now. And there were some negative sides, of course there were, but there's negative sides in every profession. But these women were dedicated. They were so focused and really good, in certain orders — certainly my order. I've never heard a bad word from any of my school friends about them.

Q: Are you religious?

A: I'm not religious at all. I'm an atheist now.

Q: What changed your view?

A: Thought — independent thought. It wasn't necessarily the Catholic Church — it was just organized religion in general. Certainly when I went to Ethiopia in 1984 to cover the famine there that really opened my eyes to what religion couldn't give you.

Q: What that a turning point?

A: I was already on that path but it certainly was profound what I saw there. That famine was basically man-made. Now there was a terrible drought. It was unnecessary for millions of people to die. Absolutely unnecessary. The same is happening still in various parts of the world.

Q: It must've been difficult trying to get back into the rhythm of everyday life after such an experience?

A: It was extremely difficult, particularly as I began to see socially how expectations of life were so inappropriate here. Vincent Browne always goes on about this being a rich country, but compared to what I saw it's mega rich. People talk here about Third World conditions in our hospitals and Third World roads — I suspect that they have never been to the Third World. So, I don't tolerate that kind of conversation.

Q: Did you experience any nightmares?

A: No, no. But I'd a lot of anger and I channeled it into a book. When I came back, I wrote a book in ten days! It wasn't a book — it was a rant! I was facilitated by Vincent Browne, who was my editor, who persuaded all of the people who were periphery — printers, distributors, etc, etc — to do it all for free and all the money went to Concern. And it sold-out. Five thousand copies were printed and it sold out in about a week and I was able to give a check — I can't remember exactly how much, but it was either 34 or £37,000 to Concern. I was very pleased with that.

Q: Do you think everybody lost the run of themselves with the Celtic Tiger?

A: What I think is: everybody had a big party. I think we had some many years of — it wasn't called austerity then — being poor. Not poor — I'm lying now. Not poor. But, you know, stretched and having to be thrifty. And, all of a sudden, this money was splashing around and I know people say, "It never reached me." But in some ways it reached everyone: the roads, the transport, all of those things. Everybody benefited from those. The opening up of the universities to people, all of that. All of that happened in the era. So, it wasn't all bad. You know, there were some very good things that happened, infrastructurally and stuff.

So, we all had a big party. I think there is always going to be people who stay on too long at the party and get too giddy at the party. There's always going to be those people. And there's also going to be the people who stay outside and say, "Well, I'm not going to partake in that." But even those people would have to admit that really there were a lot of improvements in our lives, in the life of Ireland in general. Now, look at us now. But it's not that bad now, either. It's terrible what's happening at the moment, the austerity thing. But I feel quite optimistic that over the next few years we will start (again) — and more sensibly this time.

Q: Are you more reflective as you grow older?

A: No. I'm not a "look back" sort of person. But what I do find getting older is that I think that the early memories are very vivid.

Q: You look fabulous for your age.

A: Thanks very much. No, I don't look after myself at all — maybe that's why!

Q: Do you have any regrets in life?

A: No, actually, because I always tried to be aware as I could be and I tried to live by the principals — I mean, they're quite Christian principles actually — of, "If you can't do good, do no harm," that kind of stuff. Love thy neighbor, all of that. I tried to do that. So, I can't really think of anybody I traduced, or anything like that.

My actions were not planned — ever. The only job I ever actually applied for was the Aer Lingus job. When I came back from America, I needed a job to support the family and I applied — I'm qualified for nothing — to join the RTE. They had an ad in the papers. Now, I didn't get that but I was offered a continuity announcer.

So, no, I really haven't (any regrets). I regret I'm not a millionaire! Of course I regret that. I regret I didn't win the lotto. I'm not good at holding onto money though!

Oh, there is one thing I regret — I do regret not listening to my mother, in particular. In fact, I've done a little column for a magazine in the Indo (*Irish Independent newspaper — JOT.*), 200 words, where the premise was: *What does your present self feel about looking back at your 21-year-old self?*

So, I regret that I thought my mother's stories were boring and I didn't listen to them and paid no attention. And now when I want to know things there's nobody left to ask. They're all dead. And all her contemporaries are dead. And she was a very, very interesting woman. I knew she was a very interesting woman. And all her friends — and everybody who met her — said she was a very interesting woman. But I just kind of parked that and I do regret that because she had some very interesting stories. She would be telling these things and I would be thinking something and pretending to listen. So, that I do regret.

— 2013

233

Chapter Seventeen: Mannix Flynn

Gerard Mannix Flynn is one of Dublin's most famous sons. This was evident when I met him weeks after he had first been elected as an independent candidate to local government in 2009. As we strolled through the city center that day on our way to a hotel to conduct this interview, he was constantly approached by well-wishers wanting to congratulate him on his election victory.

Prior to getting into electoral politics, Mannix was most renowned for his work as an actor and writer. Apart from appearing in many films — such as *Cal*, *Excalibur* and *When The Sky Falls* — Mannix has been critically acclaimed for his work in the theater with his one-man play, *Talking to the Wall*, which won the Fringe Festival award at the Edinburgh Festival back in the 1990s. He also won an Irish Times Theatre Award for his play *James X* in 2004. According to his Wikipedia entry, "His novels are translated into German, Italian and Polish, and are currently being translated into Chinese."

Born in 1957, Mannix's writing is mostly semi-autobiographical, with his deeply personal work exploring the harrowing issue of child abuse. Before he was even in his teens, the young Mannix was in trouble for truant and petty thief, such as stealing chocolates and a bicycle. The State decided to send him to St Joseph's Industrial College in Letterfrack, which was a so-called "correctional institute for children." While here, Mannix — just like countless others — was abused by the clergy.

After his release from this hell, Mannix understandably struggled in the outside world and was in and out of other institutions and prison. He also had to face up to his own alcoholism. The fact that he managed not only to successfully overcome all these terrible setbacks — but to also establish himself in the arts — is a testament to the man's inner strengths.

Q: Why did you decide to throw your hat into the political ring?

A: I've always been involved. There's different ways you go about your business. The reason why I went down this road is because I'm involved in political and social issues within the arts for almost 30-odd years. It was always there. It manifested itself and materialized and actualized within the arts — and then in recent years with the challenge to the Church and the State in relation to issues of torture in the institutions. I felt in myself that everybody was thinking about change but nobody was doing anything about it. I'm not an activist, I'm an actionist. I also felt that my class — the people that I come from; the community that I came from; and the constituency of thought that I've been around in the last 30-odd years, contemporary, modern talk — is not represented anywhere in Irish society. The face of the individual has been closed down.

Q: I read you were abused by the Christian Brothers on your first day in St Joseph's Industrial School.

A: I think one has to be very careful about issues relating to the personal stories. I think we are way beyond that at this stage. I would just say this to you: I was in at least seven of the institutions and that was the life that was had. These institutions were allowed to run amok, with no regulations. They were run by zealous, violent — extremely violent — men.

Q: What type of abuse was inflicted upon you?

A: What was inflicted upon me was torture in all its shapes and forms. What was inflicted upon me was extreme violence in every form.

Q: Obviously, this included sexual assault?

A: Once you put a sexual marker on it you then sexualize the act. To start putting extra tags in it — sexual tags — is not necessary. What that does is: it sexualizes the act. And it diminishes the act. When the act is actually one of violence. If you sexualize the act it does a disservice to the person it was perpetrated on. The person who it was perpetrated on doesn't see it as a sexual act. It's highly important to understand this: even though there's body betrayal within the act itself, it's got to be really clear that that is a violent act.

If a person decides they are going to chop your ear off, and they're getting sexual gratification out of it, it's not remarked (on) as a sexual crime. It doesn't come in under that. The actions perpetrated — what would be known as sexual abuse — are acts of violence. They are not acts of love; they are not acts of tenderness — they are acts of extreme fucking violence. One has to remove the word "sexuality" because that portrays the action. The action is not sexual — the action is violent. So, what I would say to you is: acts of gross violence were perpetrated upon myself and other individuals.

Q: I read an interview with you in a newspaper in which you described the acts as rape.

A: Which newspaper was it? (*I mentioned name of newspaper — JOT.*) Those quotes were taken from *James X.* It was taken from my work. The journalist took all that and said I'd said it to her. I haven't spoken to her since.

Q: In that article you talked about children being murdered in these institutions.

A: I didn't see any particular part of murder. And again, you're taking this from the interview, which is a bogus interview because it never actually happened. Nothing that I spoke about actually went in. There are certainly situations where I believe that the deaths of young men — boys — were hastened by acts that were perpetrated on them.

Q: You are talking about suicide, right?

A: There's a huge amount of taking of one's life. I do know that for a fact. I know a lot of people who took their own lives. Whether I can contribute any particular deaths to any (*pauses*)... I can certainly contribute the murder of the soul. They murdered the souls of thousands of children — boys and girls. There's no question about that. And, in turn, that situation then began to have a very dark shadow on a large proportion of communities in our society today.

Q: Were you ever suicidal?

A: I think human beings always have that measure. You always have that measure of self-sabotage — whether it goes into a desire to die and whether it goes into a real attempt to commit suicide and to really die (*pauses*)... certainly, my life had elements of that in it. There's no question about that whatsoever. The idea of contemplating suicide was there and would have been an option. Man has always had that option.

Q: Did ever have any hatred or thought about seeking revenge?

A: What's the point? You don't have the luxury of that. Remember, the inner fury of addiction of alcoholism — that's a serious damaging thing. So, all of that become interlocked into alcoholism, so it became internalized. So, I had my run-ins with the police; I had my run-ins with publications, and stuff like that. But, no, I didn't particularly feel like I was going to take revenge on them. It didn't manifest itself in that way. But it manifested itself in self-sabotage. So, you had self-fury.

But I sat with these people — I sat with the Oblate Fathers and the Christian Brothers — and I asked them would they like to apologize and they weren't interested. The only people interested in making any sort of a revised apology were the Sisters of Mercy. They actually began realizing that they did cause damage. They caused enormous damage.

Q: Many are hurting still...

A: People are coming from a hurt place. A genuine hurt. This isn't some kind of hocus pocus statement. People are fucking hurt in this country. People are closed down in this country. This is an institutionalized place masquerading as a republic!

The recent revelations of the Church and State and what happened in those institutions on that scale — you can imagine what was going on in middle class society. They won't even open their fucking mouths. What happened when a woman in a middle class society had a child out of wedlock? What happened to that baby? Nobody even asks this!

They think it was all just one-sided; that it was all got to do with the disempowered, the working classes, the poor. This is a moral diktat.

This was the fucking Ayatollah gone bananas. This was the Taliban. This is what was running this country. Not that far off the Taliban. This is where your knuckles were broken by drumsticks. Where you were kicked within an inch of your life, in full view of everybody.

It's amazing that the powers-that-be, who are constantly rabbiting on about the rest of the world and the injustices around the rest of the world, haven't opened their mouths about the injustices that are taking place here. If this occurred anywhere else, Amnesty International and all of the Trócaire's would be there. But they are not here! We've got bodies of women from the Magdalene Laundries — 60 of them unaccounted for; no names, no death certificates. Anywhere else there would be a major UN investigation. Not here! But that same gang (politicians) can fly out and make comments about Sarajevo, Iran and Iraq, etc, etc, but not about here.

Q: Why do you think there's a cover up in Ireland?

A: I think there's a terrible fear. We have a terrible fear of responsibility. We love the idea of irresponsibility. We drink a lot. In actual fact, we're borderline alcoholics. We sedate ourselves in an enormous amount here and it's all swill. So, it's all over the top; it's all energized — but not in any particular direction. So everybody else thinks, "Oh, the Irish are great. Fantastic!" We are constantly trying to get people to think well of us. We hate people to think bad of us. That's a condition. That's people pleasing. So, in actual fact, what we are is: we are all kind of compulsed here. And we're compulsed into a bogus identity.

Q: What makes you say that?

A: We are trying to compete as a city with the rest of the world. It's fucking ridiculous. Ireland can't compete with the rest of the world, but the talk is good and the jargon is good. How many bridges do we need along the Liffey? They are building a privatized world here; they are building a privatized city. That's what they are building.

We have this situation of: "We'd rather deal with it tomorrow!" So, we backup to crisis. We take an enormous amount of unnecessary backlog, irresponsible responsibility. So, what our big responsibility — at the end of the day — is our lack of responsibility.

And we are not that honest. Look at the way RTÉ and the media treated the Ryan Report. The way they sentimentalized the whole thing. They all got emotional around it when they should have been clear-cut. And the clear-cut way is the political way. But remember, all these people's careers are on the line; there's a whole other business.

We haven't one fucking decent cultural building in the fucking whole of the kip! That's extraordinary. I want to keep people awake. I want to represent and awake Ireland — an Ireland out of bed. I do not want them to try to get people back into bed, back to sleep — because that's what they're trying to do. They are trying to get people back to sleep and back to this bogus idea of traditional Ireland and "weren't we great they way we where? Wasn't it fantastic?"

I believe the spirit of the Irish people is a very interesting spirit. I believe it has enormous capabilities and possibilities. If we can excel outside of our country why can't we not excel in our country? There's something wrong here. Something seriously the fucking the matter — and it's the Nanny State, the institutionalized state, and the way they operate our lives. We've got to throw that off.

Q: What's the solution?

A: It can only be dealt with by change and by ownership. It can't be dealt with some kind of hocus pocus business. It's got to be dealt with in a really appropriate manner. It can't be dealt with like some kind of major monument to misery because we have to come out of the misery. We have to get way, way beyond all of this situation. We come from a punished place. The whole of this society is coming from a punished place. Our possibilities are fucking curtailed by the State and the Church.

Q: What's your assessment of the Ryan Report?

A: The Ryan Report was fly tipped into our society. It was like opening the back of a truck and throwing it out there. It was completely inappropriate to do that. The Ryan Report is a document of horrendous proportions. What makes it even more horrendous is the fact that nothing was done with it. It was thrown into the media the same way that everybody was thrown out of the institution — with no experience and with no backup to cope with the situation. So, society is trying to cope with being fly tipped with this information.

I met the Christian Brothers. I met the Oblate Fathers. I met these individuals. And they are not one bit repentant. They don't give two flying fucks about the report. But the problem with the report was that the State — rather than begin criminal investigation immediately, right across the whole sector, and immediately seek to confiscate the documents they were still withholding — they didn't do that. They didn't do anything. The report is an out and out right insult. The report sits alongside the Kennedy Report; it sits alongside the all of those bogus reports.

Q: What's next?

A: The Ryan Report can only be dealt with in the European context in the Courts of Human Rights, which I'm going to today. I'm going into Brussels today to meet with lawyers in order to take a case to the Court of Human Rights for torture against the Irish government and the Irish Church. I do not believe the Irish government is capable of investigating itself and capable of delivering justice. I believe the Irish State knew there was torture going on; I believe the Irish Church knew; and I believe they allowed officials to carry out that torture. That constitutes torture under the Charter of Human Rights.

With all due respects to these people, I am not their enemy. I don't have anything against any of the people who treated me the way they did. I haven't got time for that. I can't afford resentment. I'm just trying to honor myself in the process. Part of my journey in life is to do that. I do not want to hand over to the next generation a bogus state run by bogymen and women. I have as much faith as anybody else. I know the difference between faith and religion. I actually know the difference between profound belief and trust than I do about some sort of sentimentalized, spiritualized nonsense.

We need the justice system in Europe and the world to come in here to take a look at just exactly what this society did to generations of children. That's what we need to do. We need to hold our State and our Church — the Irish Catholic Church — accountable. Remember, it's across the globe that the Irish Catholic Church sent their agents and servants — and it's those who committed all those crimes.

Q: Was it ever difficult for you to form an intimate relationship considering the traumatic experiences inflicted upon you?

241

A: No, no, no. It's not difficult for me to form intimate or committed relationships. The greatest difficulty you always had is about having a relationship with yourself. I was always in that struggle. In the arts I was in that struggle. Everything was a struggle. Up to 20-odd-years-of-age I wasn't part of that struggle, I was part of the incarcerated containment and when I came out of that containment I began my struggle.

So, I've always been struggling with the problems of commitment and intimacy and relationship but with self and with others. So, yeah, no different from (what) anybody else would have had. I'm not a victim of anything and I won't be seen as a victim. Things were perpetrated on me — this is what happened — but society tends then to stick labels on you and they won't allow you to move on with your life. I've moved on enormously.

Q: Do you full comfortable in the theatre world? In a *Sunday Times* profile of you, published back in 2003, it stated that you felt the "middle-class theatrical crews were looking down" on you? Is that what happened with when you didn't perform in *Waiting for Godot*?

A: No, I never felt uncomfortable in the theatre world; I always felt extremely comfortable. In terms of *Waiting for Godot* and not turning up, I had a family crisis and I didn't make it — and that was resolved by the crew.

Q: The profile says you walked off the stage?

A: No, no, no. I never walked off stage in my life. On three occasions I didn't turn up and that was actually as a result of my life being chaotic. It wasn't about any disrespect or any disloyalty. I'm immensely proud of the theatre.

Q: Is it true that you got into acting when, after being released from prison, you approached Peter Sheridan on Dame Street, Dublin? The story goes that Sheridan gave you a part in the play when — at an audition — he asked you to intimidate an actor. Apparently, you went over to the actor, whispered something into his ear in order to terrify him.

A: No, none of that is true! There's lots of urban myths about Mannix Flynn. I've been told stories about Mannix Flynn to my face by people who didn't even know that I was Mannix Flynn! That's how bonkers it gets. I find it patronizing. They go towards giving me some sort of fraudulent image of me, which I don't buy into, because it buys into that Mannix Flynn is a hard man — all that crap that is out there. I'm as ordinary and as everyday as anybody else. I happen to get an unfair and unbalanced share of shit thrown at me, which is not very interesting.

I was always interested in the arts. In prison, I was interested in the arts. I've got work going back to when I was 15. When I came out of jail at 19 years of age — having dealt with some of the issues in my life — I realized an enormous wrong going on. When I was in Mountjoy, a group of actors performed a play. When I was out, I bumped into one or two of them and I bumped into a man named Sean Tracey, who was directing a play in Trinity College — and I started my career in Trinity College as a stage manager, stage managing *Endgame*. I then began my acting career at the Project Arts Center in a play called *Mobile Homes*.

Q: Did you have a problem with drugs? The *Sunday Times* profile claimed you had.

A: No. I never had problems with drugs. You could equally say that alcohol is a drug, but they always add these things in there because it's all about some sort of credibility. I had a chronic alcohol addiction. You couldn't get worse than that. I struggled with that for 20-odd years. I struggled to try and find answers. I struggled in therapy for years, trying to come to terms with this. They say it's a symptom of an underlining cause. And through all of that process I managed to write *Nothing to Say*, I managed to write *James X*, and I managed to build a career. I managed to build a whole load of things. But each time I managed to get a certain place my isms and my condition pulled me back down into a horrendous place.

243

Q: In the film *When The Sky Falls*, you play a gangster named Dave Hackett, which was obviously based on John Gilligan, whom I've actually interviewed. I was wondering if you were inspired in that role by the fact that your sister married the gangster Tony Felloni?

A: Well, my sister didn't marry a gangster! My sister married a man. None of that inspired me. These are people, individuals who decided that this is what they wanted to do with their lives. The character I played was a violent, criminalized individual, who operated in that world normally. They didn't operate abnormally. People who are in the criminalized world don't operate abnormally — no more than the bankers operated abnormally, or the Christian Brothers operated abnormally. And then they can't understand why this wasn't (*pauses*) ... that everybody was at this. That this is the normalized behavior. It just happens to be, you know, illegal!

The part I played in *When The Sky Falls* was based on any number of individuals who lived their lives like that. But I don't know the intimate details of who John Gilligan actually is in his private capacity. So, I can only deliver a credible performance based on the way such individuals behave. I wouldn't model it on any relation or any friend. I model it on what I'm capable of doing. It was a performance in not a great movie. It was clichéd into the bargain.

Q: But your performance was good.

A: Yes, it was a good role. It was not a biog; I wasn't asked to play a part that was credible in a particular place, in a non-credible film.

Q: I wanted to ask you about your conviction for arson?

A: It was nothing to do with me. It was this building here (*he points out window to facing building — JOT.*), but I had nothing to do with it. Again, when you're in the wrong place at the wrong time this was the way that it was. It was an automatic thing. The whole thing was so normalized. I spent five years in prison because of this building, which had nothing whatsoever to do with me.

Q: It's a funny coincidence that we came to this hotel...

A: Well, there you go. Besides the Christian Brothers being violent, so were the police. The police were extremely violent. The Gardai Síochána would kick you to within an inch of your life. That was the acceptable rule. The way business was done in the police station was a physical assault. I got beaten by police on a number of occasions as a child.

Q: But you did get involved in crime, right? Or are you saying that you were accused of things that you never did?

A: The times that I would be out of jail — the times I had breaks from them — were very, very small times. You would be arrested for loitering, you would be arrested for attempted arsenic — all of those things. This was the life. There wasn't a life outside of it. There wasn't an opportunity. There wasn't an educational opportunity for us growing up.

And the same opportunity is not being delivered today. The same crack of the whip, the same balance of society, is not befalling a whole class of individuals. You have what's been described as the underclass — the throwaway people who are sitting on the streets begging, who are out of their minds on drugs, or crammed into Mountjoy Prison, six or seven to a cell. This whole thing is bursting at the seams and no one seems to be able to deal with it. Nobody seems to be held accountable for this situation. You have people living in Corporation dwellings that are completely unfit. And no one is turning around and saying that the Dublin City Council are the greatest vandals of all!

Q: When did you stop drinking?

A: It would have been nine years ago. I have alcoholism. There's no question about that. But just because you put down the drink (it) doesn't mean your alcoholism goes away. The last thing you do when you're an alcoholic is take a drink — and then you're a drunk alcoholic. Alcoholism is about the ability to self-sabotage. I'm a recovered alcoholic, who has fully recovered, and who avails of all the support systems in order to stay in that way.

I went to a number of places. I went everywhere under the sun to try to deal with my alcoholism. I literally fucking went everywhere. I went so far as to actually flung myself into a police station one day and told them to lock me up. That's how desperate I was. I struggled very hard with AA. Eventually, I met the right people who were able to give me what I needed at the moment when I most needed it. I spent at least four years with this program. It became my primary purpose. Nothing else mattered.

Q: Was there any specific reason why you decided to stop drinking?

A: No, there was 20 years of a terrible struggle. There was 20 years of an enormously, bad, hard, very difficult struggle to stop drinking and to stay stopped drinking. I stopped drinking for a year but I didn't stop alcoholism; I didn't have a program; I wasn't dealing with the issues. I had to excavate my life. I had to reconstitute my life. I had to pull it apart and go back into my childhood, go back into generations of my family, I had to look at every single aspect and ask myself, "What happened? How did I get this way?" And I had to find out that in my life I was not a stakeholder. I was disenfranchised in my life since I was a child. Now, I'm a fully-fledged stakeholder in my life.

— *2009*

Chapter Eighteen: Michael D. Higgins

At the time of this interview, the future two-term Irish President Michael D. Higgins was in a reflective mood and admitted to being saddened as he was preparing himself to leave Leinster House after serving a lifetime in politics.

When he mentioned that his government office had once belonged to Éamon de Valera and former Labour party leader, I suggested that it was a sign that he was about to be our next president.

"I think of Dick Spring being here rather than Dev — but maybe it is," he replied, smiling. Even back then, he confided in me that he already had the private support of the then Labour Party leader Eamon Gilmore and was confident of winning the nomination to run for the presidency.

Over the next hour on tape, as we sat in that very office, Michael D. Higgins opened up and discussed with me everything from his family background to falling in love with his wife, as well as why he gave up alcohol and talked about the most painful experiences in his life which caused him sleepless nights. He also reflected on a wide range of issues such as religion, same sex marriages, abortion, and, of course, his own writing career.

Q: Can you briefly tell me about your family background?

A: My father married my mother in 1937. My sisters were twins and I was born just a year-and-a-half after them, and then my brother a year after me. So, because my father was very ill, my brother and myself were reared by my uncle and aunt in County Clare. What happened was in 1946 when I was five, my brother and I went from Limerick to County Clare to live with my uncle and aunt. Much later, my father came to County Clare with my mother and my two sisters. And we were all together in County Clare briefly for a while.

Q: Despite the hardships you went to university.

A: At that time very few people went on to third level (education) or university. But, at the same time, we were all trained to get huge marks (in the Leaving Certificate). I remember getting over 90 per cent in seven subjects in my Leaving. And then I worked briefly in Shannon in a factory with my brother John. And then I was filling in out all these forms at the time for jobs and so forth, and the ESB in Galway was recruiting. So, I took the ESB (job) in Galway. I was 19 when I went to Galway. I was a Grade A clerk on 6 pounds 14 tubance a week.

And I stayed in that job for just about three years. I was writing at that time, small bits and pieces. And a man who knew that lent me 200 pounds and I resigned from the ESB and I went to England. And when I came back I went to university in Galway. I won scholarships. I did a BA Comm. there and then I went to Indiana University in 1966. I did a Masters in Indiana. And then I went to Manchester University. And then I came back from Manchester University to stand for the Labour Party for the first time in 1969.

Q: Your strongly associated with Labour but once was a member of the Fianna Fáil party.

A: I was a member of the Kevin Barry Cumann for about six months in 1966. It was the period just before I went to America. My memory about it was: we invited ministers down to tell us about their policies. I remember Sean Flanagan. But they didn't feel that they were treated with sufficient respect and they reported the cumann. So, I think we would've been dumped — I think I was on the way out anyway if I hadn't gone to America.

Q: How did you meet you wife Sebina?

A: I met my wife in 1969 at a party that was given to celebrate Mary Kenny becoming a woman's editor at *The Irish Press*. My wife is a founding member of The Focus Theatre. Sabina was very close to Deirdre O'Connor (the playwright). She was bridesmaid at Deirdre O'Connor's wedding to Luke Kelly (of The Dubliners).

I remember the play was *The Three Sisters* they put on. And they were having a post- opening night party and I think it was at Mary Kenny's brother's flat, if I remember. And that's where I met Sabina for the first time. Sabina is a very political person. She has, as an actress, been a public person.

Q: Was it love at first sight?

A: I think it was. That was in '69, in the autumn say, and we got married in 1974. Now, in the period in between, I had gone to Southern Illinois University as a visiting professor in sociology. So, there would've been a six months period where I was in America. I think that might have been hard.

So, then I came back and we resumed again and then we got married. In fact, it was very interesting because there was a number of strikes on. There was a bus strike. And Sabina was making arrangements for the wedding and she was doing most of it on foot in Dublin. It was a great wedding.

And then Alice Mary, our first child was born just within the year of '75. And then there was a gap of four years and we had twin sons, John and Michael. And then just a year after that my youngest son was born.

Q: Can you tell me about your father's death, which inspired your poem *The Betrayal?*

249

A: There had been a bad winter and the house where we lived, which was two rooms thatched and one room slated, had run rain down in it for a lot of the time we were there studying, my brother and I. But eventually it needed to change and we changed to one of these little railway houses where you might be opening and closing the gates and so forth.

My father's health deteriorated. He had a stroke but he recovered. But then he got a form of phenomena and so on. So, he went to the general hospital and then I think my mother was very concerned about him dying at home. I have a line in that poem (*The Betrayal*) about the difficulties there would be about getting a coffin out of such a small (house), you'd have to bring it out through the window and so forth. He was cared for well. My father would've been about '68.

But, in any event, he was moved over to what would've been a poor house, in a way. And I went down to visit him and I think at that stage I was in my early twenties — I would've been really very political as well. I wrote the poem based on a set of images. I think the imagery of the poem is very strong.

Q: Do you drink alcohol?

A: I don't drink alcohol now. I really stopped, I suppose. I never took any big decision about it. I just found that it was impractical when I was minister. And also, I would be doing stuff very, very early in the morning. So, I just go out of it.

Q: Was it hard to stop drinking?

A: It was. There are many times, in fact… I still love company. There were many times but it wouldn't be worth it. I have to be able to work in the morning.

Q: Was it a case of suffering too many hangovers?

A: No, it just wasn't efficient. I loved the company but it's just not something that would work for me.

Q: Did you give it up because you felt you had a problem?

A: No. No.

Q: I'd be interested to hear your views on same sex marriage and abortion?

A: First of all, I believe people will find most of the answers if they read the poems. I don't believe in abuse in certainties to the point in which you're interfering with people's rights. I do believe that the recent legislation that we had in same-sex relationship is mad. I think if two people are entering into a commitment with each other I have no right to suggest the notion to seclude them. I think it's rather outrageous. And I have no problem whatever either with same sex-marriage. That's my person opinion. That's the question you asked me.

I also feel — you'll find it in my poems very much — the price that was paid for this terrible intolerance in Ireland are very much… there are, for example, people for whom all of it has come to late — some of the saddest people to meet. I go every year to England to met people. I do met some of those people who had to leave Ireland to express their sexuality. So, that was an incredible travesty of these people's right. I also think that if people want to live together in a marriage relationship, I do say, "Why not?"

In relation to the life of the mother I think the State has to face up to its responsibilities and legislate for the life of the mother, however complex it is.

Q: Do you agree with the women's right to chose?

A: I think it depends on the termination time. It depends on the case. I think the woman has the right to protect her health. I'm in favor of legislation that will not put any risk on the mother's health.

Q: What was the most painful experience in your life?

A: That's interesting. Well, I think, certainly the death of my father and my mother. The ones where I found myself being presented with the most horrific facts about death would have been maybe in 1981 looking at dead bodies in El Salvador.

Then, again, what I think affected me very much was the Somalia famine. It took me several weeks to recover from that. People were dying at a rate of 130 a day and the bodies were being collected every morning. I think the Somalia famine had a huge impact other than personal things in my life. It took me about six weeks. I found it difficult to sleep. These images were reoccurring.

There were different sadness's. I'm very sad of leaving the Dáil (Éireann). I've been here so long. I have 25 years (as an elected TD). I stood for the first time in 1969. I was in the Seanad (Éireann) from '73 to '77 and from '82 to 87 (as a Senator). I was 25 years in the Dáil and nine years in the Seanad. I've been a frontbench spokesperson for all of my time. And I've also been minister, as you know, from 1993 to 1997.

One of the things I haven't told anybody yet is that I'm lodging all my papers in the National Library. They've already started. I think over the years I must have about 20 chapters in other people's books; so then I would have some of the stuff from *Hot Press* (magazine), and then I have my own books as well, and I've a lot of published poems. And all that stuff is going to the National Library.

Q: You came under huge media criticism when minister.

A: I think that I was treated unfairly about two things. I was probably treated very tough. I think I had a tough time on two issues — on the abolition of the order of Section 31 (of the Broadcasting Act). The other thing, which is something I've never regretted, is my decision to establish Teilifís na Gaeilge, now TG4. I think it was extraordinary that there was one edition of the *Sunday Independent* that had five articles in the one edition attacking me on one or other of those two topics. Some of the stuff was highly personalized. For example, it was written in the *Sunday Independent* that I was the only person who wanted Saddam Hussein to have his finger on the nuclear button! It was outrageous as that.

252

Q: You fractured your kneecap last year in Columbia.

A: (In the hotel) There were tiles and there was water on the floor and I slipped and came bang down on my kneecap. So, then I had to travel for four-and-a-half hours to the nearest x-ray department.

My kneecap was fractured. So, I got a split and I had two old fashioned crutches and I went back and had a sting of meetings, so I did those in a wheelchair. When I came back, I went into hospital and I had my kneecap reconstructed. I had a cast for a few weeks. Six weeks. Then I had a brace.

Q: You are considerably older now. So, would you be up to the task of being president?

A: All that changes is the way that you work. There is no enormous disability. There is a great additional power in so far as you're more economical — you can reflect better. And also, which is discounted unfortunately, there is a wisdom that goes with it. And a tolerance. And an ability to listen as well as to speak.

But I hope to be able to continue to write as well (if elected). No, neither my age or my health are any impediment whatever. I think I can bring a very positive energy to it. I have very definite views about it. Remember, by training I'm a political scientist. I know what's the limitations are and what the possibilities are.

In addition, I've also been in nearly every elected office you have. Remember I've been on the County Council, I was a Senator and a Dáil deputy and a Minister. I was President of the Council of Culture Ministers in 1996. I know, if you like, the institutional grounds — the space, if you like.

The president can't be an organized force of opposition against the government of the day. But he or she, you know, in the oath you take which says that you dedicate yourself to the welfare of the Irish people. And in that, when you see that there you are first of all dealing with issues that are longer than a period of a government because they go both before and they also succeed. You are also able to look at themes that are not arising as problems now.

Q: For example?

A: For example, the next president will deal with some very significant dates — 1912, the founding of the Labour Party; 1913, the Lock-Out; 1914, the Great War; 1916 and so on.

If you were to take where we are now in this recession, which has turned into a depression — and I think it is a depression — and if you were trying to say to people, "Look, it's the people who really object to impunity, but that having been said, we move on from recrimination onto envisaging what you're going to do about the future."

There is scope there and the difference between different versions of the presidency is how you use your discretion. And the discretion is where you make speeches, what topics you pick. Now, your speeches are approved by the government in two circumstances — if you decide from somebody from the Council of State to address the Dáil, or if you decide to address the nation. They are actually approved by the government. But everything else in relation to where you might want to go; the issues you might want to address in terms.... I'm a person who has always driven on a kind of public discourse on the issues in relation to what I call building a real Republic that is inclusive.

Q: You must regret Labour not running a candidate — you — for the presidency in 2004.

A: My main concern in 2004 — and I think I've been proved right — was the discourse that we should be having. I was aware that Ireland had changed and also that we were at a very vulnerable stage. In the period between 1997 and 2004, a whole series of things were beginning to shift and McCreevy-ism, for example, and you also had a kind of radical individualism in the country that was beginning to change everything and the assumption was you'd have opening to growth and so on. I saw the great dangers to that and I actually wrote pieces about it. So, what I wanted to do in 2004 was a campaign in which you would have a debate about what kind of Ireland you wanted. And I feel that we missed an opportunity there.

Q: So, it upset you?

A: Yes, it did.

Q: If elected, would you take a wage cut?

A: Oh, yes, I would. I'm not in it for the salary. The salary was never my concern. I think what it should be is an appropriate salary. It shouldn't be an excessive salary.

Q: Are you religious?

A: I'm a spiritual person. I attend Catholic ceremonies. I don't think that anyone who is serious could say that they weren't a spiritual person. I don't think the world we live in can be reduced into a simple material for expression. If you like, rational world can only bring us so far; there is a transcended aspect to our existence — things that move you and so forth.

I have great respect for the humanist tradition and I know many of them. But I'm not simply a humanist myself. I feel there is an inheritance that comes through the culture of belief systems. So, when you say to me, "Are you a practicing Catholic?" I wouldn't know what it was, what these rules are.

Q: But do you believe in heaven and hell?

A: I don't. What I think about it is that they don't enter into my thinking very much. What I think that you do is: you live ethically and your spirit...does life end in the moment of physical? We'll continue to speculate on it, but I think that there is a spiritual dimension to our existence that is not turned into physically. I think that's as far as I would go.

— 2011

Chapter Nineteen: JP Donleavy

The old adage about truth being stranger than fiction was certainly apt when it comes to describing the colorful, bohemian life and times of the enigmatic best-selling author JP Donleavy.

It sounded like something straight off the pages of one Donleavy's risqué novels when his second ex-wife Mary Wilson Price publicly dropped the bombshell in 2011 that two children born during their marriage were fathered by two brothers from the Guinness brewing dynasty.

But Donleavy insisted to me that it was never really a case of life imitating art for him because — unlike the type of belligerent and bawdy characters peppered throughout his novels — he never felt any animosity towards his ex-wife or the scions of the Guinness dynasty when he discovered the shocking truth.

And it was clearly a measure of the gentleman that JP never once screamed at his wife or contemplated striking one of her lovers in rage — even when DNA tests showed he wasn't the biological father of Rebecca and Rory.

"My principal concern was always just the children and their everyday welfare," he said when we met for our final ever chat at his 180-acre estate in Co. Westmeath, back in late August 2011. The secret about the children's true biological identity had only been revealed a few days earlier and, unsurprisingly, JP had been inundated with media interview requests, but flatly turned them all down. However, I was allowed to call out to interview him because I was a neighbor, much to the surprise and delight of my then editor. I stand to be corrected, but, as far as I'm aware, this was the only in-depth interview JP conducted about the scandal.

Sadly, James Patrick Michael Donleavy — born in 1926 in New York to Irish emigrants — was no stranger to heartbreak. He admitted that he "simply wouldn't know" where to begin if asked who was the great love of his life because there were many "lady friends," as he liked to describe the women in his colorful and controversial past.

In 1946, having been in the U.S. Navy, JP secured a grant to study in Ireland through the GI Bill of Rights given out to World War II veterans. It seemed the earliest woman to break his heart was his first wife, Valerie Heron, whom JP met through her brother Michael when they shared a room at Trinity College.

It was, JP recalled, love at first sight when he met the Englishwoman. "Anyone who met her immediately fell in love with her," he said. "People regard her as one of the most beautiful women in the world. This was often said about her. But she had no sense about her beauty. It would embarrass the life out of her when you'd say: 'You're beautiful.' She never wanted to be in the limelight. She was a little bit shy, but very wonderfully mannered and charming."

It was a whirlwind romance and they married in 1948 while JP was still studying. He dropped out of university without completing his degree and the newly-married couple moved back to the US. There, they struggled financially as Donleavy pursued his dream of one day becoming a writer. The financial woes increased when the first of their two children, Philip, was born in 1951.

"I had to find places where the rent was so low they almost always were in a sort of down-market area, like a slum in Boston. That was always a problem. And, having children, I realized immediately one really had to get to the countryside somehow," he said.

"Valerie was a speech therapist and she was able to get a few clients, but not that many. We managed our way around between friends and we got invited up to Connecticut for Valerie to look after somebody's grandchildren. They gave us this wonderful cottage out in the woods to stay in."

But Donleavy insisted that monetary woes never put a strain on the marriage or caused the couple to squabble. "She had a very luxurious background. She went to a very elegant finishing school and they had servants when she grew up. But she actually liked being poor — as strange as it sounds to say that!" he said, smiling at the memories.

"She enjoyed herself. And then she'd make a fuss over being scrupulous with money. She quite liked it. Once I thought: 'God! This woman has never complained about anything.' Yes — amazing."

They moved back to Ireland and, one year after their daughter Karen was born in 1954, JP began skyrocketing towards global fame with the publication of *The Ginger Man*. His salacious debut novel, which was banned in Ireland, has sold a staggering 45 million copies and was selected 99th out of the Modern Library's Best 100 Novels of the 20th Century.

"I guess that's better than a kick in the arse, as they say!" He then laughed.

Despite his phenomenal success, Donleavy's marriage fell apart and the couple divorced in 1969. So where did it all go wrong?

"Oh, it didn't particularly go wrong. I suppose, everyone who met her would fall in love with her and some people never gave up chasing her. Finally, she decided to marry someone else and we got a divorce," he said.

It must have been an upsetting experience?

"Yes, it would have been. But, of course, one had a fairly tough background. I came out of the U.S. Navy. I coped with it pretty well. I had lot of girlfriends over the years and, as I say, it was after the war and you saw a lot of life already, so it wasn't that upsetting."

A year after the divorce, he married Mary Wilson Price in 1971. He first noticed her when she was shown on TV emerging from a nightclub with Andy Warhol. "She was the Mexicana [a now defunct airline] Girl. You would see her on billboards all over America. She was pretty stunning," he recalled.

"I know that if you went to Texas or Mexico, you would be going along the road and you would see her on great big billboards, ten feet high. They used to call her The Mighty Wonderful. They probably still do. She's a very good horse woman."

At the time, the legendary author Norman Mailer was eagerly pursuing Mary. But, from the moment they met, she only had eyes for JP. The hell-raising Mailer even talked about challenging Donleavy to a televised boxing match. But Mailer later learnt that Donleavy — an accomplished boxing champion with an impressive record of never losing a fight — could throw about "seven punches a second." Mailer later quipped at a party: "Donleavy, you're too fast and tough for me!"

Is it true that Mary was the one who pursued Donleavy? "Yes. I suppose that entered the equation," he admitted.

The couple met at a dinner in New York. He recalled: "In passing, she said: 'What do you do when you're in New York?' I said, 'I generally go out walking in the city for miles every day, from two o'clock until five.' She said: 'Would you like some companionship?' 'Yes,' I said, 'I'm walking tomorrow. I'll meet you in Central Park at a bench.' She turned up and that was the beginning of the relationship."

Was he quickly falling in love with Mary?

"Well, yes, I suppose."

After that initial brief romance in New York, Mary followed JP across the Atlantic to London. Flushed with success, he had three properties in the city, as well as a place in the Isle of Man and his estate in Westmeath.

Laughing, he recalled that she only had one of his addresses and found it difficult to track him down! When she finally did, she didn't yet want him to know she was in London.

"She used to take a taxi in Fulham to my address and go back and forward in the taxi looking at it," he recalled. "But I didn't even live there. I lived in what we called Tax Dodgers' Towers, which was a pretty sumptuous place on the 17th floor of a skyscraper."

At the time, Donleavy was in a relationship with an Austrian woman called Tessa Sayle, who was one of "London's most distinguished and distinctive literary agents," according to her obituary in the *London Independent*. She passed away in 1993 at the age of 60.

Donleavy once remarked that being with Tessa — he lived with her for five years — was "the happiest time" of his life. "She was a marvelous woman. There was no question that she was someone I was immensely attached to. She became a well known figure in her own right," he said.

However, he left Tessa and moved back to Ireland with Mary. When I ask Donleavy what made him decide to settle down and marry again, he admitted: "I'm not sure. She had a lot of admirers."

He made it sound as though he married quickly because he feared losing her to someone else if she wasn't officially spoken for. If this was his plan, then sadly the wedding ring never deterred others from seducing his second wife.

The couple based themselves at Donleavy's massive 180-acre estate, Levington Park, which is adjacent to the picturesque Lough Owel on the outskirts of Mullingar. Mary set about establishing herself on the social scene by throwing lavish parties.

With the estate's breathtaking views of the lake as a backdrop, she would organize now-legendary soirées with roaring bonfires, live music and a pig roasting on a spit.

"The tents would be set up down at the lakeshore, with great big bonfires lit. There was one principle — the champagne never ran out. Yes, it was expensive enough. Even to this day she's extremely adept at holding social matters and conducting things," he said.

However, Donleavy was a reluctant attendee of these infamous gatherings at his sprawling estate — even though he was picking up the tab. "I would just make an appearance for five minutes and walk around and then just come back to the house. I was never really around any of the parties when they were going on," he recalled.

"I find that the conditions that come up in a party don't interest me. I'm not rude or anything and I try to be as well behaved as I can. But I did realize that I had a tendency to always look for the exit when I came into a room. That was an instinctive thing. I'd find myself slipping away."

Would his wife not complain about him sneaking off from such splendidly prepared parties?

"No, she wouldn't mind that," he insists. "She would know that's what would happen. She always enjoyed company and liked having a gathering."

JP Donleavy dismissed the presumption that he — like the protagonist Sebastian Dangerfield in *The Ginger Man* — was a heavy drinker. Instead, he says he "loved having a sip of wine."

He explained: "I wasn't that serious a wine drinker, although I was serious about my wine. I wasn't that heavy a drinker. There's a wine cellar here, so the wines were always present. I'd bring a bottle on the trains in a container I had specially made for me to keep the wines chilled while we were travelling."

I'd heard rumors that JP was frugal, even Scrooge-like, from a couple of other Irish writers. But just to highlight how "lavish" Donleavy's lifestyle was during his halcyon days, several years ago a journalist visited his pile and noted that there was an empty bottle of Château Mouton Rothschild '63, which had apparently once sold at auction for £70,000 (€80,000) at Sotheby's.

"I probably wouldn't have known that it was £70,000," Donleavy said, laughing, recalling that he had drank that particular bottle with one of his "lady friends" named Rachel. He was referring to Rachel Murray who was in her 20s when she lived with her young daughter Galena at Donleavy's home for a couple of years back in the mid-Nineties. In an interview after she left Levington Park, Rachel insisted that their relationship was a platonic one.

So, who would Donleavy describe as the great big love of his life?

"Oh, God! I simply wouldn't know."

Is it a case of simply too many to count?

"Yes, there would have been over one's years."

I mention that I heard that Mick Jagger and his then-wife Bianca attended one of Mary's parties.

"Yes, that's right. He popped in here and we were having a chat in another room in the house that we call the library. We spent some time chatting in the house, where you were able to hear yourself talk," he said.

Who else would have attended these parties?

"Practically all the people who seemed to have some sort of status. They would have been all the conspicuous names around at the time. The Guinness clan ..." his voice trailed off.

Ah, the Guinness scions — the elephant in the room following Mary Price

Wilson's bombshell revelation that, during her time with Donleavy at Levington Park, her first-born child Rebecca, 32, was fathered by Kieran Guinness and her son Rory, 30, was fathered by Kieran's brother Finn. Mary eventually divorced Donleavy in 1989 and married Finn.

Was it a case of Donleavy being set in his ways and Mary feeling her biological clock was ticking and she desperately wanted children?

"Yes, that probably did come up and, you see, I already had children. I think that was probably the situation. It would be unrealistic not to expect a woman to have fulfilled her life and have children and so on."

However, JP admitted that he had no idea the he wasn't the children's biological father until a DNA test in 1988 revealed the astonishing news. "These things were contentious. It was a bleak time when these things had to be known and no one could be absolutely sure," he said.

He must have had his suspicions.

"'I'm not sure if I considered [it] ... I didn't dwell on it. Those things didn't enter into it. I just wanted to make sure the children were safe and happy, which they were."

He insists that the DNA results didn't change his love for Rebecca and Rory. "I realized they were vulnerable, innocent people who would grow up and be people and be concerned. My concern was always to look after the people," he told me.

But did he sit the children down for a big conversation about it all?

"No, no. They weren't like that. They never brought it up. It found its own way in terms of importance and communication of matters."

But it must have been emotionally difficult to explain to the children that they would be leaving the estate?

"Well, it would all be gradual things that would grow on everybody. Nothing was done out of the blue. Somehow it would just grow on people and the plans would finally get known, and they would just go off. I can remember them going down to the front gates here. The children really did find it tough; they'd break down. They were driven away sobbing, I guess. So, there were some unhappy moments."

It was, according to dispatches at the time, a messy divorce and there were rumors that JP's ex-wife was looking for his beloved estate as part of her settlement.

"I'm not sure what that was all about simply because she was marrying into the Guinness folk, who weren't short of land anywhere," he said, laughing.

"But the one thing she did miss in a sense was this place had wonderful stables and so on for horses. And that was her big interest — riding and hunting. So, this place was pretty suitable if you wanted to build up a stable or hunt. But, luckily, she was joining a clan, as we all know, who weren't short of money or land.

"When the court hearings had stopped and all the things were finally settled and worked out and so on, I remember my lawyer said: 'Do you know what you are Mr Donleavy? You are a gentleman.'"

I mentioned that Mary Wilson Price told the *Daily Mail* that she was planning to write her memoirs.

"Oh, my God! I better make a run for it! It's good to be warned about it," he joked, adding: "Yes, she'd have a lot to offer the public, I think. An exciting background."

Donleavy had written a memoir himself about the period surrounding *The Ginger Man*'s publication, but would he consider writing a proper autobiography?

'No — most of it is unprintable!"

How did JP feel about such revelations coming out into the public domain now, all these years later?

"I don't encourage it. Well, I preferred to be discreet because other people's lives — like young children — get involved and it affects them differently with their friends and contemporaries."

Rebecca once said: "When we moved to England we became different people, we changed our names, we changed everything."

Donleavy could see why that was. "Yes, I can understand that in children because they have to behave in a certain way to make life, you know, for them amenable. To me, it doesn't make any difference," he told me.

"I welcome the fact that they can find the way of dealing with any of these things to make things easier. But the association with the family itself — the

Guinness dynasty is very high profile — is always difficult to deal with. And, also, my name is known. So, they're dealing with little difficulties but they're very skilled, both of them. They're both professionals and skilled."

JP insisted he was never jealous when he discovered that his wife was having affairs.

"No, I didn't have any kind of jealousy at all. My attitude was I wouldn't want anyone around me who didn't want to be there. So, the fact that they would go off with somebody else would mean that I wasn't..." He paused to laugh. "Particularly interested that they come back! My policy was always let people do what they want to do. You just absolutely don't make any attempts to interfere with anybody or change their intentions. I never did that."

Nor did JP ever contemplate using his boxing skills on his love rivals. "Well, it never occurred to me because you can't change people's inclinations if they want to do something. I accept the fact that that's what they want to do and let them. Just go ahead," he said.

I tell him that most men would have at least screamed at their ex-wife. "Oh, really? I've no tendency [to do that] at all," he said.

Even in 2011, JP remained a true gentleman and won't utter a negative word about Kieran, who started an affair with Mary after renting the gatehouse on the estate.

"I knew him, but not that well. He was around here and so on. But he was always a gentlemanly figure, always well behaved. He was kindly as well, considerate," JP said.

After everything that has happened between their two families, anyone else would have probably banned it from their house, but surprisingly Donleavy still enjoyed the occasional glass of Guinness. "I get it but I have it brought back in the house here," he said.

Did the first or second divorce affect him more?

"I think all of them are kind of painful in their way because I can say that none of the women were unpleasant," he admitted. "All of them were very attractive."

This was where the first part of my two-part interview with JP when it ran in the *Irish Daily Mail* in 2011. I began the second part by observing:

I was sitting with JP Donleavy in front of the turf fire in his sprawling pile discussing vignettes from his extraordinary life. So far, as we talked for hours during this revelatory interview, the controversial author had confessed that he never once went into a jealous rage when confronted by the fact that DNA tests in 1988 proved he wasn't the biological father of the two children he had loved and raised as his own during his marriage to his second wife Mary Wilson Price.

If I was truly taking aback by such a surprising confession of how he maturely handled such a shocking betrayal, it's also true to say that I was also taken aback to discover one of the world's most successful authors was sitting in front of the large smoldering fire with a heavy leather jacket (which seemed to also sport some demotic-style script on one sleeve) and a red rain hat, with the tip of the cap folded upwards. He may have been a total gentleman, but perhaps it also wouldn't have been unkind to describe JP as slightly eccentric.

"I have to wear it just to keep the chill off one's head," he insisted.

Then the conversation returns once more to his extraordinary love life. JP once put an advertisement in his book, *An Author And His Image*, which read: "Slightly reclusive but anxious to get out more, gracefully older fit man... requires pleasantly attractive younger lady of principle"

And, he insisted, it wasn't a joke although he couldn't recall if it was successful or not. Nevertheless, he did have a string of romances following its publication in 1997. However, twice bitten with two failed marriages, JP said he never seriously contemplated tying the knot again after his second divorce to Mary Wilson Price.

As JP revealed in the first part of this deeply personal and touching interview, he remained a true gentleman throughout the messy saga, but — understandably — he did miss the children, Rebecca and Rory. He said that having the children of some of his "lady friends" — as he liked to describe the women in his life — running around his mansion helped him "cope" with it all.

"One copes with that. Remember that I had an association of children living here with a girlfriend, so they would take up most of your attention," he told me, while putting turf on the fire, as we sat in one of his extensive parlors.

Such was his generosity that JP once took in one of his old flames and her two children and allowed them to stay at his estate while she got back up on her feet.

"Yes, she was quite an important person in this house. She was marvelous. She had two children and they spent a few years here growing up because she was having trouble," he said.

"I remember she phoned me and as the conversation went on I realized she was in deep trouble, destitute or something. I remember getting into the car and going down to one of the big shops and just filled it up with food — strawberries, jelly beans, loafs of bread, all kinds of things. I arrived there to this little council house and the children were sitting on the stairs, hungry, crying, and suddenly this bonanza turns up. They never forgot it. Ever after that, whenever they saw me they would just break into great big grins.

"And then she was getting evicted and I said, 'There's plenty of room out here. Put them in the car and drive them out.' So, she did.

"I remember the children getting up early in the morning and I was down in the kitchen and they were just there mesmerized with all the food around. It worked out well with a big house. I was always conscious of anybody being in trouble like that, especially lacking food and that type of thing."

The children staying with him even became close friends with Rebecca and Rory. "I saw them running at each other, throwing arms around each other," he said.

JP loved organizing parties for the children. He recalled: "It would be just for them, no adults. I would go up to the Shelbourne (Hotel) and take practically a floor in the hotel and then I would give them the rooms to have. And I would say, 'I'll leave you to it. And you can have a little party for yourselves.' I got a call from the kitchen in the Shelbourne saying, 'Mr Donleavy, I don't want to interrupt but I thought we better ask if the following is permitted; They've just ordered six bottles of champagne!'"

We both laughed and then I asked, "How old were they?"

"They were about 13 or something like that. I said, 'Yes, bring them up a few bottles and warn them that it's intoxicating.'"

He paused to laugh again and I told him that it was clear to see that he loved being around children.

"Oh, yes. I find children pretty fascinating because they don't have any bias and they respond to things directly and quickly. So, they've always been a source of information and entertainment... just having conversations emotional moment when Suzanne and her children finally left his home," he said.

"When they were moving away — they lived in one of the gate houses — and they came to say goodbye and the little girl was standing there and her mother was saying, 'Go ahead, ask him.' She was so shy; the little girl wouldn't say anything. I had to speak up and said, 'What does she want to ask me?' And she said, 'She wants to give you a hug.'"

It seemed that most people really warmed to JP when they get to know him. The comedian Billy Connelly once came to visit and ever since he religiously sent JP a Christmas card each year.

"He's a great old pal, Billy. He came here and I was giving him a lift down the countryside. He had made an appearance on Irish television the evening before. I was giving him a lift and he had to relief himself, so he got out of the car and went off to find a place where he could urinate and wouldn't attract a lot of attention," he recalled.

"He got well off the road and was beginning to urinate into a sort of ravine or something and suddenly a man looked up — and urine was coming down on him, but fortunately he wasn't hit with any urine. But when he looked up and saw Billy he said, 'Ah, it's himself!' He did! Those very words — because he saw him on television the evening before."

Aged 85-years-old when we last spoke, JP then spent his days mostly painting, writing, walking and looking after his "cattle of about 60" — including a bull, which he warned me to be careful of when I was leaving his grounds.

How was his health holding up?

"I've never been — touch wood — really been sick. I've never actually been sick. In the Navy once, I got some kind of infection, a stomach bug, but it was one of the few times I had to be in a bed for a few days."

After a couple of hours talking, JP then took me, once again, on a tour of his mansion to show me his collection of paintings. Since his Trinity days, JP had many exhibitions of his art; his watercolors today can fetch several thousand euro. Walking through the vast rooms, we eventually come across some nude portraits.

"Sometimes people posed (naked), but usually I did them from my imagination quicker," he said, laughing.

After showing me his sauna and an idle swimming pool badly in need of maintenance, we eventually found ourselves back in the main parlor. I was struck by how much JP remained me of the protagonist from his Darcy Dancer novels about a writer living the life of Reilly in his country estate.

We sat back down in the massive parlor with the turf fire, which was full of old newspapers and magazines because JP detested throwing out reading material.

The room consisted mainly of a big open fire, two chairs, an ancient floral sofa, and a grand piano in the far corner. And like the rest of the house, which was built in 1742 by the third Baronet of Parwich, Sir Charles Levinge, the walls were adorned with works of art — and endless photographs of all four of his beloved children.

"James Joyce walked through that door. He wrote about his visit in one of his books [*Stephen's Hero*]," JP said, pointing to a door at the end of the room."

How did JP make all his money?

"The only income I've ever had all my life is as a professional author." Of course, there was the small matter of how he ended up the proprietor of one of the world's most famous publishers, Olympia Press after suing them over the copyright of his debut novel, *The Ginger Man*, and managing to bring the publisher to his financial knees.

"I'm the owner now of the Olympia Press in Paris. So, this came up where I was in effect publishing myself! It still has titles that make some royalties, but not much. Some," he said, modestly.

The legal case with JP forced the publisher of Olympia Press, Maurice Girodias, to wind down the company. But when he tried to pull a fast stroke by buying it back on the cheap at what he thought was a closed auction in Paris, he was shocked to find JP's second wife Mary Wilson Price there to outbid him.

They may have gone through a bitter divorce but, always the gentleman, JP gave credit where it's due and proclaimed his ex-wife deserved credit for this ingenious, tactical piece of revenge.

"Somehow she was instrumental in a way of getting it simply because she measured out exactly what she thought might happen and she went on with sufficient funds. That was the big point. That was her. She was very careful in figuring out what she thought would happen at the auction," he said.

"Girodias was trying to buy the company. It had gone bankrupt, deliberately, I suppose. He was just buying it back cheap and it got rid of its debts. But she attended the auction and it came as a enormous surprise.

"At the auction itself, people held their breath because every time Giodrias put in a bid she would bid higher until he absolutely didn't know what was happening and suddenly she found herself owner of the Olympia Press."

Did it bother him that despite writing many critically acclaimed books that he is mostly remembered for *The Ginger Man*?

"No, I suspect that this is the case. It makes no difference to me at all."

At that moment, he was putting the finishing touches to his latest opus, *The Dog On The Seventh Floor*, which he'd worked on for several years. It has yet to be published. The novel *A Letter Marked Personal* was posthumously published in 2019.

He wrote in longhand and then has his secretary, who worked in a different wing of the house, type it up for him. They could go days without seeing each other.

"We generally contact by phone because I'm on one wing of the house and she's on the other wing. She has her own office and conducts business accordingly. So, it could be periods of time when I wouldn't see her face to face but we'd be on the phone."

JP rarely ventured outside his property, but he dismissed the suggestion that's he was a reclusive figure like other literary giants such as JD Salinger. "No, it probably isn't true. As you can see from coming into this place, you're naturally isolated right off the bat. It's just the availability of people to be around," he said.

Did he get lonely?

"You do and you don't. Every time you walk out the door you're looking at a plant or an insect and your attention is caught up, so you don't feel any loneliness any time you move around," he answered.

"This is why this house is so marvelous because you have all these windows.

I'm out and around the house. I take an interest in watching things and looking out windows and studying the landscape.

"Another big interest is going for walks. Plus the fact that you can walk miles in this house without noticing it. I often spent time at the front door here where I generally wear clothes that allow me to work on the place. I had quite a long conversation (recently) with — what do you call the people who live on the side of the road—a tinker?"

"A 'Traveller,'" I proffered.

"I think a 'Traveller' man came up and by the way I was dressed and working on the road he assumed I was the workman to the place. And I played this role. And he said to me, 'Would you ever be able to get anything out of the people up there in the big house?'

"And I said, 'Oh, they're as tight as they come. You couldn't get anything out of them.' He'd go away a little bit subdued thinking, "What a waste of time this was that the gardener couldn't even get anywhere with them!'"

Did he think much about coming to end of his life?

"Yes. You actually don't seem to mind much thinking that either. I'm not tired of life, but you realize there's an end to things."

Finally, did JP have any regrets in life?

"Not particularly. No, no, no. I've always found myself quite pleased and happy enough. It does occur to me to be grateful to be able to live in the countryside. I wondered often if I'd be able to hold out in the city for too long — even thought I did live in London in my Tax Dodgers Towers," he concluded.

"I sometimes have to stop and think, 'How on earth did I manage not having to do something else and I always stuck it out in the writing game?' I was very lucky with this."

— 2011

NOTES

Chapter One: JP Donleavy. This interview was published September 2007 in the Irish Daily Mail.

Chapter Two: Sebastian Barry. It appeared December 2017 in Hot Press *magazine.*

Chapter Three: Patrick McCabe. The interview appeared in Hot Press, *October 2017.*

Chapter Four: Jennifer Johnston. This previously unpublished Q&A was conducted in April 2011. Some of the quotes appeared in a 2,000-word profile published in the Irish Daily Mail, *November 2011.*

Chapter Five: Dermot Healy. A significant shorter version of this interview was published March 2011 in the Irish Daily Mail.

Chapter Six: John Boyne. This interview was published April 2017 in Hot Press, *but a few additional quotes included in it are taken from an interview conducted in April 2013 with the author for a feature published in the* Irish Daily Mail.

Chapter Seven: Emma Donoghue. A significantly shorter version appeared in the Irish Daily Mail, December 2009.

Chapter Eight: Joseph O'Connor. It was published July 2008 in Hot Press.

Chapter Nine: Donal Ryan. A slightly different version of this interview appeared December 2018 in Hot Press.

Chapter Ten: Leland Bardwell. This previously unpublished interview took place in March 2011.

Chapter Eleven: Peter Sheridan. The interview with Peter Sheridan was published January 2013 in the Irish Mail on Sunday.

Chapter Twelve: Derek Landy. This previously unpublished Q&A was conducted in September 2010, but some of the quotes were used in an article published that same month in the Australian publication The Irish Echo.

Chapter Thirteen: Ian Gibson. It was published April 2017 in Hot Press *magazine.*

Chapter Fourteen: Ulick O'Connor. This chapter is a hybrid of an interview published in the Irish Daily Mail in September 2009 and my column in the Irish Sunday Mirror *in October 2019, along with additional quotes from my taped conversation with Ulick.*

Chapter Fifteen: Lee Dunne. Some of the qoutes in this Q&A appeared February 2007 in Hot Press *magazine.*

Chapter Sixteen: Deirdre Purcell. This previously unpublished Q&A was conducted in October 2013. Some of the quotes were used for a feature that appeared in the Irish Daily Mail *on November 1, 2013.*

Chapter Seventeen: Mannix Flynn. This previously unpublished interview was conducted in June 2009

Chapter Eighteen: Michael D. Higgins. This Q&A article was published in the Irish Daily Mail, *November 2011.*

Chapter Nineteen: JP Donleany. This article was originally published as a two-part feature in the Irish Daily Mail *on September 3 and September 5, 2011.*

Acknowledgements

I'd like to thank the following for their support and encouragement: Eva Prat, Darren Kinsella, John Drennan, Linda Langton, Sylvia Pownall, Frank Tighe, Niall Stokes, Mick McNiffe, Pat Flanagan, Demelza de Burcha, Ronnie Haughey, Linda Maher, John Lee, Valerie Hanley, Eric Bailey, Trevor O'Rourke, Declan Cassidy, Stephen Agnew, Vincent Smith, David Gilna, Jason Barry, Daniel Landon, Anthony Fox, Frank Bambrick, Brian Brannigan, Angela Kerins, Amy O'Toole, Lorraine O'Toole, Keith O'Toole, Marianne O'Toole, Olga Prat, Caridad Prat, Jesús Elices, Juana Prat, Ascension Gonzalez, Fernando Prat, María Teresa Sevilla Maté, Jose Álvarez, Alejandrio Ciriiano Cervantes, and Ben Ohmart and all at Bear Manor Media.

I want to give special mention to my old mentor and dear friend Paul Drury, who sadly passed away from cancer at the relatively young age of fifty-seven in 2015. As a cub reporter, I first wrote for him when he was the editor of Dublin's *Evening Herald* in the early 1990s, and then later when he hired me on two occasions in the noughties to work for the *Irish Daily Mail/Irish Mail on Sunday*.

During those last five years working together, Paul, first as my editor and then as a colleague when he switched posts to become a fine columnist, went out of his way to champion my work. I've fond memories of Paul offering me much-needed guidance over frequent long boozy lunches at plush Dublin restaurants on his expense account. My writing vastly improved under his tutelage for which I will be eternally grateful, but, more importantly, I gained a confidante who will forever hold a place in my heart. He's deeply missed.

A few days prior to writing this acknowledgments section, my former editor at the same paper, Paul Field sadly died from a suspected heart attack at only aged forty-eight. He also deserves special mention and my gratitude for hiring me, solely on the recommendation of Paul Drury, to write my own weekly two-page slot called *The Jason O'Toole Interview*, which resulted in many of the interviews in this collection.

Finally, I want to pay tribute to my old friend Lee Dunne who passed away at the grand old age of eighty-six in April 2021. We'd been close friends ever since he took me under his wings as a budding scribbler in my teens in 1991. We talked regularly for over twenty-five years, but the calls had dried up in recent years due to his battle with Alzheimer's. We weren't embarrassed to tell each other, "I love you, pal" during our last conversation, which brings me some comfort now.

I'll leave the last words to Lee. He once told me, "Death holds no terror for me since I see it as a natural part of life. The all important thing is not to die in a bad humour!"

About the author

Born in Dublin, Jason O'Toole is a best-selling author, playwright and journalist who has been hailed as "Ireland's best interviewer". He studied for both his BA in Humanities and MA in Political Communication at Dublin City University (DCU). O'Toole is columnist with *Irish Sunday Mirror* and a music writer for the *Irish Daily Mirror*. He previously worked as a senior editor for *Hot Press* magazine and a staff writer with the *Irish Daily Mail/Mail on Sunday*. His journalism has also appeared in *The Sunday Times, Irish Independent, Empire, Playboy,* and the Italian titles *La Republica* and *Panorama*. *The Writing Irish* is his ninth book. He resides in Madrid.

www.ingramcontent.com/pod-product-compliance
Lightning Source LLC
Chambersburg PA
CBHW070444030726
47503CB00004B/886